THE GREEK WORLD

The Making of the Past

The Greek World

Roger Ling

Peter Bedrick Books
New York

Advisory Board for
The Making of the Past

Frontispiece: restoration of the sanctuary of the Great Gods at
Samothrace, drawn by G. Niemann in the 1870s.

AN EQUINOX BOOK
First American edition published in 1988 by
Peter Bedrick Books
2112 Broadway
New York NY 10023

First edition © 1976 Elsevier Publishing Projects SA, Lausanne
Second edition © 1988 Equinox (Oxford) Ltd

Library of Congress Cataloging-in-Publication Data
Ling, Roger,
    The Greek world/Roger Ling.— 1st American ed.
      p. cm.— (The Making of the past)
    Bibliography: p.
    Includes index.
    ISBN 0-87226-301-0
    ISBN 0-87226-229-4 [PBK.]
    1. Greece—Civilization—To 146 B.C.   I. Title.   II. Series:
Making of the past (New York, N.Y.)
DF77.L45 1988
938—dc19   88-819
                                            CIP

Printed in Yugoslavia

5   4   3   2

First paperback edition, 1990

Contents

Maps

Preface to the Series

This book is a volume in the Making of the Past, a series describing
the early history of the world as revealed by archaeology and related
disciplines. The series is written by experts under the guidance of a
distinguished panel of advisers and is designed for the layman, for
young people, the student, the armchair traveler and the tourist. Its
subject is a new history – the making of a new past, uncovered and
reconstructed in recent years by skilled specialists. Since many of the
authors of these volumes are themselves practicing archaeologists,
leaders in a rapidly changing field, the series is completely
authoritative and up-to-date. Each volume covers a specific period
and region of the world and combines a detailed survey of the modern
archaeology and sites of the area with an account of the early
explorers, travelers, and archaeologists concerned with it. Later
chapters of each book are devoted to a reconstruction in text and
pictures of the newly revealed cultures and civilizations that make up
the new history of the area.

Preface

The Greek world is much more than Greece. In the Classical age of the 5th and 4th centuries BC it extended from Spain to Syria, and from southern Russia to the coast of Libya; in the Hellenistic period that followed, it spread eastwards to India and south to the Sudan. But it is the area focused on the Aegean Sea – Greece, the Greek islands and the Turkish coast – that we associate with the greatest days and the most splendid achievements of Greek civilization. A land of mountains and sea, often barren but invariably beautiful, it is best seen in the long summer months, when the brilliance of the sunlight and the luminous clarity of the air combine with the browns and blues of its rocky coasts to leave an unforgettable impression. Such a landscape seems tailor-made for the sharp-fluted marble columns which are the most characteristic material remnants of Greece's former glory.

When the present-day visitor sees remains like the temple on the promontory of Cape Sunium or the great theater carved in the side of the hill at Pergamum, he will admire the extraordinary gift which the ancient Greeks had for fitting their buildings to the natural environment. But, above all, he will be conscious of history. The stadium at Olympia where generations of athletes competed in the ancient games; the sanctuary at Delphi where Apollo's priestess uttered her enigmatic oracles; the majestic Parthenon in Athens, the religious focus of a great maritime empire – all are pregnant with historical associations. And this was no ordinary historical period. Classical Greece provides one of those felicitous moments – one thinks also of Augustan Rome, itself heavily indebted to the Greeks, and of Renaissance Italy – when great men have come together under enlightened patronage in a wonderfully beneficial intellectual climate to add a new dimension to the story of civilization. The statesman Pericles, the playwrights Aeschylus, Sophocles, Euripides and Aristophanes, the historians Herodotus and Thucydides, the philosophers Socrates, Plato and Aristotle, the sculptors Phidias and Praxiteles, the orator Demosthenes – these are but a few of the names of the period. All are among the greatest geniuses that the world has ever produced. More remarkable still, all lived within the space of two centuries, and all were born in or attracted to Athens. Has ever one city – and a city with less than a quarter of a million free inhabitants – produced a record to compare with this?

It was a passion for the cultural achievements of the Athenians and the other Greeks which prompted the growth of an interest in their archaeological monuments. Already in the first centuries AD, when the Greek world had been absorbed into the Roman Empire, wealthy tourists were visiting the Aegean to see attractions like Praxiteles' statue of Aphrodite at Cnidos, and antiquarian authors were composing works like Pausanias' guidebook to Greece. In the 15th century, at a time when the revival of Classical learning was in full swing, the Italian merchant Cyriac of Ancona traveled all over Greece and the islands, writing descriptions and making drawings of the antiquities which he saw. Interest gradually mounted till in the late 18th and early 19th centuries the architectural drawings of Stuart and Revett and the sculptural acquisitions of Lord Elgin, coinciding with the heyday of the Neoclassical art movement, put the remains of Classical Greece squarely before the eyes of the educated public in western Europe. From then on Greece became a regular port of call for artists and scholars. The desire for Greek artworks inaugurated the era of excavation, and after the middle of the 19th century there was a great spate of digging culminating in the massive German campaigns which laid bare the monuments of Olympia, Pergamum and Miletus. During this period the aims of archaeology gradually changed and techniques gradually improved; and since World War I the evolution has continued. Nowadays we are no longer content simply to hunt for spectacular finds but seek to extract information from a site – information which can be used, in conjunction with the literary evidence, to build up a picture of how the Greeks lived and worked.

It is the object of this book to follow the progress of archaeology over the centuries and to outline the picture of Greek life to which the antiquarians and archaeologists have contributed. The picture is in many respects imperfect; for instance, we know a great deal about Classical Athens but very little about other important cities like Byzantium or Hellenistic Antioch. But every year brings new evidence. It may concern housing conditions, or trading patterns, or agricultural practices; it may deal with the career of an athlete, the date of a temple, or the wages of a plasterer on Delos. Whatever the case, it is one more small contribution to our understanding of the Greek world.

Chronological Table

BC	Political History	Literature, Science and Philosophy	Art and Architecture
480	Formation of Delian League 478 Pericles comes to prominence at Athens 461 Athens at war with Peloponnesians 459 Treasury of Delian League moved to Athens 454 Peace between Athens and Sparta 445 Pericles in ascendant 443–430 Great Peloponnesian War begins 431 Athenian expedition to Syracuse 415–413 Fall of Athens 404	Pindar (lyric poet) 518–438 Aeschylus (tragic playwright) 525–456 Sophocles (tragic playwright) c. 496–406 Herodotus (historian) c. 484–c. 425 Euripides (tragic playwright) c. 485–c. 406 Thucydides (historian) c. 460–400 Socrates (philosopher) 469–399 Hippocrates of Cos (physician) c. 460–c. 377	Polygnotus of Thasos (painter) active c. 475–c. 450 Temple of Zeus at Olympia c. 470–457 Myron of Eleutherae (sculptor) *fl.* c. 460–450 Phidias of Athens (sculptor) active c. 460–c. 430 Parthenon at Athens 447–432 Propylaia at Athens 437–432 Polyclitus of Argos (sculptor) active c. 450–c. 420 Temple of Apollo at Bassae c. 425 Erechtheion at Athens 421–405
400	Ascendancy of Sparta 404–371 Ascendancy of Thebes 371–362 Philip II king of Macedonia 359 Battle of Chaeronea 338 Alexander the Great 336–323 Ptolemy takes control of Egypt 323 Wars of Successors begin 319 The Successors take the title of King 306–305 Lysimachus and Seleucus win Battle of Ipsus 301	Aristophanes (comic playwright) c. 450–c. 385 Lysias (orator) c. 459–c. 380 Xenophon (historian) c. 430–c. 354 Plato (philosopher) c. 429–347 Isocrates (orator and educationalist) 436–338 Demosthenes (orator and statesman) 384–322 Aristotle (philosopher and scientist) 384–322 Theophrastus (scientist and scholar) c. 372–c. 287 Menander (comic playwright) 342–291	Temple of Asclepius at Epidaurus c. 380 Scopas of Paros (sculptor) *fl.* c. 370–350 Praxiteles of Athens (sculptor) *fl.* 360–340 New temple of Artemis at Ephesus begun 356 Mausoleum at Halicarnassus c. 350 Temple of Athena Polias at Priene c. 350–c. 330 Lysippus of Sicyon (sculptor) *fl.* c. 340–310 Apelles of Ephesus (painter) *fl.* c. 330–320 Attic red-figure pottery ends c. 320
300	Seleucus becomes sole ruler of Asia 281 Antigonus Gonatas king of Macedonia 275 First Syrian War 275–272 Pergamum becomes independent kingdom 262 Expansion of Achaean League begins 251 Bactria becomes independent c. 250 Attalus I of Pergamum defeats Galatians 230 Antiochus III king of Seleucid Empire 223 Fourth Syrian War 219–217 First war between Rome and Macedonia 215–205	Euclid (geometer) *fl.* c. 300 Epicurus (philosopher) 342–271 Zeno (philosopher) 335–263 Herophilus and Erasistratus (physicians) *fl.* c. 300–250 Theocritus of Syracuse (poet) c. 310–c. 250 Callimachus of Cyrene (poet and scholar) c. 305–c. 240 Apollonius of Rhodes (poet) c. 295–after 247 Aristarchus of Samos (astronomer) c. 310–c. 230 Archimedes of Syracuse (mathematician) c. 287–212 Eratosthenes of Cyrene (polymath) c. 275–c. 194	Temple of Apollo at Didyma begun c. 300 Tyche of Antioch c. 290 Colossus of Rhodes c. 280 Pharos at Alexandria c. 270 Statues of Gauls at Pergamum c. 230–200
200	Second Macedonian War 200–197 Rome defeats Antiochus at Magnesia 190 Demetrius invades India c. 185 Rome wins Third Macedonian War at Pydna 168 Menander king of India c. 167–c. 150` Macedonia becomes a Roman province 148 Destruction of Corinth 146 Last king of Pergamum dies 133 Pergamum becomes the Roman province of Asia 129	Seleucus of Seleucia on the Tigris (astronomer) *fl.* c. 150 Polybius (historian) c. 203–c. 120 Hipparchus of Nicaea (astronomer) c. 190–c. 126	Nike of Samothrace c. 190 Great Altar of Zeus and Athena at Pergamum 197–159 Temple of Despoina at Lycosura c. 175–150 Stoa of Attalus at Athens c. 150 Temple of Artemis at Magnesia on the Maeander c. 130 Venus de Milo c. 125–100
100	Mithridates VI of Pontus sacks Delos 88 Romans under Sulla sack Athens 86 Syria becomes a Roman province 63 Battle of Actium. Rome wins Egypt 31	Posidonius of Apamea (polymath) c. 135–c. 51	Mechanical copying of Greek statues begins c. 100 Pasiteles (sculptor and silver-worker) *fl.* c. 80–60

Introduction

During the past 12 years there has been no slackening of research and discovery in the field of Greek studies. Many issues have been clarified, others made more muddy; long-held tenets have come under attack, even more venerable ones have been resuscitated. Major projects have come to fruition, exciting finds have been announced, sites destroyed by development and looting, and scientific techniques applied to a growing range of historical and archaeological investigations.

This new Introduction is ordered, if loosely, along the lines of the main text, and numbers in brackets refer to its pages. It concentrates on new discoveries and their interpretation, but a few topics are singled out for particular detail. Now and then an alternative view is aired, to demonstrate that much of our "knowledge" of the ancient world is based on interpretation, and where evidence is slight, as it often is, such interpretations can vary.

Negative factors. The darker side of these comments should not be ignored. By definition, a countless number of archaeological sites, some no doubt of high importance, have been lost through the pace of building development, the spread of deep plowing and the "professional" use of metal detectors. Whether one would defend the preservation of all such sites or not, the fact is undeniable; if all archaeology is destruction, this is something worse. It is invidious to select examples that can be called representative, but in our period we may note that a temple site at Kardamaina on Cos was largely bulldozed for hotel foundations. Rescue excavations have taken place to reveal a Hellenistic temple foundation and a good deal of earlier material yet to be published. Near Sparta substantial terracing operations for agricultural purposes totally destroyed a farmhouse site of the Classical period. Elsewhere one gets various reports that landowners have hastened the destruction of remains to avoid the nuisance of archaeological intervention. More positively, some expeditions have set out to interest local inhabitants in their past, as at Stymphalus, home of mythical birds, in the Peloponnese, where a modest harvest of inscribed stones was brought in by farmers to a Canadian team.

Antiquities are nonetheless being illegally looted and smuggled out of their country of origin at an increasing rate. Incensed at the acquisitions of some American museums, the Turkish authorities somewhat inequitably refused excavation permits to teams from the USA in 1987. Rarely are substantial interceptions made, though one long-distance truck, late at the Greek-Yugoslav frontier, was found to have illegal emigrants aboard, including a fine Classical grave relief, now in Thessalonica Museum. Naturally, recent events in the Near and Middle East have not been conducive to the preservation of antiquities, let alone archaeological research. It was an earthquake, however, that caused the collapse of the fine tower at Aegosthena (69) in 1981.

New developments in archaeological research. Our knowledge of Olympia and its history (37–44) has developed in a variety of directions of late. Among recent finds of inscribed plaques is one that records the rejection on appeal of a condemnation of the Boeotians instigated by the Athenians; this accusation was almost certainly connected with the Persian Wars, in which the Boeotians joined the Persian camp. Further evidence of interstate aggression has come to light within the sacred precincts in the shape of trenches dug, on archaeological evidence, in the 360s BC; they are very plausibly hasty defenses dating to 364 when warfare between the Arcadians and Elis not only continued into the period of the Olympic truce, but entered the sanctuary itself. Interestingly the defenses were set up *after* the construction of a nearby building in which many stones from the great temple of Zeus were employed – a startling illustration of the violence of the earthquake which hit the Peloponnese in 373 and the extent to which the temple was henceforth a renewal. Stones from the temple were also employed in the structure of the long Echo Stoa which divides the sanctuary from the later stadium; yet it is now clear that this prominently situated hall remained a mere shell for several centuries, before it was completed in the time of Augustus, with the help of blocks from other Classical buildings.

While recent work on only a highly selected number of sites can be reported here, it is worth noting that excavation has continued in many places and has expanded significantly in northern Greece.

In Athens, a new series of campaigns in the Agora area has led to the discovery of the west end of the famous Stoa Poikile, in which the paintings of Polygnotus of Thasos were displayed from the 460s, alas on wooden boards. The ultimate decision faces future research, whether to pull down the Epiros taverna to continue the work. On the Acropolis (63–68) a major program of reconstruction works on the monuments and the rock itself has reached an advanced stage; it has involved dismantling the Erechtheion and now the Parthenon to remove the modern iron clamps that were rusting and expanding inside the blocks, and to preserve the more vulnerable surfaces, especially the sculpture, from the accelerating decay caused by atmospheric pollution. Other efforts to protect the buildings from the trample of too many feet include the provision of a new museum, below the Acropolis itself; part of it will be in one of the earliest buildings of modern Athens, the old military hospital constructed in the 1830s.

The Parthenon remains a magnet for research and reevaluation. Two striking contributions are the realization that the blinding marble surface of this and other Athenian buildings was "toned down" by a wash of such substances as milk and wax, and that there were windows high on the walls of the porches (not the only temple windows to see the light in recent years). The last point was clarified by the observation of smoke traces on the now fallen blocks that must be associated with those walls. Such close scrutiny will ever be a major aspect of the reconstruction of buildings sacred and profane. More controversial has been the suggestion that chariots framed the central group of the east pediment of the Parthenon, a conclusion based on minor differences in the measurements of fetlocks and hoofs that survive. We may also note that the discovery of an inscription in its original setting at the east end of the slopes of the Acropolis has given precious topographic evidence for a relocation of a number of shrines and features previously thought to be a compass point or more to the west.

In Attica the silver mines of Laureion continues to be explored. A continuing lack, however, is that of any smelting works, curious in view of the full sequence of processes now published. Scrutiny of the isotopes of lead ("fingerprinting") in ancient silver and bronze has helped pin an origin to a range of artifacts, though due attention has been paid to the fact that by our period many pieces must have been made at least in part from earlier melted-down materials. Study of the isotopes of more common elements such as oxygen has led to more precise identification of another mineral for which Attica was a major supplier, namely marble, though Professor Bernard Ashmole, who died at the age of 93 in 1988, felt that the tutored eye was a fair judge also. Certainly for scientific purposes a large data bank is a requisite before confident assertions about origin can be made, but good progress is being made, especially with respect to marbles from Asia Minor.

Progress of a slower kind, but highly visual, has been made down at the Piraeus, where two modern reconstructions have docked in recent years. The first was a replica of the cargo ship found off Kyrenia (60–61), which had made a round trip to Cyprus, weathering

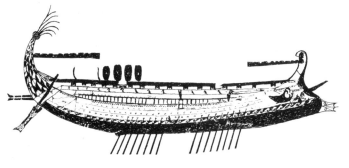

Above: fresco of a very large trireme, named the *Isis*, on the walls of a tomb of the 3rd century BC, at Nymphaion in the Crimea.

Right: the replica of an ancient Greek trireme took to the sea in summer 1987, its three banks of oars manned by a largely British crew.

three force-10 gales on the return leg. The second was the latest recruit to the Greek Navy, the trireme *Olympias*, which arrived in August 1987, after its training runs off Troizen, the refuge of the Athenians in 480 BC. The project was guided by John Coates and John Morrison, combining knowledge of naval construction and the evidence for the ancient trireme. One difficulty they faced was not unknown in the ancient world—lack of timber; an oak of suitable size for the keel could not readily be obtained and so iroko was substituted. The craft is 36 meters long and 4.5 meters in the beam; it has the stipulated three banks of oars, whose original weight has now been lightened. The ability of the crew to synchronize, even with a slight wave effect from stem to stern, was gratifying; as only the upper oars had a good sight of water they followed the lead of the other banks. A top rate of seven knots was reached with the original heavy oars.

Of considerable naval interest also is the elaborate fresco of a large trireme, or perhaps quinquereme, named the *Isis*, found in a tomb at Nymphaion in the Crimea, dating from the middle of the 3rd century BC. Among the many details given is a little cameo of one of the Dioscuri, Castor and Polydeuces, protecting the boat, with his horse, at the prow.

Politics and administration. With respect to administrative matters, we may note first that the highest financial officers at Athens were elected, not selected by lot, and from the richest of the property classes (the *pentakosiomedimnoi*, or 500-bushel men), while the first regular issues of gold coinage came from the mint of Syracuse in the period around 400, rather than from Macedon under Philip (74). The coins of Athens of the earlier 4th century are central to a recently discovered legal text on a stone from the Agora, dated to 375; the problems of recognizing and dealing with forged Athenian-type coins are tackled, and a public servant deputed to arbitrate in disputed cases. This reminds us that in general one could only use local currency in a *polis*, and needed to change other currencies. A second find of interest to the process of law at Athens is a fragment of a jar with a painted inscription stating that it contained sealed depositions for a court case, a process previously known from literary texts but not in actuality.

Such depositions remind us that Greek cities did have public archives, which increased in size and scope in the course of the 5th and 4th centuries. A range of recent finds has enormously increased our awareness of this aspect of ancient bookkeeping. In particular, several groups of clay sealings, preserved by the chance of fire, have come to light, from both official and private offices. They are of the 3rd and 2nd centuries, while earlier are the "ghosts" of texts once pinned to the architrave (and perhaps walls) of the central temple of Apollo Pythios at

Argos; the original texts, whose shape alone is preserved by the nail holes, would have been cut on bronze; this was a common habit in the Peloponnese, as best evidenced by the large number of such plaques found at Olympia. An intriguing inscription from the island of Paros, apart from giving precious details of the topography of the town, orders the copying of the city's archive, normally kept only in the sanctuary of Apollo and Artemis, on to papyrus for deposit in the temple of Hestia, a move specifically designed to counter tampering with such records.

The caches of sealings are from Demetrias in Thessaly, Delos, Callion in Aetolia and Paphos on Cyprus. The last and those from Delos, some thousands, have yet to be fully published; the 800 from Callion give an interesting insight into the "diplomatic" connections of this relatively out-of-the-way center in the period c.250–150, and throw much light on such topics as public seals, Hellenistic seal engraving and Ptolemaic interest in mainland Greece. The excavations at Callion took place as rescue work ahead of the creation of a dammed lake on the River Mornos, to slake the thirst of ever-expanding Athens, some 200 kilometers away.

Sparta (72–73) has been the object of several new studies. A major new piece of evidence had been lying in the courtyard of the museum since before 1965. It is a fragmentary stone inscription with the text of an alliance between the Lacedaemonians and a subgroup of Aetolians, dating perhaps to the very end of the 5th century. It confirms the Spartan fear of risings of the Helots, noted in preserved literature, and gives the lie to the notion that the Spartans forbade the writing down of such administrative details. Not that one text constitutes an archive.

Less formal are curse tablets, writing scratched on lead sheets, condemning enemies, normally personal, to various forms of fate, and then deposited in unpropitious places, especially wells and tombs. One of particular interest was found recently in the Kerameikos of Athens; the "named" men are prominent politicians and generals of the 310s, including Cassander, the ruler of Macedon, and the oligarchic controller of Athens Demetrius of Phaleron. Such individuals more often appear in our documentary evidence as recipients of honors. Two interesting documents of the activities of Philip and Alexander detail their redistribution of land in areas immediately east of the Macedonian territory from which their rule expanded. Alexander took Hellenism a mite further eastward, and recent finds have illuminated that expansion in a variety of ways. A sherd of a Hellenistic jug appeared in the excavations of Hafun in Somalia; an inscription found on the island of Failaka off Kuwait (ancient Icarus) shows it to have the same concerns of civic proprieties as any other Greek city (even if it was not so constituted itself); and a fine, perhaps late Hellenistic bronze statue of Heracles has been found at Seleucia on the Tigris, with an inscription in Greek and Aramaic, the local language of record, commemorating its capture from nearby Mesene in one of the local Parthian disputes of 150–51 AD. Up on the "northwest frontier" Greek gold and silver vessels of the 1st century BC have been found in Bactrian burials, alongside pieces inscribed with Chinese characters, at Tillya Tepe in northern Afghanistan.

These were excavated after 1978, the year in which work ceased at nearby Ai Khanoum, where French excavators had uncovered the remains of a typical Hellenistic city, flourishing in the 3rd to 1st centuries BC; its public monuments, stoas, gymnasia and theater differ little from those of the homeland. Here too it is a mixture of influences in the "archival" material that indicates something unusual—officials with Iranian names, texts in Aramaic and Bactrian, references to Indian coins, and one document in an undeciphered script. To the south, at Kandahar, further Hellenistic remains have come to light, above those of the earlier Persian masters of the area.

Among recent finds in more northerly areas, most striking is the hoard of nearly 200 silver vessels, many with gilt decoration, from Rogozen in inland Bulgaria, not far south of the Danube. Buried in the late 4th century, it includes a number of pieces marked as gifts from various subject areas to the kings of Thrace; pride of place belongs to a small dish with a magnificently modeled medallion of Heracles attacking Auge, probably Attic work of around 400 BC. High-quality Greek metalwork has also come to light at the far end of the Black Sea, in ancient Colchis, home of Medea and the Golden Fleece. Other finds include plentiful Greek wine jars of the Classical period, especially from Chios, but as yet no sure traces of purely Greek settlement, or of strong Greek influence on the local cultures has been reported.

Economics and society. Broadly economic aspects of the Greek world (91–98) have continued to attract the attention of researchers. To the fore are such aspects as town and country, sufficiency and surplus, trade and the state; and it is a debate that will continue with vigor. The close connection of town and country is ever to be stressed, their interdependence basic to the structure of any society. Close scrutiny has been paid to such aspects as the size of landholdings, their fragmentation and distance from the owner's main residence. The old tenet of alternate years fallowing has been questioned, and therefore a basic aspect of estimating annual crop yields. Severe drought could always cause chaos, but it does seem that our estimates of the reliance of Attica in particular on imported grain have been grossly overestimated, by up to 40 percent.

We may note that, although the major grape variety planted in the Crimean Chersonesus (92) was the hardy *Vitis silvestris*, far more developed types are also sporadi-

cally attested there. The wine trade as a whole has been investigated closely, mainly through its prime container, the amphora. Those of Rhodes are of a particular archaeological importance, since they are stamped with annually changing devices, which theoretically can give a precise date to the contexts in which they are found; the work of Virginia Grace in painstakingly pegging these stamps to years BC continues. In the meantime, on the island of Thasos, another major wine exporter of the 4th and 3rd centuries, several kilns in which amphorae were made have been investigated and have thrown up interesting results regarding the organization of the stamping system there. The official eye seems to have been on the correctness of the size of the jar, not the quality of the wine, although it remains a puzzle why only about a half of the Thasian jars (and a smaller percentage at other centers) bear the official stamp.

Individual finds of amphorae at Corinth and off Las Palmas are worth mentioning. The first are from a building near the heart of Classical Corinth, used for some 50 years as a depot. Many of the jars, including those to be attributed to a factory on the Moroccan coast, contained filleted fish, notably sea bream. While the difficulty of catching "commercial" quantities of fish with the tackle available to the Greeks has been pointed out, there is no doubt of the existence of this long-distance trade, which includes fish-salting works excavated in Greek settlements of the Crimea area.

The second, Majorcan, wreck contained a mixed cargo, as did most vessels of the pre-Roman period known to us. Included was very down-market Attic red-figured pottery, of a type already known in some quantity from finds on the Spanish mainland. Yet there is no such parallel for the remarkable range of storage amphorae from the wreck, pieces of Black Sea, East Greek, Carthaginian and also local origin: another mystery to be solved.

While at sea, we may note a recent review of Greek ferry charges, two obols to cross the Euripus from Chalcis to Oropus, for example. On a far grander financial scale it is worth stressing the fiscal divide between the Ptolemies and much of the rest of the Hellenistic world (97), in that they perpetuated and intensified the old system of a closed economy in which only local currency was valid, thus in fact obviating much of the inflation that occurred in the freer markets outside, where the Attic-weight coins of Alexander and his successors circulated liberally.

Town planning. Looking more specifically at town and country planning, we may note further areas in which the apportionment of land has been detached, notably at Agde, the colony of Agathe, in southern France, where lots of 180 square meters were gridded out in the Hellenistic period. Town plans on similar grid systems have been explored and an important contribution made to the history of the Greek house. The most promising site may well be Stymphalus in the north Peloponnese, tucked away and so spared many of the ravages of modern development, added to the fact that the land is state-owned and so less open to exploitation. Aerial photography and a resistivity survey have demonstrated the grid plan, probably of the 4th century, and a rarity in "old" Greece, though substantially forestalled by a similar plan imposed on the contours of Halieis in the Argolid (near modern Porto Cheli) in the 6th century.

More difficult to detect is the original plan of the Piraeus, laid out by Hippodamus of Miletus in the mid-5th century under the eye of Pericles. Small scraps of it lie among the modern concrete, though some of the ancient walls of the town have succumbed in recent years. Here and at a range of other sites German researchers have shown that the original town plan was based on sets of identical houses (give or take a differently sited entrance passage). It is interesting to note the gradual increase in significance of the *andron* or men's dining room in these original plans, from a side room, dependent on the main living room or *oikos*, to a central position. At Priene in particular (120) they note the considerable alterations

made to the original plans over the centuries, some houses becoming veritable clubs, mere sets of *andrones*. As a postscript we may note that the addresses given to houses tended to depend on the nearest landmark. Some recently found leases, cut on lead sheets, from Camarina in Sicily, itself a grid-plan town, exemplify this: "Dinarchus buys from Dion the house and entire retail establishment, with doors and party walls with Philoxenus and Thrasyllus, the region being that above the sanctuary of Gaos and Persephone, for 40 talents" (in Sicily about 4 kilograms of silver). The 4th-century text was actually found in the house in question, an invaluable and rare occurrence in the days of the metal detector.

A further text of high interest gives an almost complete description of the circuit of walls of Scotoussa in Thessaly in the earlier 2nd century BC, its prime purpose being to establish a free zone, inside and out, for defensive purposes. Fortifications of the ancient world have been treated in a number of publications, including one encapsulating the life-long experience of A.W. Lawrence. He and others have worried in particular about the isolated "tower houses" that dot the Greek landscape, especially in the islands. They would have been beyond the financial means of most single families, and a variety of uses must be postulated, from slave pen (on the rich mining islands of Thasos and Siphnos) to guard post and communal refuge. A variety of the mines on these islands has begun to be explored, one in fact right under the acropolis of the town of Thasos, yet largely neglected until 1978. A similar juxtaposition of town and industry has come to light at Thoricus near Laureion (93) – a mine adit cheek by jowl with the entrance to the theater. An oddity of town planning is a small sectioned-off "keep" in the north Greek *polis* of Mesembria; even the identification of the site is disputed, since it was not accepted by the magisterial French epigraphist Louis Robert, who died in 1987.

Religion and sport. Much recent work on Greek religion has concentrated on the structure of religious life in individual communities and the interrelationship of sets of deities and their functions. In a society where there was no extensive "professional" priestly class it has also been worthwhile examining the use of religion or cult for broadly political purposes. One such treatment stems from the study of a recently discovered calendar of sacrifices of about 430 BC, from the deme of Thoricus; in it we find purely local cults set alongsde those inspired from the center at Athens. Such records also give a good idea of the range of animals sacrificed, and at what time of year; it is interesting to note that in less official documents, notably scenes of everyday life on vases, there is a clear tendency to depict the sacrificial animal as the expensive bull rather than the far more commonly used sheep or goat.

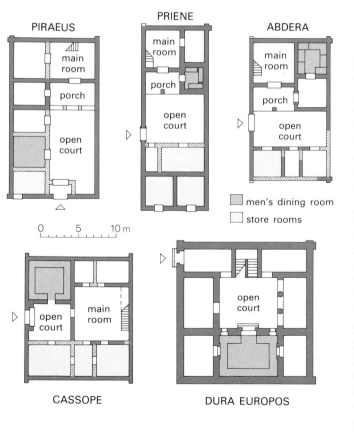

Courtyard, living room and a men's dining room of increasing importance are essentials in the plans of houses of the 5th and 4th centuries at a range of sites.

It is a sad fact that we have no contemporary manuscript texts to eke out these other forms of evidence. A severely damaged papyrus roll was discovered in Athens in 1981 in a tomb probably of the 5th century; letters were visible, but the piece seems to have been beyond conservation. The papyrus of the mid-4th century found carbonized on top of a tomb at Derveni (135) still awaits official publication. The printing of a pirated section of the text in 1982 demonstrated that it is a commentary on a "Creation" poem based on the cult of Orpheus, and also caused much ruffling of academic feathers. More weighty is the "philosophical brick" from the site of Ai Khanoum. It is a section of text of the mid-2nd century transferred to a mud-brick surface from a papyrus that had lain against it, and is part of a dialogue in the style of Plato in which his theory of Ideas and perceived objects is discussed, in northern Afghanistan.

With regard to the other major aspect of the core curriculum of Greek education, sport (110), it is the stadium that has taken the limelight. At Olympia the successive, and increasingly grandiose entrances into the stadium from the sacred Altis have been more closely examined, while it has been demonstrated that the stadium high up above the sanctuary of Apollo at Delphi was only laid out in the 2nd century BC, and that we must seek the original arena elsewhere, perhaps not near the cult center at all. At Corinth work in the center of the Roman forum has shown it to overlie the Classical stadium, a trifle short of the required 600 feet, since established roads lay at either end; also found were the postholes for temporary stands set around the boxing and wrestling ring by the start of the track. To the south, at Nemea, site of other Panhellenic games, the University of California has started major excavations. At the stadium an early example of a Greek arch has come to light, of the late 4th century, while in the nearby sanctuary of Zeus we may note the range of treasuries flanking the temple, and the probable existence of a 7th-century predecessor of the temple itself. Regrettably the site was very severely disturbed by Byzantine farming activities.

Temples elsewhere have been unearthed or reinterpreted. At Kalapodhi, in eastern Phocis, a highly interesting cult complex has yielded good evidence of continuity of worship throughout the Dark Ages. It is to be identified with the shrines of Apollo and Artemis of Hyampolis, mentioned in literary sources. A final temple in the series discovered was begun around 450 BC, after a period in which only a temporary altar was in use; the altar was deliberately buried and found with a selection of the paraphernalia of cult still upon it. We have here an illustration of the vow taken by the Greeks in 479 not to rebuild the temples destroyed by the invading Persians until full vengeance had been exacted. Both the excavation and Herodotus speak of such a destruction at Kalapodhi.

Different but equally interesting observations have been made at the temple of Didyma (122) by Lothar Haselberger. On the walls of the inner court he descried the lightly scratched outlines of architectural drawings, largely at full scale, most probably from the hand of the architect. While the full significance of the find is still a matter of debate, the meaning of "on-site planning" in the Greek world has certainly taken a new turn. Even more debate concerns the identity of a small round building found at Cnidos in southwest Turkey; is it the shrine of Aphrodite in which Praxiteles' renowned statue was exhibited (127)? Much depends on the lengthy architectural history of the structure, together with the few, not wholly consistent, ancient texts which mention the setting of the sculpture.

Sculpture. If Praxiteles' statue has not been found, there has been no lack of other new sculptural discoveries, from Baksy to Baiae. The former is a site in the Crimea, where a particularly fine, if fragmentary, Attic red-figured krater of the late 5th century was found in 1882 and published a century later. Its interest is that it gives us our earliest preserved reflections (by no means copies) of the two great masterpieces of Phidias, the gold and ivory statues of Athena Parthenos and of Zeus at Olympia. At Baiae, the Roman resort on the bay of Naples, a cellarful of fragments of plastercasts was found in 1954 and published a mere generation later. They represent casts taken from a range of famous Greek originals, ready to be copied in marble for Roman clients. Not only do they give us precious details of the originals, akin to the Hestia (126), but they are also invaluable for demonstrating methods of copying in antiquity.

Not all sculpture in the Roman world was copied, and two sets of originals have caught the eye. The famous bronze horses of San Marco in Venice have been the subject of a special exhibition and close scientific scrutiny; the 98 percent copper content has led many to doubt whether they can be of Greek origin. From Rome itself we have a new Classical Greek pediment (or respectable fragments of it), removed from its original home to grace a temple of Apollo in the principate of Augustus; excavated in the 1930s, the fragments were placed in several museums and only recently reconvened.

Not all finds are ancient, but we may pass over rapidly the episode of the Colossus of Rhodes in 1987 that made the biggest archaeological headlines of recent years; it was an engineered ploy to render a huge lump of stone like a human fist.

From the Greek mainland a most impressive find is a tomb monument of c. 340, found in the area between Athens and the Piraeus. It has figures standing in an architectural frame which itself is adorned with friezes, much influenced by the Mausoleum (35); the color is particularly well preserved. It was set up for a foreigner, from Histria on the Black Sea, but despite its pretentious size we may note that even more imposing monuments to the great Athenian dead were set up during the century, to judge from surviving literary descriptions.

The sea continues to give up bronze statuary, notably in Italian waters. A youth in the style of Lysippus is in the Getty Museum, while other pieces remain in Italy, in Reggio Calabria. Fragments recovered by police and excavators from a wreck at Porticello near Reggio include a superb mid-5th-century male head, dubbed "the philosopher," while even more exciting are two more or less contemporary over-lifesize male nudes, found, with only the slightest traces of a boat, just off the coast at Riace, around the toe of Italy. The two represent the best of Classical workmanship and have been attributed by many to Phidias himself. They are depicted as warriors of heroic status and were probably part of a larger group, from Olympia or Delphi. One has had his right arm replaced, probably in the Hellenistic period. The facial details of statue A are particularly striking, with silver teeth, copper lips and ivory and amber in the eyes. All these bronzes have naturally added immensely to our knowledge of the practicalities of ancient bronze casting, not least the mixture of casting directly and indirectly from the original maquette.

Other arts. Other arts too have seen their stock increase. New mosaics have been found at Pella (134), but finds from further south have bolstered the view that figural mosaic was a central Greek invention – small scraps from Sicyon, Corinth and Athens, and an impressive suite from Eretria, all of the late 5th and 4th centuries. Yet the north of Greece has continued to yield especially fine work in this and other fields, largely the fruit of a deliberate policy to expand archaeological research in the area. We may note the exceptional state of preservation of organic materials found in some tombs of the 5th and 4th centuries at Pherae in Thessaly. They include beds of olive twigs, woolen blankets, sandals, purple clothing and fruit.

Finds from cemeteries in Macedonia have been even more impressive. The built Macedonian tomb, with its architectural facade, has long been known, but many more have been located recently, bringing the total to some 50. Regrettably most have been looted in ancient or very recent times. They form an intriguing, very disparate architectural ensemble. One site where they occur stands apart, Vergina, which lies close to the River Haliakmon near where it debouches into the present coastal plain. It has been convincingly equated with the first capital of the tribe of the Macednes, Aegae. In the largest of the many burial mounds in the area Professor Manolis Andronikos discovered in 1977 an extraordinarily rich, intact tomb, with cremation burials in both main chamber and anteroom, male and female respectively,

One of the pair of bronze statues found off Riace. Over 2 meters high, it may well be the work of the great Athenian sculptor Phidias, about 450 BC. Reggio Calabria Museum.

with the remains of the pyre collected and placed on top of the roof; a small structure nearby is likely to have been a hero shrine. A second intact tomb was found close to the first, and a third one, looted, but with well-preserved and stunning mural decoration, notably a flowing, near impressionist rape of Persephone by Hades, a revelation in terms of mid-4th-century art. Only marginally less impressive is the battered frieze above the marble doors of the unplundered tomb, with motifs paralleled by the perhaps later original of the Alexander mosaic (132).

"Perhaps later" since there has been lively debate about the occupant(s) of this tomb. The grave goods, especially a golden diadem, point to royalty. Andronikos believes the man to have been none other than Alexander's father, Philip II, assassinated in 336; evidence to support his case, which can hardly be controverted, comes from a forensic examination of the skull found in the gold chest that contained the cremated remains. The right eye socket was nicked, the result of a wound of a type which we know Philip suffered – and for the treatment of which his surgeon gained some renown. Other circumstances support this identification and must override objections which concern the precocious date for the use of an arch roof to the chamber. and the date of some of the few ceramic vases found therein, which have been argued to be of late 4th-century date at Athens.

Finds from the tomb of Philip II at Vergina include fragments of the gold and ivory parade shield, whose cover is propped against the wall.

The cremated remains of Philip, once wrapped in purple cloth, were found in this simply decorated gold chest, 40 centimeters wide.

Most of the other objects found in the tomb and antechamber (and in the second, perhaps earlier, intact tomb) were of richer materials. Bronze is reserved largely for more functional equipment, but even here there was a surprise, with a helmet and cuirass of wrought iron. A contemporary tomb in Epirus, the home of Philip's first wife Olympias, contained similar iron armor. The golden burial caskets are particularly spectacular, with the star-shaped "symbol" of the Macedonians on the lid. Within, the bones were wrapped in a cloth of purple and gold. Carved ivory reliefs from elaborate couches were found in each tomb, one bearing what seem to be small portraits of members of the royal family, the other suitably convivial Dionysiac scenes. Ivory also appears in the *pièce de résistance* of Philip's tomb; beneath a bronze shield cover once lay a magnificent parade shield wrought of gold sheet, ivory and clear glass on a wooden frame; it had disintegrated into hundreds of fragments, but the restorers of the Thessalonica Museum have been able to recreate much of its former glory. As ever in the Greek world, weaponry and art were no strangers.

Alan Johnston

Persephone carried off by Pluto. Part of the fresco in the looted tomb under the great mound at Vergina, Macedonia. Vivid work of a master artist of 350–325 BC.

1. Greek Civilization

Historical and geographical background. The period with which we are concerned is one of four and a half centuries: from 479 BC, when the Greeks defeated the Persians at the battle of Plataea, to 31 BC, when Egypt, the last independent part of the Greek world, came under the rule of the Romans. A short period in cosmic, or even historical, terms – but one of immense significance in the saga of western civilization. It was in these four and a half centuries that the astonishingly precocious developments of the previous age were brought to maturity in a cultural climax such as had never occurred before and has rarely been equalled since. And it was in these four and a half centuries that the foundations were laid for most of the artistic and literary, even scientific, achievements of the modern world.

First, we must define our historical terms. The story of the Greeks from the end of the Bronze Age to the coming of the Romans is conventionally divided into four main phases. The first is the so-called "Geometric" period, lasting from the 11th to the 8th century: a veritable dark age in which the art of writing, known in the Bronze Age, seems to have been lost, and the only chinks of light to pierce the gloom are the stiff figurines and abstract vase decorations that have given the period its name. In the second ("Archaic") period, dating from 700 or 650 to about 500, came the awakening. Trade and colonization carried the Greeks over much of the Mediterranean, bringing them into contact with other, older civilizations, notably those of Egypt and the Middle East; writing was reintroduced; Greek literature and science were born; social and political institutions were gradually perfected; monumental stone buildings were erected; large-scale stone statues were carved. In short, the Greek world acquired the political and cultural features that were to be characteristic of its apogee.

The other two phases are represented by our four and a half centuries. The "Classical" period, occupying the 5th and 4th centuries, was the great age of the independent city-state. It was ushered in by the wars in which the Greeks halted the westward expansion of the Persian Empire and thereby established a freedom to develop unhindered by foreign interference. The city of Athens, in particular, benefited from the discomfiture of the Persians to enter upon a golden age of power and prosperity; it was now that she completed the evolution of her democratic form of government and produced her remarkable series of statesmen, thinkers, writers and artists. Her intellectual importance continued in the 4th century, but her political and economic standing declined after the disastrous Peloponnesian War in which she was defeated by her great rival, Sparta. Sparta now enjoyed a brief spell of preeminence, but further wars led to a general exhaustion of all the Greek states, and to the ascendancy of the northern kingdom of Macedonia, which effectively conquered continental Greece by 338.

The fourth and final ("Hellenistic") period was in-augurated by the conquests of the Macedonian king Alexander the Great (336–323) who led the Greeks in a war of aggression against the Persian Empire and extended their world to include Egypt and the whole of western Asia as far as Afghanistan and northwest India. Though Alexander's empire split up after his death, much of it continued to exist in the form of independent kingdoms till they were absorbed piecemeal by the Romans during the 2nd and 1st centuries. During this fourth period Greek history entered a whole new dimension. The independent city-state was now overshadowed by vast monarchical states with mercenary armies; Greek civilization now became the unifying element in a cosmopolitan world embracing a large part of the Middle East.

The Classical and Hellenistic periods are, then, our historical compass. What of the geographical background? The chief point to stress is that there was never a single nation of Greece (even Alexander did not rule every part of the Greek world), still less a nation corresponding in area to present-day Greece. Ancient Greece, or more correctly Hellas (for the terms "Greece" and "Greeks," derived from the Latin "Graecia" and "Graeci," have never been used by the Greeks themselves), was an abstract concept, like "Christendom" in the Middle Ages or "the Arab world" today, embracing a large number of independent states. And these states were not confined to the Greek peninsula but were scattered in various parts of the Mediterranean, around the Black Sea and eventually throughout the Middle East.

There were often considerable differences between one state and another. The inhabitants might speak different dialects, use different weights, measures and coinages, live under different political systems and different laws, put the emphasis on placating different gods or goddesses within the Hellenic pantheon. But to a Greek the similarities far outweighed the differences. Wherever he lived, he was conscious mainly of the bonds which united him to his fellow Greeks: their common race, common language, common alphabet, common religion and common customs. As a corollary to this he looked upon all other races as being in a separate class. Whether civilized Persians or wild northern tribesmen, they were described as *barbaroi* ("barbarians") – that is, those who could not speak Greek and made sounds like "bar-bar-bar." It was not necessarily a pejorative term, but many Greeks used it in a way which implied a firm belief in the cultural superiority of their own race.

The homeland and heartland of Hellas was continental Greece. This is a land of high mountains, narrow plains, and a deeply indented coastline; it has no navigable rivers; and the climate shows considerable variation, being hot in summer and severe in winter in the mountains, and temperate all the year around in the coastal lowlands. These factors contributed to two essential characteristics of the Greek world. One was its division into small, independent states: the difficulty of overland com-

A typical Greek landscape, from the air over Loutraki near Corinth. The mountains are broken by narrow plains and sheltered bays.

munications and the tendency of the population to concentrate in certain geographically and climatically favorable centers militated against political unity. The other was its use of sea transport. No part of the Greek peninsula is much more than 60 miles from the coast, and conditions in the summer months are generally favorable to sailing, particularly in the Aegean basin, where the winds are steady and sheltering islands are never far away. So the Greeks found it natural and convenient to become a race of seafarers. A third aspect of Greek life may also be attributed specifically to climatic factors: its predilection for the open air. The long, dry Mediterranean summers meant that much of the business of life, from political assemblies, religious festivals and theatrical performances to gymnastic training and mere conversation, could be conducted out of doors.

Political geography. The political geography of the Greek peninsula in Classical times may be summarized area by area, beginning with the Peloponnese. This, the southern part of Greece, can be divided, on the basis of the dialects spoken (which reflect the pattern of early tribal settlements), into three parts. The central, mountainous area, Arcadia, was a pastoral region, remote from the mainstream of Greek politics; it preserved its own individual dialect, and its chief cities, Mantinea and Tegea, lay on its eastern fringes. To the north and west lay the cantons of Achaea and Elis, the latter containing the great Panhellenic religious center of Olympia. In both these areas the predominant dialect is now known as Northwest Greek. The remainder of the Peloponnese was dominated by four powerful states where the Dorian dialect was spoken: Sparta in the south, Argos, Sicyon and Corinth in the northeast. Of these Corinth enjoyed by far the most advantageous position. Situated at the southern end of the isthmus which links the Peloponnese to central Greece, and controlling ports on both coasts, she had long been one of the foremost trading cities in the Greek world.

The Dorian-speaking sphere extended along the isth-

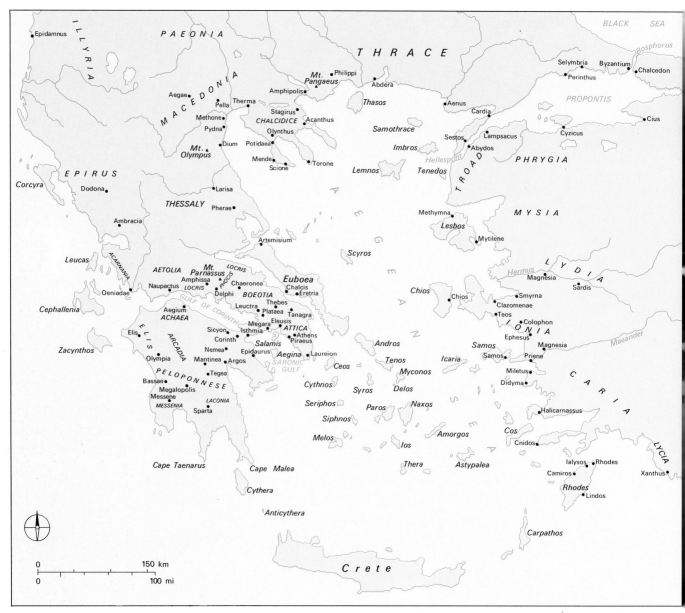

Greece, the Aegean Sea and the Turkish coast during the Classical period.

mus to the city of Megara and into the Saronic Gulf to the east, where it included the island of Aegina. Beyond, occupying the southeastern projection of central Greece, lay the province of Attica, whose urban center was Athens, the richest and most important commercial city in Hellas. Like the large neighboring island of Euboea, Attica was an Ionian state, and its inhabitants spoke a version of the Ionian dialect. The Ionians and the Dorians were the most important tribal groups in the Greek race; and much has been made of a supposed lingering Dorian–Ionian rivalry. There was certainly a cultural distinction between the two groups, a distinction expressed, for instance, in their architecture, social structures and mental outlook; and in certain parts of the Greek world this ran to an outright antipathy; but in continental Greece it is doubtful whether the old tribal divisions still exercised much influence on people's feelings.

Northwest from Attica came Boeotia, an agricultural region containing a confederacy of cities under the leadership of Thebes; and beyond Boeotia lay a group of mountainous provinces including Phocis and Locris. In Phocis the most notable spot was the oracular shrine of the god Apollo at Delphi, situated on the southern slopes of Mount Parnassus. These mountainous areas, like Arcadia in the Peloponnese, tended to lag behind in cultural and political development; and the same applies to the cantons further west, Aetolia and Acarnania. To the northeast lay the extensive plainlands of Thessaly, famous for horse-breeding and long ruled by a small nucleus of baronial families who kept the bulk of the population in a state of subjection. In all these central districts the chief dialect was Northwest Greek, but western Acarnania spoke Dorian, while Boeotia and northern Thessaly contained descen-

The sanctuary at Delphi. The columns are those of the third temple of Apollo, built after the previous temple was destroyed by an earthquake in 373 BC.

dants of the Aeolian tribes, who had their own dialect.

Further north two huge semi-Greek areas straddled the peninsula. Epirus in the northwest, famous for the oracle of Zeus at Dodona, was inhabited by numerous tribes which were not effectively unified till the 4th century. Macedonia in the northeast, a land of hardy peasant folk, had a greater degree of unity, and this was consolidated by the vigorous military leaders who eventually elevated her to the greatest power of the Balkans. Along her coast, however, and particularly in the three-pronged peninsula of Chalcidice, there were several purely Greek settlements, mostly planted by Ionian emigrants from Euboea.

From mainland Greece we may pass to the islands. Those off the west coast were of limited importance, apart from Corcyra (Corfu), a stepping-stone on the maritime route to southern Italy and Sicily. More in the mainstream of things were the islands of the Aegean, which both served as ports of call on the routes from Europe to Asia and yielded important natural resources. The southernmost group, running across from the Peloponnese to the southwest corner of Asia Minor, was Dorian-speaking; it included Cythera and Anticythera, Melos, Thera, Crete (which played a surprisingly small part in the history of the Classical and Hellenistic periods), Carpathos, Cos and Rhodes. The last-named occupied an especially important position at the meeting-point of the Aegean and Levantine trade routes; its three independent communities Ialysos, Camiros and Lindos eventually formed a union with a new federal capital, the city of Rhodes, at its northern tip.

The mid-Aegean islands, including most of the Cyclades, were Ionian. Several of them, notably Paros and Naxos, contained valuable marble deposits; while Samos and Chios, large islands adjacent to the Anatolian coast, were rich in agricultural produce. A historical significance out of all proportion to its size and resources was enjoyed by the tiny Cycladic islet of Delos, which served first as the religious center of the islanders and later as the chief exchange-mart of the Aegean area.

In the north Aegean, the islands off the coast of Asia Minor, Lesbos and Tenedos, were Aeolian, while those further north, Lemnos, Imbros, Thasos and Samothrace, were predominantly Ionian-speaking. Thasos was particularly wealthy: not only was it an important wine-producer, but also, like the adjacent coast of Thrace, it had gold mines and valuable supplies of shipbuilding timber. Samothrace was famed for its cult of the *Kabeiroi*, a pair of non-Hellenic deities commonly known as the "Great Gods."

The west coast of Asia Minor was lined with Greek communities. Their dialects belonged to the same three groups as the islands: the northern part of the littoral spoke Aeolian, the central stretch Ionian, and the southwest corner Dorian. The Ionian sector, or "Ionia" as we generally call it, contained all the finest sites and in the 6th century, before its absorption by the Persians, had been one of the most prosperous and culturally most advanced areas of the Greek world. Its richest cities were Ephesus and Miletus, which controlled the exit of the main trade routes from the interior.

The settlements of western Asia Minor were among the first Greek colonies overseas and they clearly marked the pattern to be adopted by all the waves of colonization before Classical times. Wherever they were founded, colonies clung to the coast. This was partly because the sea

was their lifeline, the means by which they maintained contact with the mother-cities from which their founders had sailed, but mainly because the colonists sought to reproduce the conditions to which they were accustomed at home. As they generally came from maritime cities, they tended to look for sites with good harbors and with the mild coastal climate on which their agricultural systems were based. Their relations with the peoples of the hinterland varied. Where these latter were uncivilized tribes like the Sicels and Sicans in Sicily, the Greeks normally dominated the natives; but where their neighbors were advanced and well organized, as in Asia Minor and Egypt, the settlers often had to accept an overlordship.

By the 5th century Classical Hellas had taken shape. Its nucleus remained continental Greece, the Aegean islands and western Asia Minor. But its outliers extended far beyond. In the north, colonies were dotted along the coast of Thrace, on either side of the Hellespont (Dardanelles), the Propontis (Sea of Marmara) and the Bosphorus, and all round the Black Sea. In the east, there were settlements along the south shore of Asia Minor and particularly in Cyprus, which was rich in copper, timber and cereals, and played an important role as a staging-post for Levantine trade. In the south, Greek states existed along the coasts of Egypt and Libya; the most important was Cyrene, which derived great wealth from the production of corn, wool, dates and the drug *silphion*. In the west, the coastal areas of Illyria, southern Italy, Sicily, southern France and Spain were all colonized. Some western cities, notably Taras (Taranto) in the instep of Italy and Syracuse and Acragas (Agrigento) in Sicily grew to be among the largest and most powerful states in the Greek world. Others, notably Neapolis (Naples) and Massilia (Marseilles), have survived to be leading ports of modern times.

With the conquests of Alexander the Greek world was

The Mediterranean and Black Sea in the Classical period, showing Greek and other settlements.

Sophocles (*c.* 496–406 BC), the great Athenian dramatist who wrote the tragedies *Antigone* and *Oedipus Rex*. A Roman copy, in the Vatican Museums, of a statue set up in Athens between 440 and 430 BC. 2·04 meters high.

acme as early as the 9th or 8th century, when Homer wrote down the *Iliad* and the *Odyssey*, two of the world's masterpieces. But drama and history were evolved and perfected in the 5th century. The former developed gradually from choral songs sung in honor of the god Dionysus at his Athenian festivals. In the hands of the three great tragic playwrights, Aeschylus, Sophocles and Euripides, all of whose careers belong to the 5th century, the new art form became a vehicle for creative reinterpretations of well-known myths, through which the author sought to examine man's fate and his relationship to the gods. In the hands of the comic poet Aristophanes, active in the years before and after 400, it became an instrument for pouring ridicule on contemporary personalities and ideas. Later, Menander adapted it to a new form, the light-hearted domestic farce. Drama has since, of course, become one of the major branches of western literature. While no writer has ever recaptured Aristophanes' unique blend of uproarious obscenity and soaring lyric odes, Greek tragedy has served as an inspiration for modern playwrights from Racine to Anouilh, while the "new comedy" of Menander is the ultimate ancestor of our comedy of manners.

History is indissolubly linked with two great names, Herodotus and Thucydides. Herodotus, who came to Athens from Halicarnassus in Asia Minor, wrote a history of the Persian Wars, a prose epic in which great deeds are set against a rich background of geographical, sociological and anecdotal information. Though naive in many ways, he was the first major writer to break away from the traditional grip of myths and legends, and to reconstruct the past by the careful analysis of documentary records, oral traditions and eye-witness accounts, collected in the course of his long travels through Hellas and the Middle East. For this he is justly termed the "Father of History." The less colorful, more matter-of-fact Thucydides chose as his canvas the Peloponnesian War, in which he had served as an Athenian general. As a contemporary of the events described he was able to set new standards of scientific accuracy; but, more than this, he sifted the important from the unimportant; he examined the causes of events; and, above all, taking something from the dramatists and something from the philosophers, he drew universal lessons regarding human nature and its influence on the course of history. Once again the new literary genre was bequeathed to posterity. Livy, Tacitus and Gibbon have all, in their different ways, been the successors of the Greek historians.

Drama and history were not the only fields of literature in which our period excelled. In lyric poetry the Boeotian Pindar wrote lofty odes in honor of victorious competitors in the Panhellenic games. Oratory was perfected by the 4th-century Athenian speech-writers Lysias, Isocrates and Demosthenes. And philosophical writings were raised to a major art form by the dialogues of Plato.

Philosophy was, indeed, another main sphere in which

vastly expanded and assumed a much more continental character. At the same time its center of gravity moved eastwards: the capitals of the new Hellenistic kingdoms – Alexandria in Egypt, Antioch in Syria, and Pergamum in Asia Minor – became the focuses of Greek civilization.

The Greek legacy. No account of the Greek world would be complete without some reference to the Greek achievements in literature, thought and science. What was the general contribution of the Classical and Hellenistic periods to western culture?

Here the astounding thing is that, in almost every field of their intellectual endeavor, the Greeks were pioneers. In literature, for example, the genres of epic poetry, drama and history were all Greek creations. Epic had reached its

Socrates (469–399 BC), the Athenian philosopher, mentor of Plato. The head is copied from a full-length statue of the 4th century BC. Naples, National Museum.

the Greeks made a pioneering contribution to western culture: metaphysics and ethics both began with them. Here the first outstanding figure was the Athenian Socrates (died 399), who never wrote a word, but whose constant discussions with the young men of his native city turned philosophical inquiry from speculation about the nature of the universe to the study of man and of moral values. His teaching was developed and transformed by his pupil Plato, the author of the theory of "Ideas," the doctrine that the only true realities are concepts like Beauty, Love, Wisdom and Goodness, of which all sense-objects are mere reflections or imitations. Plato was followed by Aristotle, a philosopher much admired in the late Middle Ages, who argued that reality was to be found less in generalities than in particulars. Finally came the great philosophical schools of the Hellenistic Age – notably the "Stoics," whose idea of a brotherhood of man ruled by a Supreme Being, all-wise and all-good, who is the source of all that exists, was remarkably prophetic of Christian teaching. Indeed the cornerstone of Stoic ethics – that virtue, and therefore happiness, consisted in living according to the Divine Will – exercised a profound influence on the evolution of Christianity.

In science the Greeks again achieved revolutionary progress. The "Hippocratic" school of physicians on the island of Cos began the scientific practice of medicine. Aristotle, who established the principle of collecting data as a necessary preliminary to understanding the physical world, founded the study of biology. The Hellenistic age, in particular, saw a spate of brilliant achievements. In geography Eratosthenes of Cyrene measured the circumference of the earth to within 200 miles; in astronomy Aristarchus of Samos realized that the planets, the earth included, revolved around the sun, and that the sun was much larger than the earth; in mathematics Archimedes of Syracuse calculated the value of π. Mechanical inventions of various sorts exploited the principles of water pressure, air pressure and even steam power, and employed transmission devices like the screw and the cogwheel. As an example we have fragments of an "astronomical clock" with a system of cogwheels and dials designed to show the risings and settings of the sun and stars throughout the year.

In art, architecture and government, too, the Greeks took giant steps. They produced the western world's first truly naturalistic sculpture and painting, and, in works like the Parthenon statues and the red-figured pottery of Athens, attained a sublimity of conception which is timeless in its appeal. Their colonnaded buildings created the "classical" orders which were to become a fundamental factor in the architectural styles of subsequent periods, Roman, Renaissance, Baroque and Neoclassical. And their political constitutions introduced the idea that the whole, or a large part, of a state's citizen body should have a voice, and sometimes the overriding voice, in its government. Indeed, without the Greeks, the whole science of politics might never have been invented. It was the peculiar nature of the Greek democratic state, in which every citizen was a potential politician, and thus the business of government became a matter of general interest, that led to Plato's and Aristotle's studies on political theory and the ideal state.

The city-state and its features. The main factor which distinguished the Greek state and enabled the ordinary citizen to play a part in public affairs was its small size. There were some big rural areas, like Thessaly and Aetolia, which retained a tribal organization during the Classical period, and others, like Messenia in the southwest Peloponnese, which lived in a state of political subjection to a powerful neighbor; but the characteristic community in the Greek world was a compact, self-governing territory with a single urban center. This was the *polis* (from which come our term "politics" and its derivatives). Hellas contained hundreds of *poleis*, of which the largest, Athens (i.e. Attica), was about the size of modern Luxembourg, with an area of 1,000 square miles and a population of 300,000 or so. The vast majority were much smaller: populations of 5,000 or less were quite common.

We generally translate *polis* "city-state," but this glosses over the point that the territory of a state included both town and country and that country-dwellers formed an integral part, and sometimes the more numerous part, of the citizen body. Thus all the inhabitants of Attica of freeborn native stock, wherever they lived, were members of the "*polis* of the Athenians." But the government was concentrated entirely in the town, a situation which tended to give the urban population greater political influence than the country folk. And in both town and country there would be a large number of slaves and others who lacked the franchise: even in a democracy the citizens were something of a ruling elite.

Being a member of the *polis* meant far more than just having political rights. Citizens were expected to conform to the religious observances of the state and to carry out such duties as the state demanded, especially military service. They were also bound to obey the laws, which had sacred authority over the whole political life of the state. Government was normally based on three main elements: the Assembly, which consisted of all, or a large proportion, of the citizens; the Council, a smaller body which prepared business for the Assembly; and the magistrates, the chief executive officers. The emphasis given to the different elements varied according to the nature of the constitution. If it was a democracy, the Assembly carried the greatest power; if an oligarchy ("rule by the few"), the Council. In most states there was friction between the supporters of oligarchy and the supporters of democracy – a friction which could lead to sedition and to violent changes of government. Corcyra suffered from particularly bloody factional struggles at the start of the Peloponnesian War.

Even in the Hellenistic period, when it was over-shadowed by the new kingdoms, the *polis* continued to play an important role in the Greek world. Some states, such as Rhodes, remained fully autonomous and exercised

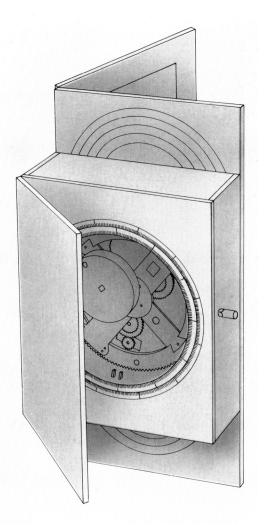

A reconstruction (after de Solla Price) of the astronomical clock from Anticythera. Made of bronze dials and cogwheels set in a wooden case, it plotted the movements of sun, moon and stars.

A fragment of an astronomical clock, found in a ship which was wrecked off the island of Anticythera in the second quarter of the 1st century BC. Now in Athens, National Archaeological Museum.

considerable power in international politics. In the Asiatic kingdoms *poleis* were deliberately propagated as an instrument of "Hellenization." These new cities obviously had no freedom of action in the field of foreign policy, but they were granted a large measure of local autonomy: they possessed their own territory, lived under their own laws and administered their own finances; they were governed by the traditional Council and magistrates, and frequently had an Assembly too; they even suffered at times from the age-old problem of inter-party strife. At the same time the title of *polis*, previously confined almost exclusively to Greek communities, was conferred upon native cities, like Sardis in Asia Minor, which were deemed to have acquired a suitable degree of Hellenism.

Religious life in the *polis* revolved primarily around the cults of the "Olympian" gods, i.e. those whose traditional abode was Mount Olympus in northern Greece – Zeus, Hera, Poseidon, Athena, Aphrodite, Demeter, Artemis,

An ox being led to sacrifice, a detail of the Athenian religious procession depicted on the frieze of the Parthenon, carved about 440 BC. British Museum.

Detail of a Panathenaic amphora, the prize for a victory in the athletic *agones* at Athens, in this instance for boxing. British Museum, 336–335 BC.

Apollo, Hestia, Hermes, Ares and Hephaestus. Other deities, notably Tyche (Fortune) in Hellenistic times, were also the subject of civic worship, but generally one or other of the Olympians predominated, being adopted as the patron god or goddess of the state. They were honored with offerings of various forms, from animal sacrifices to splendid two- or three-day festivals.

Education was distinctive in its choice of subjects. In militaristic states the main concern was training in the art of war; elsewhere the curriculum was based for a long time on the twin arts of music and athletics, proficiency in which was indispensable to the young aristocrat; it was only in Hellenistic times that the emphasis came to be placed on grammar and literature, and at a higher level on rhetoric and philosophy.

Entertainment was provided chiefly by contests (*agones*) of various forms – dramatic, choral and athletic – which were organized in connection with the great religious festivals. The "agonistic" spirit was a hallmark of the Hellenic way of life and inspired many of the Greeks' finest achievements.

Physically, the *polis* was distinguished by the layout and buildings of its urban center. This was generally provided with fortification walls and contained a citadel (the "acropolis"), a system of streets which was often (especially in the newer towns) laid out on a grid pattern, and a central square (the *agora*) which formed the focus of civic and commercial life. Around the *agora* lay *stoai* (porticoes containing shops and offices) and public buildings like the *bouleuterion* (the chamber in which the Council sat). Here, too, would be found some of the city's numerous temples, each containing the image of the deity to which it was dedicated, and each decorated with an external screen of columns in the Doric or Ionic styles. Otherwise the principal monuments were all connected with education or entertainment and were all open to the air. The *gymnasion* was a sports and cultural center containing an exercise ground (the *palaistra*), running tracks and bathing installations; the *stadion* (stadium) was the main arena for competitive athletics and particularly for foot races; and the theater, with its distinctive curving auditorium, provided the venue for dramatic performances. The bulk of the remaining structures in the town were, of course, private houses and shops – unpretentious buildings, often constructed of inferior materials like unburned brick.

Perhaps the most splendid of the Classical-Hellenistic cities was Athens. Its walls, pierced by some 15 gates, enclosed an area of about one square mile, in which the streets sprawled haphazardly around the rocky mass of the Acropolis. This was now a sacred precinct, which contained the city's most illustrious shrines and temples, three of which – the Parthenon, the Erechtheion, and the tiny temple of Athena Nike, all dating to the second half of the 5th century – are relatively well preserved. Its entrance was spanned by a monumental gateway, the Propylaia, whose north wing contained a rest house decorated with paintings – the Pinakotheke ("Picture Gallery"). To the west of the Acropolis rose the Areopagus, a rock which served as the meeting place for the old aristocratic court which tried cases of homicide; and further west lay the

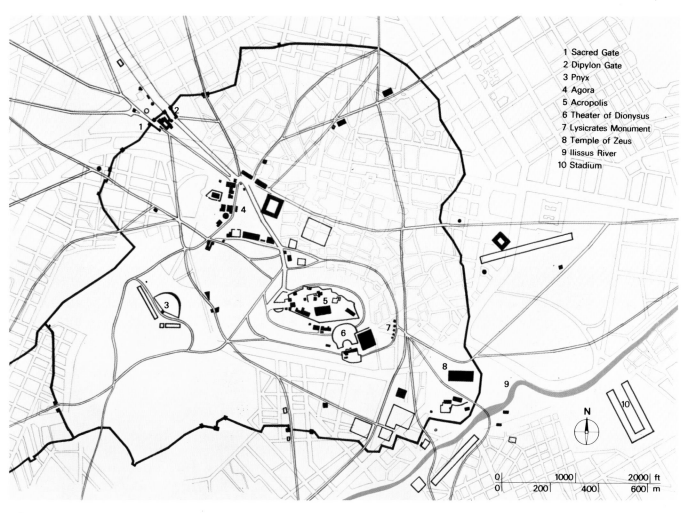

1 Sacred Gate
2 Dipylon Gate
3 Pnyx
4 Agora
5 Acropolis
6 Theater of Dionysus
7 Lysicrates Monument
8 Temple of Zeus
9 Ilissus River
10 Stadium

Above: Classical Athens, imposed on a streetplan of modern Athens. After Travlos.

Below: the "Theseum" on the hill of Kolonos Agoraios overlooking the Athenian Agora. It was dedicated to Hephaestus. 449–444 BC.

The Tower of the Winds in Athens, an octagonal structure containing a water-clock (mid-1st century BC). Each of the eight faces was decorated with a sculptured personification of one of the eight winds.

Pnyx, the semicircular arena where the citizens' Assembly held its debates. To the northwest was situated the Agora, surrounded by the usual quota of public and commercial buildings – the Bouleuterion, the Tholos (the headquarters of the chairmen of the Council), the mint, the law courts, further temples (including the finely preserved temple of Hephaestus, now popularly known as the "Theseum"), public fountain houses, and several *stoai*, of which the one on the east, donated by the Hellenistic King Attalus II of Pergamum, has recently been reconstructed. Close at hand rose the octagonal "Tower of the Winds," built in the mid-1st century BC to house an elaborate water clock.

To the south of the Acropolis stood two buildings connected with entertainment – the theater of Dionysus, home of Athens' dramatic contests, and the Odeion of Pericles, a concert hall designed for musical contests. Victors in these competitions set up commemorative monuments in the nearby "Street of the Tripods," and an exquisite little example, the cylindrical monument of Lysicrates, is still standing today. A short distance away rose the largest of Athenian temples, that of Olympian Zeus, begun in the 6th century BC but not finished till the time of the Roman Emperor Hadrian. Inside the north-west ("Dipylon") gate, in the district known as the "Kerameikos" ("Potters' Quarter"), stood the Pompeion, the building from which the great Athenian ceremonial processions started for the Acropolis. Houses and shops, finally, existed in various parts of the walled area, and several have been excavated, notably in the quarter south-west of the Agora.

Outside the walls came the cemeteries. One of the most important, the "Kerameikos cemetery," containing numerous monumental tombs of the 5th and 4th centuries, lay outside the Dipylon gate. Other extramural features included a small Ionic temple which stood, till the 18th century, by the River Ilissus southeast of the city; the Stadium, which was built in the 4th century in the same

area; and the famous suburban *gymnasia* where philosophical schools were founded – the Academy to the west, the Lykeion to the east, and Kynosarges to the southeast.

The role of archaeology. Our knowledge of Athenian buildings, whether within or without the walls, is based partly on the actual remains, partly on the evidence of ancient writings. The Tower of the Winds, for example, in addition to being excellently preserved, was described by the Roman writer Vitruvius, who reveals that it was set up by one Andronicus and was surmounted by an ornamental bronze weather vane (now missing). It is this unique combination of well-preserved remains and abundant literary testimonia that has made Athens so important in the history of Greek archaeology.

But what is true of Athens is true, to a greater or lesser degree, of other centers too. Indeed the whole progress of Greek archaeology has been conditioned by an embarrassment of riches. The study of the Greek world in Classical and Hellenistic times is dominated on the one hand by written texts, and on the other by art and architecture. For political history our primary sources are, of course, the historical and political writings of men like Thucydides and Aristotle, in conjunction with the stone-cut inscriptions which record decrees, lists of public expenditure and so forth. For social and economic history we have evidence scattered through the pages of countless ancient authors, from comic playwrights to geographers; and we have the Egyptian papyri, preserving everything from private correspondence to school exercises. Art and architecture, on the other hand, speak for themselves. They are represented by copious and often glamorous remains: great stone buildings, large-scale stone sculptures, painted pottery, metalwork and jewelry.

Much of this evidence, even the inscriptions and papyri, is archaeological, in that it consists of material relics directly bequeathed from antiquity. But precisely because it is so informative, so monumental, so glamorous, it has tended to distract students from the more mundane aspects of archaeology – e.g. the examination of apparently trivial relics; the analysis, in minute detail, of the circumstances in which an object is discovered; the development of scientific methods of dating. The importance of these aspects was first realized by researchers into other epochs and other cultures, notably prehistorians, who have no written records to help them and very few spectacular finds to seduce them. Our period has, not surprisingly, lagged behind.

Even so, much progress has been made, especially over the last 50 years. The centuries-old antiquarian tradition, essentially literary and art-historical in its coloring, has slowly given way to a much more scientific approach, in which techniques like stratification, the construction of type series, aerial survey, and chemical analysis are part of the archaeologist's stock-in-trade. In the course of the next two chapters we shall see how this change came about.

2. The Early Progress of Archaeological Research

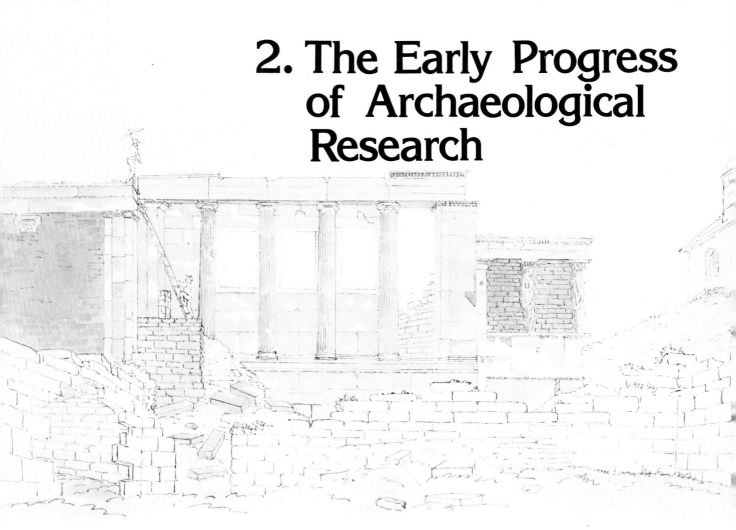

Antiquarians in antiquity. An interest in the material remains of Classical Greece goes back to the ancient world itself. Perhaps the earliest example is Thucydides' account of the city walls which were hastily erected at Athens after the retreat of the Persians in 479 (two generations before Thucydides was writing) and contained tombstones and other worked stones thrown together higgledy-piggledy. Later, as the Romans absorbed the Greek world, there developed a mania for things Greek, particularly works of art. Roman generals plundered the cities of Greece and Magna Graecia for sculptures and paintings to decorate their houses; enterprising artists set up workshops to produce copies of famous statues and "Old Masters" for the Italian market; new works were created in a consciously Classicizing manner. Such a climate naturally fostered a spirit of "archaeological" inquiry. We hear from the Roman statesman and orator Cicero how he located the tomb of Archimedes at Syracuse, hidden (unknown to the Syracusans themselves) amid the nettles and brambles of the cemetery at the Agrigento gate: "so the noblest state of Greece would have been unaware of the monument of her wisest citizen, had she not learned of it from a man from Arpinum."

But the most important antiquarian of Roman times was the Asian Greek Pausanias. Writing in the third

Elgin's trusty henchman Lusieri, umbrella in hand, working on the Erechtheion, whose remains are incorporated in the ruins of a Turkish house. Watercolor by Willam Gell in the British Museum.

quarter of the 2nd century AD, Pausanias composed an ancient Baedeker: a catalogue of the monuments of Greece, arranged as a traveler might come to them, riding along the routes between city and city, walking along the roads which linked a city center with its gates. It is a dry, matter-of-fact account; and it is by no means all about the past – modern buildings are interspersed among the old. But most of the time Pausanias is talking about monuments which were as much anterior to his own day as, say, the Black Death is to ours. He deals, too, not just with standing buildings but also with ruins, sometimes mentioned not without a touch of color – thus of a sanctuary in Boeotia he writes, "Thick, powerful ivy has grown on it, breaking it loose joint by joint, tearing it apart stone from stone." None of this, of course, is rediscovery: Classical Greek culture had lived on, unsubmerged, into Roman times, and Pausanias was an observer rather than an explorer. His antiquarian interest is confined mainly to the historical or mythological interpretation of what he saw. But as a traveler with an eye for the past Pausanias is the true ancestor of the modern pioneers of archaeology.

Dancing girls. A frieze from the Propylon (gateway) of the sanctuary of the Great Gods at Samothrace (4th century BC). Paris, Louvre.

The Renaissance. When we come to our next personality, the situation in the Greek world had totally changed. Nearly 1,300 years had elapsed; barbarians and Christians had wrought havoc among the Classical monuments; the Byzantine Empire, which had survived the fall of the Roman Empire in the west, was now on its last legs; Asiatic Greece was largely in the hands of the Turks; European Greece, itself menaced by the Turks, was divided into a number of separate states, mainly Greek, Florentine or Venetian.

It was against this background that the genial Italian merchant Cyriac of Ancona (1391–1455) spent the best part of 30 years touring Greece and the Levant. Although the main motive of his travels was trade, Cyriac lost no opportunity of sketching and recording ancient remains, especially inscriptions; he collected the results of his research in six volumes of Commentaries, combining his drawings with descriptive passages in Latin. Only one brief section from Cyriac's own hand survives; otherwise we are dependent on more or less inaccurate copies made after his death. They suggest, when carefully weighed against other evidence, that he could be a remarkably faithful reporter by the standards of his time. For instance, in recording the remains of Hellenistic ship-sheds at Oeniadae in Acarnania, he saw details which eluded the eye of Leake in the early 19th century: namely an inscription "Aristidas" (still discernible in 1903) carved in the rock-face, and the fact that a series of pilasters at the back of the building were not constructed of masonry but cut from the natural rock. In transcribing inscriptions, he was capable of misreading or omitting letters, or even of altering words which he did not understand; but we must remember that the science of recording antiquities was in its infancy and be prepared to marvel at the degree of Cyriac's accuracy rather than to cavil at his mistakes.

Despite the influence which his work exercised on humanists and artists of the late 15th century, particularly in northeast Italy, Cyriac of Ancona was to all intents and purposes an isolated phenomenon. The interest of the Italian Renaissance, now in full swing, focused on the art and monuments of the Romans. This failure to awaken to the legacy of Greece was largely a matter of taste; but there were soon additional factors at work. With the capture of Constantinople in 1453, of Athens in 1456, and of the Morea (Peloponnese) in 1458, the Turks became masters of most of the Greek world; and the long-standing antipathy between Christian and Muslim put an effective barrier between western Europe and Greece. Italian merchants and explorers turned their attention from the Levant to the western trade routes.

In the 16th century, therefore, the Greek world was virtually a closed book. Although the loquacious Ogier Ghislain de Busbecq, ambassador of the Hapsburg Emperor at Constantinople, toured Asia Minor between 1555 and 1562, collecting coins and inscriptions, most of the material with which he was concerned seems to have been Roman in date. So dark was the gloom surrounding European Greece that in the 1570s and 1580s Martin Kraus (Crusius), professor at Tübingen, had to write to correspondents in Constantinople and Greece to find out whether Athens still existed as a city. He was assured that it had a population of 12,000, with the Acropolis ("on which stands a temple to the Unknown God") occupied by Turks, and the lower town by Christians.

The 17th century. It was only in the following century that a fuller awareness of Greek antiquities began to reach the west. As early as the 1620s, Thomas Howard, 14th Earl of Arundel, formed a major collection of Greek sculpture and inscriptions from Athens and Asia Minor – a collection which turned Arundel House into an "anticipatory British Museum," but which was sadly neglected and within a few decades dispersed. Then, in the third

Cyriac of Ancona's drawing of the Samothrace frieze. He interpreted the dancing girls as muses.

quarter of the century, a spurt of activity took place in Athens. Aided by the sympathetic consuls François Châtaignier and Jean Giraud, a number of visitors, both French and English, toured the monuments and left accounts of what they saw. At the same time the priests of the religious orders lately established in the city applied themselves to the elucidation of antiquities: the Capuchins produced a panoramic plan of the city about 1670, while the Jesuit Father J. P. Babin sent his *Relation de l'état présent de la ville d'Athènes* to the Lyonnais physician Jacob Spon, who published it in 1674.

It is amusing to read some of the fanciful or erroneous ideas current at this time. The Parthenon is the "Temple of the Unknown God"; the Propylaia is the "Arsenal of

A metrological relief from the Earl of Arundel's collection, now in the Ashmolean Museum, Oxford. It gives an otherwise unknown standard for the fathom, ell and foot. 5th century BC.

Lycurgus"; the temple of Olympian Zeus is the "Palace of Hadrian" or "Theseus," raised aloft on a podium of 120 (or 366) mighty columns; the Tower of the Winds is the "Tomb of Socrates"; the monument of Lysicrates is the "Lanthorn of Demosthenes." According to Babin, Demosthenes retired to his "lantern" to cut his hair and beard; his nearby chambers must have been burned down, because "I cannot believe that he was always shut up in this little tower as if in a dungeon." Amid this welter of tomfoolery it comes as a surprise to learn that the Prussian Georg Transfeldt wrote a manuscript in 1675 in which he both read the inscription of the Lysicrates monument and correctly identified the ruins of the temple of Olympian Zeus. This manuscript remained unpublished for 200 years.

One of the problems which faced visitors was gaining admission to the Acropolis, now a Turkish fortress. Nicholas, Sieur du Loir, who came in 1641, did not succeed; the Turks were "so jealous that they hardly permit the local inhabitants to enter, and absolutely forbid foreigners to do so. We had to be content, therefore, with

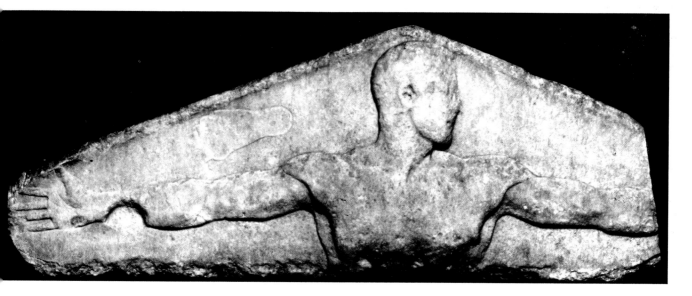

what showed from the outside and what people told us about it." Thus his account of the Parthenon is vague and totally underestimates the temple's size. In 1669 a French priest, Robert de Dreux, was at first arrested as a spy but eventually bribed the Disdar (the commander of the Turkish garrison) into admitting him; the priest was sent an ivory ring which would act as a passport for himself and six companions. In similar fashion, seven years later, Jacob Spon and George Wheler were to gain admission by gifts of coffee.

Within the Turkish fortress the ancient buildings had been effectively adapted to new purposes. The Parthenon, which had already done duty first as a Greek Orthodox, then as a Catholic church, had now become a mosque, with a minaret rising at its southwest corner. The Erechtheion was a Turkish house. The Propylaia had served as a powder magazine, with the Disdar's quarters above it; but an unfortunate explosion during an electrical storm in the 1640s had caused so much damage (besides disposing of the then Disdar and most of his family: "They were carried so far away that nothing was ever found of them," comments Spon laconically) that the armory had now been transferred to the temple of Athena Nike. Crammed in between and around these reused ancient buildings were the remaining houses and gardens of the Turkish community.

In the autumn of 1674 Charles-François Olier, Marquis de Nointel, the recently appointed French ambassador to the Sublime Porte, visited Athens bringing with him a young painter, almost certainly Jacques Carrey of Troyes, who spent 15 days on the Acropolis drawing the sculptures of the Parthenon. These drawings, invaluable since they are the most complete record of the sculptures to have survived, are remarkably accurate, considering the date at which they were produced, the shortage of time at the artist's disposal and the difficulties under which he had to work. Spon, who met Nointel in Constantinople during the following year and examined the drawings, reports: "His painter . . . almost ruined his eyesight, because he had to draw everything from the ground, without scaffolding." Anyone who has attempted to study the remains of the west frieze today, even in the far more favorable lighting conditions which have obtained since the loss of much of the ceiling, will appreciate Carrey's achievement. His vantage-points would, moreover, have been restricted by the presence of Turkish houses, not to mention the mistrust of Turkish householders.

In all, something like 55 drawings were produced in the 15 days; 35 are extant. Executed stylishly in a combination of red and black pencil, they show the sculptures of the two pediments, the south metopes and over half the frieze, exactly as they were in 1674 – cracks, missing limbs and all. We learn that the central part of the east pediment was already lost (it had probably fallen victim to the apse of the Christian church) but that the remaining figures were still largely intact; that the west pediment lacked only Poseidon's chariot team and other minor elements; that the south metopes were all in place and well preserved; and that most of the frieze too had survived unscathed. The drawings acquire additional importance from the fact that the next century or so saw the destruction or removal of most of the sculptures which they portrayed. We are fortunate to have them; of all Carrey's other drawings of Greek antiquities a mere handful remain.

Of scarcely less importance than the Carrey drawings are the records of the visitors who came to Athens in the following two years. In 1675 Francis Vernon made notes and drawings which were never published. Then in 1676 came Spon and Wheler, who were engaged in a grand archaeological tour of Greece and Asia Minor – a tour whose outcome was the publication of two books, Spon's *Voyage d'Italie, de Dalmatie, de Grèce, et du Levant fait aux années 1675 et 1676* (published in 1678) and Wheler's *A Journey into Greece* (1682), which inaugurated a whole new genre of literature on Greek antiquities: the antiquarian travelogue. The two travelers report their journeys from place to place, describe the monuments and inscriptions which they saw, illustrate them with more or less schematic engravings, and launch into etymological and historical digressions in a manner which would have pleased Pausanias. Outside Athens, they provide valuable information on the archaeological remains then existing at various important sites, such as Delos – even though they were not always successful in their searches for particular monuments. At Ephesus, like many travelers after them, they were led into the ruins of a Roman bath complex in the belief that it was the temple of Artemis. At Delphi they failed to find any clear indications of the temple of Apollo: "The thing which I found the most bizarre," writes Spon, "is that the most famous place in the world has suffered such a reversal of fortune, that we were obliged to look for Delphi in Delphi itself, and to ask where the temple was when we were standing on its foundations."

It was at Athens that their most important contributions were made. Spon often falls into error, but his is the first detailed study of the Athenian monuments by a writer who combines a good knowledge of ancient literature with some idea of critical method. So he dismisses the nonsense that the "Palace of Hadrian" was raised in the air on a podium of columns, and he reads the inscription on the Lysicrates monument and realizes that it commemorated a theatrical victory. On the Acropolis, he identifies the temple of Athena Nike and the Erechtheion, and gives the most detailed description of the Parthenon yet to appear, complete with fairly accurate measurements. The work of Spon remained the basis of all discussions on Athenian antiquities for a century or more.

Eleven years after Spon and Wheler climbed the Acropolis, disaster struck the monuments. Threatened by a Venetian attack, the Turks had strengthened the fortifications of the Acropolis, dismantling the temple of Athena Nike to build a new bastion in front of the

Propylaia, and removing their powder store from this temple to the north porch of the Erechtheion. But some powder and munitions were also stored in the Parthenon, and on 26 September a well-aimed cannonball from the besiegers ignited it, causing an explosion which blew out the central part of the temple, wrecked the surrounding houses and started a fire that raged for two days. The Erechtheion, too, seems to have been damaged, though the main powder store was spared. After the inevitable Turkish surrender, the victorious Venetians moved in. Their occupation produced a flurry of reports and other documents which either glossed over or sought to excuse the destruction of the Parthenon; but at the same time several drawings and engravings were made which depict the bombardment with obvious relish.

The effects of the siege on the Parthenon sculptures had been disastrous: on the north and south flanks of the temple long stretches of the frieze and all the central metopes were blown to smithereens. To make matters worse, the Venetian general Morosini later made an attempt to lower Athena's horses from the west pediment, no doubt desiring to emulate a predecessor who had taken to Venice the great bronze horses from the Hippodrome in Constantinople. His tackle snapped and the horses were smashed. By April 1688 the occupation force had withdrawn from Athens, leaving the Parthenon a ruined shell, with its remaining sculptures "continually exposed to the vandalism of stone-robbers, lime-burners, curio-hunters and religious iconoclasts."

The temple of Olympian Zeus in Athens, begun in the 6th century BC but not finished until the time of Hadrian. The ruins were correctly identified by Georg Transfeldt in 1675.

The 18th century. The first half of the 18th century was a quiet period. The Turks regained control of the Morea; but Greek antiquities continued to arrive in western Europe, and travelers continued to visit Greek archaeological sites. J. Pitton de Tournefort, for instance, toured the Aegean islands between 1700 and 1702, writing a description of the remains on Delos; Richard Pococke saw

The bombardment of the Athenian Acropolis during the siege of 1687. In this engraving published by Fanelli in 1707 we see the trajectories of cannonballs fired by the Venetian batteries.

VEDUTA DEL CAST: D'ACROPOLIS DALLA PARTE DI TRAMONTANA
308

the islands, the Asian sites and European Greece in 1739 and 1740 on the way back from a tour of Egypt and the Near East; and Richard Dalton went to Asia Minor and Athens during a similar wide-ranging trip in 1749. Both Pococke and Dalton presented plans and views of the monuments in Athens, though Dalton's most notable contribution is, perhaps, to have been the first to publish drawings of the reliefs from the Mausoleum at Halicarnassus which were built into the walls of the castle at Bodrum in southwest Turkey.

From the 1750s, however, Greek art and architecture began to overtake Roman as the focus of antiquarian study. The personalities with whom we associate this development are, in Italy, the German Winckelmann and, in Greece, the Englishmen Stuart and Revett.

Johann Joachim Winckelmann (1717–68) was a self-made man who in his spare time acquired a phenomenal knowledge of the ancient writers and applied himself with fresh eyes to the study of ancient art. To him belongs the credit for having distinguished stylistic phases in Classical art and for having realized that a large proportion of the works of art in the great Italian collections were Roman copies or adaptations of originals produced by the Greeks.

His ideas were embodied in his magnum opus, *History of Ancient Art* (1764), in which he also studied the political, social and intellectual background to creative activity in ancient Greece. Although Winckelmann never visited Greece and was brutally murdered at a hotel in Trieste while still at the height of his powers, his work can be said to have done more than almost anything else to arouse western Europe to the true importance of Greek art and archaeology. Thus artists and scholars now became aware of the long-neglected Greek temples at Paestum in southern Italy, which Winckelmann himself had admired; the great engraver Giovanni Battista Piranesi (1720–78) made drawings there in the year of his death. And art-historians now began to recognize copies of the Greek statues famed in ancient literature – the Tyche of Antioch, Praxiteles' Cnidian Aphrodite, Myron's Diskobolos.

At the same time an ideal climate was created for the reception of the drawings made by Stuart and Revett. James Stuart (1713–88) and Nicholas Revett (1720–1804) met in Rome while studying painting, and together with Gavin Hamilton in 1748 they formulated their "Proposals for publishing an accurate description of the Antiquities of Athens." Assisted by financial support from Lord Charle-

Opposite: drawing by Piranesi of the temple of "Poseidon" (actually Hera) at Paestum (1778).

Right: Stuart's drawing of the Monument of Lysicrates, incorporated in the house of the Capuchin friars in Athens. The hollow upper part served as the Superior's library.

mont, the Earl of Malton and other wealthy backers, they spent the years 1751–55 in Athens and other Greek centers carrying out a program of detailed measurement and drawing, the fruits of which were the great folio volumes *The Antiquities of Athens* which began in 1762 and were only completed in 1816.

Stuart and Revett were primarily architects rather than archaeologists, and their main concern was to provide exemplars for the British architects of their day, a principle which left no room for romance or approximation. For each building considered, the editors showed a view of its present condition and the actual modern setting (they had no time for the evocative landscapes employed by Dalton and the French architect Le Roy); elevations, sections and plans with measurements in minute detail; and individual architectural elements, including any sculptural adornment which survived. Throughout, they laid down rigorous standards of scientific observation and recording, making a careful distinction, for example, between visible and conjectural features. They even indulged in some excavation when this was necessary to obtain a full elevation: "We have carefully examined as low as to the foundation of every building that we have copied, tho' to perform this, it was generally necessary to get a great quantity of earth and rubbish removed; an operation which was sometimes attended with very considerable expense." The lengths to which Stuart and Revett were prepared to go is shown in the chapter on the Tower of the Winds, where Stuart reports that they demolished a house which obscured two of the monument's reliefs and built a new one with a window specially positioned "to give

future travellers a distinct view of those figures."

The text of the early volumes, written by Stuart, contains its mistakes and misinterpretations, but the importance of the *Antiquities* lies in Revett's architectural drawings. As a corpus of information on certain Greek buildings, these have never been wholly superseded. Volume I includes the temple on the Ilissus, the Tower of the Winds, and the monument of Lysicrates; volume II the Parthenon, the Erechtheion and the Propylaia; volume III the "Theseum," the temple of Olympian Zeus, and various remains on Delos. The full value of their records was amply illustrated by the destruction in 1778 of the little temple on the Ilissus to provide building material for the city walls.

As an example to their age, the *Antiquities* achieved everything that the authors could have wished. English architects began to look for inspiration in the austerity of the Greek ideal; Stuart and Revett themselves were commissioned to carry out a number of projects in imitation of Greek buildings – one may cite Stuart's replica of the Tower of the Winds at Shugborough in Staffordshire. At the same time, the impetus was given for further exploration and recording of the Greek monuments.

One of the prime moving forces in this work was the Society of Dilettanti. "In the year 1734, some gentlemen who had travelled in Italy, desirous of encouraging, at home, a taste for those objects which had contributed so much to their entertainment abroad, formed themselves into a society, under the name of the Dilettanti, and agreed upon such regulations as they thought necessary to keep up the spirit of their scheme." Spurred on by the success of Stuart's and Revett's expedition, the Society resolved in 1764 to send an expedition of their own "to some parts of the East, in order to collect informations, and to make observations, relative to the ancient state of those countries, and to such monuments of antiquity as are still remaining." The result was Chandler's expedition to Ionia and Greece from 1764 to 1766. Richard Chandler, 26 years old at the start of the trip, was an Oxford don who had just made a name for himself by his publication of the ancient sculptures owned by the University; he was accompanied by Revett, who was to act as the mission's architect, and William Pars, the mission's painter. Together they inaugurated the *Antiquities of Ionia* (the Dilettanti's answer to the *Antiquities of Athens*), which began in 1769 and continued through five large folio volumes to 1915. Among the important monuments to receive a scientific treatment in volume I were the temple of Athena Polias at Priene and the temple of Apollo at Didyma.

Chandler also produced a continuous account of the mission's journeys in his *Travels in Asia Minor* and *Travels in Greece*, books which are among the most readable of their genre and contain vivid word-pictures of the sites, as well as many valuable contributions to the study of Greek topography. Chandler was the first to locate the site of Olympia; and in Athens he correctly identified the Pnyx (previously regarded as the 2nd-century AD Odeion of Herodes Atticus), the Odeion of Herodes Atticus (previously regarded as the theater of Dionysus), and the theater of Dionysus (previously overlooked). He also obtained permission for Pars, who seems to have spurned all discomfort and danger in his professional zeal (he eventually died of a chill contracted while standing in water to do a drawing in Italy), to make the first close-up drawings of the Parthenon sculptures. "His post was generally on the architrave of the colonnade, many feet from the ground, where he was exposed to gusts of wind, and to accidents in passing to and fro." As with Elgin's draftsmen 35 years later, there were Turkish objections to this lofty vantage-point. "Several of the Turks murmured, and some threatened, because he overlooked their houses, obliging them to confine or remove the women, to prevent their being seen from that exalted station." Objections notwithstanding, Pars "designed one hundred and ninety-six feet of bass-reliefs in the Acropolis." He also drew the sculptures of the "Theseum." His drawings, accurate and beautifully executed, are reproduced in volumes II and IV of the *Antiquities of Athens*, where, however, much of their subtlety is destroyed by the metallic harshness of the engraver's technique.

In the years following Chandler's journeys the passion for Greek antiquities grew apace in west European artistic and scholarly circles. For the first time, collectors began to take serious note of painted vases. Sir William Hamilton, British envoy at Naples from 1764 to 1800, made two large collections, mostly of south Italian red-figure ware,

Stuart's replica of the Tower of the Winds at Shugborough, Staffordshire, England. Built in the 1760s.

and saw that they were presented to the world with lavish illustrations in two *de luxe* four-volume publications. His object, again, was to furnish models for practicing craftsmen, and indeed Josiah Wedgwood was duly inspired to launch his famous "Etruscan" pottery; but, as with Stuart and Revett, the new standard of recording and publication also marked a turning-point in the study of antiquities for their own sake.

But it was in Athens, cultural capital of ancient Greece, where bribery could circumvent a Turkish embargo on the removal of ancient stones from the Acropolis, that the collectors were primarily interested. Chandler relates how, in the winter of 1765–66, he purchased inscriptions from Turkish householders, including two which were brought down stealthily, with the connivance of the Disdar, while the Turks were at their devotions in the mosque. Similarly, fallen fragments of the Parthenon sculptures found their way to various parts of western Europe.

But the most avid collectors were ambassadors. While Sir Richard Worsley, British ambassador in Venice, acquired a few sculptures during a visit to Greece in 1785, the newly appointed French ambassador at Constantinople, the Comte de Choiseul-Gouffier, took advantage of France's influence with the Turkish Empire to obtain permission for his agent, the painter Louis François Sébastien Fauvel, to draw and make casts of antiquities in

Above : watercolor by William Pars of the remains of the temple of Apollo at Didyma. British Museum.

Right : drawing of Lord Elgin, about 1795, when he was 28 or 29. By G. P. Harding after Anton Graff. British Museum.

Athens. He added a specific brief to plunder. "Remove all that you can. Don't neglect any opportunity to pillage all that is pillageable in Athens and its territory. Spare neither the dead nor the living." Fauvel did his master proud. Though not allowed to remove any sculptures still in position on the Parthenon, he bribed the Disdar into letting him have a frieze slab and a metope which had been dug up among the ruins, and in 1788 bought a metope which had fallen during a storm. He also acquired sculptures from many other sources and shipped them back to France for Choiseul-Gouffier's collection.

Elgin. Then in 1801 it was the turn of the British ambassador Lord Elgin, benefiting from an improvement in relations between Britain and Turkey. He had already sent a team of artists, draftsmen and cast-makers to the Acropolis under the Italian landscape-painter Giovanni Battista Lusieri, but they had been harassed in their work by the Disdar and his troops; now Elgin procured a *firman*, a letter of authorization from the Grand Vizier, which removed all obstacles from their path. It instructed the Voivode (civil governor) of Athens: ". . . as long as the said painters shall be employed in going in and out of the said citadel of Athens, which is the place of their occupations; and in fixing scaffolding round the ancient Temple of the Idols there; and in moulding the ornamental sculpture and visible figures thereon, in plaster or gypsum; and in measuring the remains of other old ruined buildings there; and in excavating when they find it necessary the foundations, in order to discover inscriptions which may have been covered in the rubbish; that no interruption may be given them, nor any obstacle thrown in their way by the Disdar or any other person; that no one may meddle with the scaffolding or implements they may require in their works; and that when they wish to take away any pieces of stone with old inscriptions or figures thereon, that no opposition be made thereto."

Elgin's enthusiastic chaplain, Philip Hunt, who took the *firman* to Athens, made sure, by a combination of threats and bribes, that a liberal interpretation was put on the document's terms, and within 10 days metopes were being removed from the Parthenon itself. The next four years saw the lowering of almost all the more presentable sculpture which still remained on the temple – a task which inevitably caused much damage to the surviving fabric, notably to the cornice, which was virtually destroyed. Travelers of the period were scandalized by what was going on. A French visitor was moved to write,

"It is a sad thing to remark that the civilized peoples of Europe have caused more harm to the monuments of Athens in the space of 150 years than all the barbarians together over a period of several centuries. It is hard to think that Alaric and Mahomet II respected the Parthenon, yet it has been overturned by Morosini and Lord Elgin."

It was not only the Parthenon that attracted the attention of Elgin's minions. Elements were taken from the Propylaia and the temple of Athena Nike; while Hunt even conceived the idea of removing the whole Erechtheion and shipping it to England. But no ships were available, so Lusieri's men had to be content with one of the caryatids from the south porch, one of the columns from the east portico, and a few other specially selected architectural members.

Nor was the program of work limited to taking pieces from upstanding monuments. A good deal of excavation was undertaken in the environs of the Parthenon and in other promising spots. Not, of course, excavation of a scientific nature, but hole-digging in search of further sculptures and other antiquities. It proved profitable enough, yielding fragments of statues from the west pediment of the temple, as well as coins and a fine haul of painted vases.

The ethics of Elgin's treatment of the Parthenon have long been debated. In his defense it may be said that much sculpture was spared from the lime-burners and the shellings during the Greek War of Independence. At all events, after a long series of mischances, including the wreck and subsequent salvaging of a shipload of marbles off Cythera, and the imprisonment of Elgin himself in France on his way back to England, the sculptures were eventually sold to the British government and exhibited in

the British Museum. They thus gave a tremendous boost to what was fast becoming one of the foremost of all collections of Greek antiquities. Founded in 1759, at a time when royal and public museums were growing up in various parts of Europe, the British Museum had already acquired Hamilton's first vase collection and the sculptures from the temple of Apollo Epikourios at Bassae.

Bassae. The excavation at Bassae, along with that of the Archaic temple of Aphaea on Aegina, was the first truly international enterprise in Greek archaeology. The site, isolated in the Arcadian hills, had been discovered in 1765 by a French architect, Joachim Bocher, who had described it to Chandler, and returned in 1770 to carry out a fuller investigation, only to be murdered by bandits. Now it aroused the interest of a group of young architects and travelers which included the Bavarian Baron Carl Haller von Hallerstein, the Britons C. R. Cockerell and J. Foster, the Estonian Baron Otto Magnus von Stackelberg, the Dane P. O. Bröndsted, and the Württemberger J. Linckh. After a preliminary visit in the late summer of 1811, during which they made some measurements and drawings, and Cockerell by dint of crawling into a fox's lair among the rubble found one of the carved slabs of the frieze, members of the team returned in 1812 to complete their work. Armed with an authorization from the governor of the Morea, Vili Pasha, who stipulated only that he should receive one half of the proceeds, they overcame local opposition and spent three months at Bassae, with a work force of 50 to 80 laborers living in a temporary village of huts covered with oak-branches. Both Cockerell and Stackelberg have left colorful accounts of the folk-dances, the rustic music, the roasted lambs and kids and "the generous contributions of Bacchus, proffered to us, as is still the custom, in the primitive goat's skin" which helped to enliven their weeks of labor.

The results of the excavation were spectacular. On the one hand, the temple's unusual plan was recovered, along with most of the architectural elements (including the earliest known Corinthian capital, and possible fragments of two more). All of these were recorded with the scientific exactitude which had been laid down by Stuart and Revett, and, as a consequence, it was possible to attempt detailed reconstruction drawings of elevations and sections – drawings bedeviled, however, by the notion, common in the 19th century, that the *cella* (the central hall) of this and other temples must have been open to the air.

On the other hand, the excavators procured a rich haul of sculptures – the continuous frieze, 31 meters long, which ran round the interior of the *cella*; fragments of the cult statue which stood behind the *cella*; and parts of the metopes from above the front and rear porches. Vili Pasha was so disappointed to find that they were not gold and silver that he sold his interest in them and sanctioned the

Above: the temple of Apollo at Bassae (last quarter of 5th century BC). Designed by Ictinus, the architect of the Parthenon, it contained the earliest known Corinthian capital.

Below: drawing of excavations in progress at Bassae. From C. R. Cockerell, *The Temples of Jupiter Panhellenius and of Apollo Epicurius* (1860).

export of the whole lot; they were carried the 13 miles to the coast by 150 peasants, six to eight men to a slab, and loaded on to a British ship which conveyed them to the island of Zacynthus, then under British occupation. On the way they narrowly escaped the efforts of Vili Pasha's successor to stop the export taking place. According to one story, the sculptures were still being loaded on the shore when the Turkish troops arrived, and the Corinthian capital had to be abandoned in the rush. But this is probably a highly colored version of events (there is some evidence, for instance, that the capital had been left in the ruins of the temple). At Zacynthus the sculptures were auctioned and bought by the British government for 60,000 dollars.

19th-century travelers. The first 20 years of the 19th century were something of a heyday for travelers in both European Greece and Asia Minor (despite the ever-present dangers of fever, insurrection, bandits, pirates and shipwreck to which their writings bear witness). Edward Dodwell, who toured Greece twice between 1801 and 1806, excavated eagerly in Attica and the Corinth area, amassed a large collection of antiquities and made many drawings of "Cyclopean Remains in Greece," including Classical and Hellenistic fortifications. He also offered one or two useful contributions to the study of the Athenian Acropolis, rejecting the long-standing idea that two of the figures in the Parthenon's west pediment represented the Roman Emperor Hadrian and his consort Sabina, and observing the molded blocks of an earlier temple in the Parthenon's foundations. William (soon Sir William) Gell accompanied Dodwell and carried out topographical researches; then in 1811, along with the architects J. P. Gandy and F. Bedford, he was sent on the Society of Dilettanti's second Ionian mission, with instructions to correct errors in the work of Chandler's mission and to examine the buildings in more detail by means of excavation. The result was a new and better edition of the first two volumes of the *Antiquities of Ionia*. Meanwhile, some interest was being taken in the monuments of Greek Sicily. In 1812 Cockerell, discoverer of the Bassae sculptures, studied and measured the fortifications at Syracuse and collected material for an attempted reconstruction of the temple of Olympian Zeus at Agrigento.

But the most important traveler of the period was Colonel William Martin Leake (1777–1860). Journeying almost continuously in Greece and Asia Minor between 1800 and 1810, and collating information from the accounts of other travelers, he became the leading authority on the topography of the Greek world and can be regarded as the true founder of the science of ancient topography. The nucleus of his work was its maps, compiled with unprecedented detail and precision. His map of the Peloponnese, for example, was "the result of more than fifteen hundred measurements with the sextant and theodolite, made from every important geodaesic

station, which circumstances would admit of my employing, corrected or confirmed by a few good observations of latitude."

His examination of the topography of Athens, too, provides an object lesson in sound scholarly method. Working without preconceptions from a thorough knowledge of Pausanias and other ancient writers and of the existing archaeological remains, he carried out the most far-reaching survey of the Athenian monuments yet undertaken. The Athenian Agora was correctly located (though extended too far to the southwest); the positions of the Kerameikos, the Dipylon gate and the Piraeus gate were all correctly deduced; the case for placing the temple of Athena Nike to the south of the Propylaia and putting the Pinakotheke in the Propylaia's north wing was argued with irrefutable logic. Henceforth Leake's work was the inevitable starting-point for all studies of the Athenian monuments.

The liberation of Greece. In 1821 began the bloody War of Greek Independence, which dragged on till 1832; archaeological studies were hampered, and the antiquities suffered new casualties. But one positive benefit was the occupation of the Morea by a French force which brought with it a scientific expedition. The archaeological section of this expedition, under the leadership of Abel Blouet, toured the peninsula from 1829 to 1831, compiling data for a detailed new map, making drawings of the monuments, copying inscriptions, and carrying out excavations, notably at Olympia, where they partially cleared the buried remains of the temple of Zeus. The published drawings of this excavation show that the trenches had an irregularity which would be unacceptable today, but the temple's plan was recovered, drawings of elevations and sections were attempted, and the first fragments of the sculptured metopes were unearthed.

After its liberation from the Turks, the new kingdom of Greece came under the rule of the Bavarian Otho I (1832–62) and a new impetus was given to archaeology. The first major effect was the removal of the Turkish structures on the Acropolis and the almost symbolic freeing of the Periclean monuments – a task carried out under the direction of the volatile Ludwig Ross (1806–59). Born in a village in Holstein, Ross had first studied medicine (he gave it up after fainting at his first section), had then turned to ornithology, and finally to philology and epigraphy; he had received a travel grant from the king of Denmark and in 1832 went to Greece, where two years later, at the age of 28, he was appointed Ephor-General of Antiquities in Athens. It was Ross who prevented the erection of the royal palace on the Acropolis and began the conversion of the rock from a fortress into a

Opposite: the temple of Athena Nike in Athens (c. 427–424 BC). The tiny Ionic temple on the southwest corner of the Acropolis had been dismembered by the Turks and was completely reconstructed after Ross had begun clearing the Acropolis in the 1830s.

showpiece of ancient architecture. The steps of the Parthenon were uncovered, the Propylaia was freed from its blocking-walls and bastions, most of the members of the Nike temple were retrieved and the building was reconstructed on its original foundations. Later, after Ross's resignation in 1836, the Erechtheion was similarly disentangled and rebuilt. The excavations which accompanied these projects yielded a number of important discoveries. In addition to finding more Parthenon sculptures and fragments of many inscriptions, including the lists recording Athena's share of the tribute paid by Athens' subject states in the 5th century BC, Ross confirmed that the foundations of the Parthenon incorporated the substructure of an earlier temple and established the existence of an older Propylon beneath the Periclean Propylaia. He also discovered sherds of red-figure pottery in the debris caused by the Persian sack of the Acropolis in 480 BC – a find which was crucial for the chronology of Attic vase-painting, but which was for a long time largely neglected.

The first archaeologists. An event of importance in the emergence of an archaeological awareness in Greece was the foundation of the Greek Archaeological Society in 1837. This society was destined to play a leading role in the study of Greek antiquities – a role which it still performs today.

While the new nation was cutting its archaeological teeth, a series of major explorations began in Turkey. Their primary object was to acquire material for European museums. Thus Charles Texier, who had carried out a survey of the monuments of Asia Minor on behalf of the French government between 1833 and 1837, returned in 1842 to superintend the excavation of the frieze sculptures of the temple of Artemis at Magnesia and saw them transported to the Louvre in Paris. But the chief beneficiary of the work in Turkey was the British Museum. In 1846 it received, as a present from the British ambassador at Constantinople, Viscount Stratford de Redcliffe, the Mausoleum reliefs which had been built into the walls of the castle at Bodrum; and soon afterwards its stock of 4th-century material was greatly swollen by the excavations of Newton, Pullan and Wood.

Charles Thomas Newton (1816–94), who investigated several sites, including Cnidos, whence he procured the famous statue of Demeter, is best known for his discovery and excavation of the Mausoleum at Halicarnassus, a project rendered romantic by the monument's status as one of the Seven Wonders of the Ancient World. Plundered and destroyed by the Knights of St John in the 16th century, the Mausoleum had disappeared almost beyond trace. Different visitors located it in different places. Newton, however, working from a passage of the Roman writer Vitruvius and a scatter of Ionic architectural fragments visible on the surface, plumped for a spot covered by Turkish houses and gardens and, armed with

Statue of Demeter from Cnidos, discovered by Newton. The seated goddess, 1·53 meters high, was carved from Parian marble, perhaps by Leochares, c. 340–330 BC. British Museum.

men and money from the British government, started digging in January 1857. Within a few days,

"I came to several small fragments broken off from a frieze in high relief. One of these, a foot, had a piece of moulding attached, which I at once recognized as identical with that of the slabs of frieze removed from the castle in 1846. This was enough to convince me that I was on the right track, and that the site of the Mausoleum could not be far off."

What he found was in fact the western edge of the great sunken quadrangle in which the Mausoleum's foundations and basement had been set. Further to the north, digging by means of tunnels to avoid the objections of the landowners, he found the monumental staircase which had descended to the tomb chamber of Mausolus and the great block of green stone which had closed the chamber's entrance. To the south, he came upon the southwest corner of the foundation, and, computing the lengths of the sides from information given by the Roman encyclopedist Pliny, he located the northwest and southeast angles. He was now able to purchase and demolish the houses which stood on the site and lay bare the whole area.

Although all but the lowest courses of the foundations had been taken for building-material by the knights and the Turks, a rich harvest of sculptures was recovered, including several frieze slabs and fragments of the chariot group of Mausolus and his queen Artemisia which crowned the monument. There were also sufficient architectural fragments for Newton's architect, Richard Popplewell Pullan, to make, with the aid of Pliny's description, detailed drawings for a suggested reconstruction. To his credit, Newton did not regard the site merely as a quarry for works of art, but published the scanty remains of the architecture with a thoroughness exemplary for his time. Careful plans and sections of the site itself were accompanied by drawings of individual stone blocks and lithographs made from photographs taken during the excavation.

Pullan was later put in charge of the Society of Dilettanti's third Ionian mission and, between 1862 and 1869, carried out surveys and excavations in the temples of Dionysus at Teos, Apollo Smintheus in the Troad, and Athena Polias at Priene. It is encouraging to learn that he "made his excavations with care, dividing up the ground into squares of 10 feet and noting the position of fragments found." A huge quantity of these fragments came to the British Museum. From Priene alone 91 cases were carted away on horseback and 20 on camelback.

Pullan was a paragon of virtue compared with John Turtle Wood, the excavator of Ephesus. Wood was an

Left: portrait statue of Mausolus from the Mausoleum at Halicarnassus (mid-4th century BC). Found together with a female statue and the remains of a marble chariot on the north side of the Mausoleum, this figure was originally ascribed to the chariot group which crowned the monument. It now seems more probable that they occupied a lower position, perhaps in the interior. Twice life-size (2·99 meters high). British Museum.

Below: the great blocking stone at the entrance of the tomb chamber in the Mausoleum at Halicarnassus, along with two of Newton's team of sailors from the British fleet. From C. T. Newton, *A History of Discoveries at Halicarnassus, Cnidus and Branchidae* (1862).

The discovery of the temple of Artemis at Ephesus. Wood's archaeological methods are well illustrated by this woodcut from his *Discoveries at Ephesus* (1877).

engineer whose life's dream was to discover the temple of Artemis, another of the Seven Wonders of the World. His long quest and eventual success have been aptly described as "one of the romances of archaeology."

Although no trace of the temple survived, ancient writers revealed that it lay outside the Hellenistic and Roman city, to which it was connected by a road running from the Magnesian gate. Wood's obvious policy was to locate the Magnesian gate, but for some reason he did not immediately investigate the Magnesia (southeastern) side of the city. Starting to dig in 1863, he eventually located an inscription telling of an annual procession from the temple to the theater which entered the city through the Magnesian gate and left via the Coressian gate. In 1867–68 Wood found the Magnesian and Coressian gates on the east side of the city and pursued the roads outside them till in 1869 he struck the wall which enclosed the precinct of Artemis. Its identity was conveniently corroborated by a pair of inscriptions. By the end of the year he had located the temple itself. From then until 1874 Wood concentrated on clearing the temple and trying to elucidate its plan and structural sequence, in so far as the adverse conditions and the chaotic state of his excavations permitted.

Wood's account of his work makes absorbing reading; one cannot help but admire his fortitude in the face of constant difficulties. He broke his collarbone when his horse fell in a ditch; he narrowly escaped death when knifed by a maniac in Izmir; he faced several threats of violence, suffered numerous bouts of fever, endured repeated interference from the Turkish authorities. His workmen went on strike, engaged in violent brawls, even buried a dead man in the excavations. Wood's perseverance and resourcefulness amid these trials and tribulations are quite remarkable. But as an archaeologist he committed some of the cardinal sins. He dug holes more or less at random, often without the landowner's permission; he rarely bothered to fill them in; he left his workers without the supervision of a trained archaeologist; he failed to shore up the sides of his trenches adequately (one man was killed by a collapse). Worst of all he never published a precise account or proper plans of his work. It was left to later researchers to examine and survey the site in a more scientific manner and to correct Wood's errors of interpretation.

It would be wrong, however, to regard Wood's excavations as typical of the third quarter of the century. The work of Ross in Athens and Newton at Halicarnassus had set better examples; and the excavations at Olympia in the 1870s were to make considerable progress towards the modern ideal.

Olympia

Olympia was the site of the most celebrated of the Greek religious festivals. Situated in the fertile valley of the River Alpheus, about 20 kilometers from the west coast of the Peloponnese, it was neither centrally placed nor easily accessible to the majority of Greeks; so its rise to preeminence in Hellenic religious life was as irrational as that of, say, Canterbury in the English Church. Every four years delegates and visitors from all over Hellas came to attend the festival, and more particularly to watch and compete in the athletic contests which were offered to the sanctuary's presiding deity, Zeus. These games, the ancestors of our modern Olympics, included chariot- and horse-racing, foot-races, jumping, wrestling and boxing; and there were events for both men and boys. In view of its ancient role, Olympia is a unique archaeological site. It was not a city-state (in fact it lay, in Classical and Hellenistic times, within the territory of Elis, which administered the festival), and it contained no domestic buildings in the normal sense: the buildings identified in the excavations are all connected, to a greater or lesser extent, with religion or athletics. In the reconstructed model (*below*), which shows Olympia in Roman times, the central building (white-roofed because it was tiled with marble) is the temple of Zeus; above it is the smaller temple of Hera; and at the top right is a row of treasuries in which various states placed devotional offerings. Dotted around are innumerable statues in honor of victorious athletes. Further out, outside the sanctuary proper, lie the purely secular buildings – the Palaistra and Gymnasion (top left) the Leonidaion (bottom left) and the Bouleuterion (bottom). The Stadium is off the picture to the right.

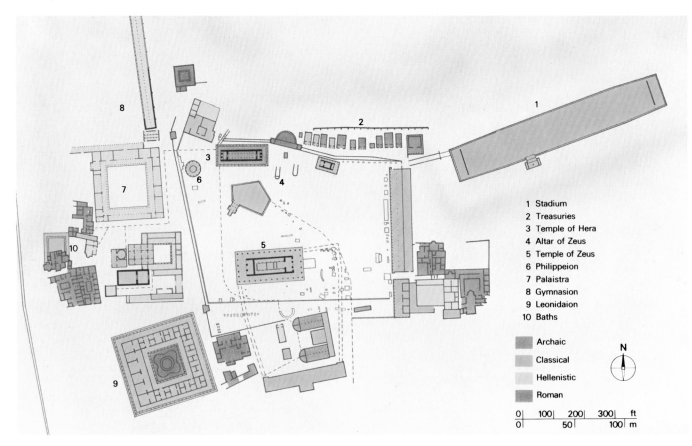

1	Stadium
2	Treasuries
3	Temple of Hera
4	Altar of Zeus
5	Temple of Zeus
6	Philippeion
7	Palaistra
8	Gymnasion
9	Leonidaion
10	Baths

Archaic
Classical
Hellenistic
Roman

N

| 0 | 100 | 200 | 300 | ft |
| 0 | | 50 | | 100 | m |

Above: plan of the excavations. Many of the structures recovered date from Roman times, notably from the time of Nero, who competed in the chariot-race.

Below: aerial view. The Stadium, which originally started near the temple of Zeus, was pushed further east in the 4th century BC and separated from the sanctuary by a *stoa*.

The temple of Zeus, erected between 470 and 456 BC, was the religious focus of Olympia. The largest Doric building of continental Greece at the time of its construction, it was elaborately decorated with sculptures and is often regarded as the canonical Doric temple. *Above:* a cross-section illustrates the structure of the building. Seated at the back of the *cella* is the colossal gold-and-ivory statue of Zeus, the masterpiece of the Athenian sculptor Phidias. Recent excavations in Phidias' workshop show that this statue was not executed till 20 or 30 years after the temple was completed. *Below:* the sculptures of the east pediment, which showed the prelude to the chariot-race between Pelops and Oenomaus, the legendary antecedent of the chariot-races in the Olympic Games. The arrangement of the figures shown here is probably incorrect in some details.

Above: head of Apollo, the central statue in the west pediment of the Zeus temple. Apollo presides, unseen, over the legendary battle between the Lapiths and the half-horse, half-human centaurs – a conflict which symbolized the victory of civilization (Lapiths) over barbarity (centaurs) and was thus popular in 5th-century art as an allegory of the Greek victory over the Persians. The west pediment is a landmark in the history of Greek sculpture, because of its experiments with drapery in movement and with overlapping and interlocking postures. Apollo himself, austere and aloof, is one of the most impressive statues of the early Classical period.

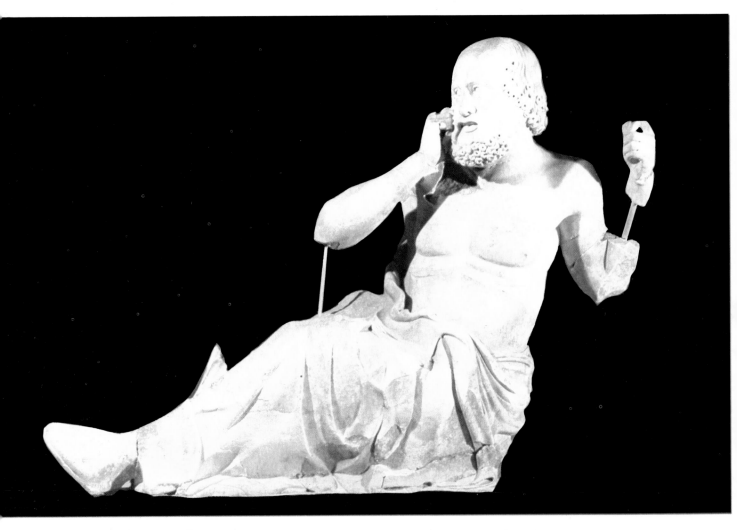

Above: the figure of a seer from the east pediment of the Zeus
temple. Foretelling the fate of his master Oenomaus, who is
about to be defeated and killed in the chariot-race with
Pelops, the old man draws back in alarm and raises his right
hand to his chin; this gesture, together with his creased brow
and part-open mouth, shows an interest in the portrayal of
expression which is characteristic of the period. The left arm
was supported on a staff, which would have been made of
bronze. *Right:* one of the sculptured metopes of the temple.
There were six metopes above the inner porch at either end,
so the space available was ideally suited to the subject chosen:
the 12 Labors of Heracles. Heracles, traditionally the founder
of the Olympic festival, was given a series of 12 daunting
assignments which included plucking the golden apples from
the dragon-guarded tree at the world's end, overcoming the
triple-bodied monster Geryon and stealing his cattle, and
going down to the Underworld and bringing back the three-
headed watchdog Cerberus. Using much ingenuity, the
master-sculptor rang the changes on the traditional artistic
versions of these episodes and created a varied pageant of
reliefs, some showing restful compositions, others
representing violent action. Here Heracles brings Athena, his
patron goddess, the dreaded Stymphalian birds, which he has
shot down with his bow.

Above: the Stadium, where athletic events took place. A rectangular area about 190 meters long and 30 meters wide, its shape was dictated by the oldest of the Olympian athletic events, the foot-races. These were contested, like the field- and combat-events, by naked athletes who had rubbed oil in their skin to keep dirt out of the pores. The runners were released from a starting-gate and ran from end to end. The shortest race was one length (the *stadion,* or "stade," which gave the course its name); but there were also three longer events – the two-length race (*diaulos*); the long-distance race, of 20 lengths (*dolichos*); and a two-length race for men wearing helmets and carrying shields. In these longer races the competitors had to round a turning-post at either end, with all the attendant risk of thrills and spills. Here the starting line is visible in the foreground, and the Hellenistic tunnel which leads to the sanctuary in the background. *Below:* the umpires' tribunal, midway along the side of the Stadium. Its foundations were uncovered when the German excavators peeled away the banking around the Stadium.

Statue of Nike (Victory) carved by the sculptor Paeonius, from Mende in Chalcidice. The figure originally stood on a 9-meter-high triangular pillar before the temple of Zeus and was represented leaning forward to be better visible from the ground. The forward lean was brilliantly balanced by the heavy marble masses behind her – her wings (now missing) and her billowing drapery. An inscription reveals that the Nike was executed in the years after 424 BC and that the artist had won a competition for the *akroteria* (roof-sculptures) of the temple of Zeus.

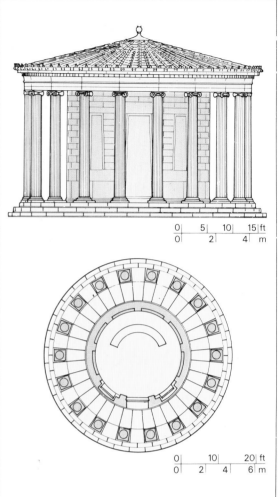

Above: the foundations of the Philippeion, a small *tholos* at the northwest corner of the sanctuary, begun by Philip of Macedon in 338 BC and completed after his death by his son Alexander the Great. The interior, framed by a ring of Corinthian half-columns, contained gold-and-ivory statues of members of the Macedonian royal family. *Right*: a restored elevation and ground-plan of the Philippeion. *Below*: a model of the buildings to the south of the sanctuary. In the middle is the Bouleuterion, the seat of the Council which administered the sanctuary. On the left is the South Stoa, a kind of grandstand from which spectators watched the arrival of the procession which inaugurated the festival.

A necessary concomitant to athletics were facilities for bathing, and the Greek baths at Olympia have yielded unique evidence of the development of such facilities from simple wash-houses to the Turkish-style baths characteristic of Roman times. *Right:* remains of hip-baths in the 5th-century bath-house. *Bottom right:* a partial reconstruction of the bath-house built about 100 BC. The floor of the main room was raised on small pillars so that hot air channeled from a nearby furnace could circulate beneath it. The same source heated the water in a bath at one corner of the room.

Below: the remains of the Leonidaion, a hotel built by Leonidas, a rich citizen of Naxos, in the 4th century BC. It was probably intended to provide accommodation for the better-off visitors to Olympia, notably contestants in the horse- and chariot-races.

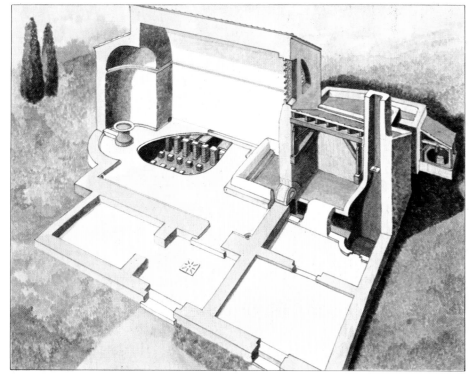

View of the Palaistra, the exercise-ground in which boxers and wrestlers trained. Built in the 3rd century BC, it consisted of an open court, 41 meters square, surrounded by a colonnade (which has now been largely reerected) and by the necessary ancillary rooms. These included storerooms, a hall for indoor training in bad weather, and a lecture room for the teachers of philosophy and rhetoric who were an essential feature of Hellenistic sports centers.

Life-size bronze head from a statue of a victorious athlete. This is the only remnant to have survived from any of the victor statues at Olympia; it probably dates from the 4th century BC, and the flattened nose and swollen ears suggest that the subject was a boxer. The combat events in the games had no classification by weight, so that big men tended to predominate; but a referee was on hand to ensure adherence to strict sets of rules. Boxing went on continuously till one of the contestants raised his hand in acknowledgment of defeat. Boxers wore leather thongs or gloves to protect their hands and could apparently strike with the flat or side of the hand as well as the fist.

3. Archaeological Research in Modern Times

The great excavations (1830-1914). With the excavations on Samothrace and at Olympia in the 1870s, Greek archaeology moved into a new phase: the recovery of the plan and history of whole complexes, not just the identification and excavation of single buildings, or the securing of individual specimens for European museums. Techniques and publication also became much more scientific.

On Samothrace the sanctuary of the Great Gods was studied in 1873 and 1875 by two Austrian expeditions under the leadership of Alexander Conze (1831–1914). Finds were shared with the Turkish government, to which Samothrace then belonged: Conze's main concern was not to look for art-treasures but to carry out a scientific study of the buildings of the sanctuary, making a full photographic and architectural record as the structures were uncovered. The two volumes of the publication were promptly produced and contained full visual documentation, including measured drawings of all the significant architectural blocks, and the first actual photographs to appear in an archaeological report.

More important was the excavation of the sanctuary of Zeus at Olympia, a project planned by Winckelmann and Ross but finally realized by the historian Ernst Curtius, who enjoyed close links with, and financial support from, the Prussian royal family, from 1871 the ruling family of the German Empire.

The excavations, supervised from Berlin by Curtius and the architect Freidrich Adler, lasted for six winter seasons (1875–81), employed up to 250 workmen at a time, and resulted in the clearance of most of the buildings in the sanctuary. Starting from the temple of Zeus, whose remaining architectural sculptures were found scattered where they had fallen or built into Byzantine houses, the excavators fanned outwards to find the more important buildings described by Pausanias – the Archaic temple of Hera (still containing Praxiteles' statue of Hermes and the child Dionysus), the treasuries, the Metroon, the Philip-

Above: Fougères' excavations at Mantinea. In addition to the structures uncovered, there are traces of unexcavated foundations, revealed by scattered stones and stunted growth of the overlying grass.

peion, the Palaistra, the entrance to the Stadium, the Prytaneion, the Bouleuterion and the Leonidaion. In charge of the work was a small team which included some of the ablest archaeologists and architectural historians of the day: notably two young men of genius who served their apprenticeships at Olympia – Adolf Furtwängler (1853–1907) and Wilhelm Dörpfeld (1853–1941). Furtwängler brought order to the bronzes and other small finds; Dörpfeld interpreted the architectural remains, diagnosing the phases and putting together the elements of the superstructures with marvelous insight.

From the first the excavations were conducted with close attention to scientific standards. A daily journal of the work was kept; an inventory of all finds was made; find-spots were carefully recorded; the sculptures were drawn upon discovery, often before they were removed from their finding places. At the same time a yearly report kept the interested world informed of the work's progress. The whole project was crowned by the official publication, again sponsored by the German government, which comprised five parts – topography and history; architecture; sculptures; bronzes and small finds; inscriptions.

This publication reveals how the Germans were beginning to tackle questions of chronology. Thus the first volume includes surveys of the site in Roman and Byzantine as well as Greek times; while the second volume sketches the chronological development of individual buildings. In the Bouleuterion, for example, the north wing is dated to the 6th century; the south wing to the 5th century; and the central building and front portico to a later period. To aid such analyses Dörpfeld adduces the evidence of architectural style and the forms of the clamps used to fasten the masonry; and to justify them he presents architectural drawings showing plans of the buildings as excavated, down to the last clamp. Of stratification, however, little use was made. Like Ross before him, Dörpfeld produced simplified sectional drawings of earth deposits to show the relationship between different periods of building, but made no systematic attempt to exploit the material found in the layers to date them. For this reason pottery plays little part in the publication: Furtwängler reveals that most of the sherds were packed in boxes and baskets without being cataloged. The dating of Greek pottery, which was still studied from an art-historical rather than an archaeological standpoint, was too uncertain to provide chronological criteria; and in any case most buildings of the Classical and Hellenistic periods could be dated, at least approximately, by other means – inscriptions, information in ancient writers, or architectural factors.

The importance of Olympia, however, extended beyond its excavation and publication. For one thing all finds were ceded by treaty to the Greeks. For another they were not removed to Athens but left, alongside the uncovered remains, at Olympia itself, where a special

Drawing made in 1879 of Ernst Curtius (1814–96), the excavator of Olympia. Curtius won royal support for his plan to carry out the project first conceived by Winckelmann.

museum was opened for them – a bold venture at a time when Greece had no railway and no developed network of roads.

Olympia afforded the pattern for several undertakings on Greek soil during the following years. The Greeks, unlike the Italians at this time, welcomed foreign excavators, provided only that they dug under Greek supervision and agreed to surrender all finds. It was in this climate that foreign schools for archaeological research grew up in Greece and gradually took over the administration of foreign excavations.

The French School, founded in 1846, had already existed for a generation and had engaged in archaeological and architectural work at Athens. Now it began to take on larger projects. From 1877 to 1894 it conducted somewhat haphazard excavations on the island of Delos, uncovering the precinct of Apollo and various public and private buildings within the city, including the harbor installations. In the late 1880s it carried out investigations in the cities of Mantinea and Tegea, and from 1892 to 1901, after long delays caused by official prevarication and local resistance, it completed the clearing of the sanctuary of Apollo at Delphi.

In 1874, in the great upsurge of German archaeological activity which followed the establishment of the Empire, the German Archaeological Institute set up its branch in Athens. This too soon became a focus of archaeological work in the Greek world, not only sponsoring its own projects at various sites, but also sending able young scholars to support the teams working at Olympia and Pergamum. It prospered particularly under the direction of Dörpfeld, who was First Secretary from 1887 to 1911.

Apart from his famous guided tours of the Peloponnese and the Aegean islands, he carried out a great deal of research into Classical Athens, digging in the theater of Dionysus and the Pnyx-Areopagus area, and acting as architectural adviser to almost everyone else's excavations.

The American School of Classical Studies, founded in 1882, excavated in the sanctuary of Hera near Argos from 1892 to 1895 and launched its long-running program at Corinth – a program which proved more informative for Roman times than for the Greek period – in 1896. The British School came into existence in 1885 and examined the theater and Thersilion at Megalopolis between 1890 and 1892. The Austrian Institute was formed in the 1890s; the Italian School in 1909.

The Greeks themselves and in particular the Greek Archaeological Society also carried out a number of large-scale operations. The sanctuary of Asclepius at Epidaurus was cleared in two major campaigns between 1881 and 1903; the sanctuary of Demeter at Eleusis was excavated between 1882 and 1890; and the Athenian Acropolis was systematically uncovered between 1885 and 1890. In all cases the indispensable Dörpfeld was called in to study and interpret the architectural remains. Among his more notable contributions were the reconstruction of the original plan for the Propylaia in Athens, and the unraveling of a veritable maze of foundations at Eleusis.

In Turkey too large-scale excavations were undertaken, chiefly by the Germans, who enjoyed almost a monopoly

Remains of the Hall of the Mysteries at Eleusis. In its final form it contained six rows of columns and four banks of seating.

Present remains of the Great Altar of Zeus at Pergamum. Most of the material from Humann's excavations of the late 1870s and early 1880s was transported to Berlin.

of the Classical and Hellenistic sites. Here, since Turkey did not yet insist on retaining all the finds from archaeological explorations, the German government financed the work partly if not primarily to secure material for the Berlin Museums. Nonetheless it had become inevitable that any treasure hunt should be accompanied by a scientific program of investigation.

The first of the German campaigns in Asia, the excavation at Pergamum, well illustrates this dual approach. It began as an exercise to retrieve the sculptures of the Great Altar of Zeus and ended up as a major program of research into all aspects of the city and its development – a program which is still continuing today.

The story of the finding and excavation of the Great Altar is perhaps the greatest of all the romances in Greek archaeology. It centers around the colorful character of Carl Humann (1839–96), an engineer who had originally come to Turkey on doctor's advice in 1861 and had got to know Pergamum in the course of road-building operations for the Turkish government. While there, he discovered fragments of a great high-relief frieze built into a Byzantine wall on the acropolis and in 1871 sent two of them to Berlin. He was hoping that the Berlin Museums would mount an excavation to recover further reliefs, but it was not till 1877, when Alexander Conze became

director of the sculpture gallery, that he persuaded the Museums to act. It was now realized that the reliefs came from the battle of gods and giants portrayed on the "great marble altar" mentioned by the Roman writer Ampelius, and in the late summer of 1878 Humann began his search for this altar.

"There was no point in my looking for it up here at the north end, nor indeed on the actual crown of the acropolis, for in that case I should certainly have spotted a mound of debris from the massive building; nor was there any point in looking below the Byzantine wall, for such was the abundance of building-material that no one would have hauled the great blocks uphill. There remained only the space between the Byzantine wall and the third defensive wall above. In fact a mound-like heap of debris rose near the western edge; it offered distant views to east, south and west, and, though about 40 meters below the summit of the acropolis, it was still a commanding position. Here I determined to begin work next morning and at the same time tackle the western part of the Byzantine wall.

"On Monday 9 September 1878 I climbed up with 14

workmen, took a pickax and said: 'In the name of the Protector of the Royal Museums, the happiest and most beloved of men, the warrior who has never been vanquished, the heir to the most illustrious throne in the world, in the name of our Crown Prince, may this work be attended with fortune and success.' My workmen thought that I was reciting a magic spell and they were not far out.

"Four workmen drove a couple of trenches into the mound of debris, one from the south and the other from the east, while 10 men worked to clear the western part of the Byzantine wall of the debris which had accumulated against it. The next day was a Greek holiday and I had only four workmen, but by the same evening two reliefs were visible, each over 2 meters long; they were in the inner face of the wall, set on edge, with the undecorated side of the slabs outwards. The next evening 11 of them were visible, while the excavators in their trenches had struck the compact masonry of a foundation, where they found broken-off pieces of fish-tails and other fragments."

In three days Humann had discovered the Great Altar. He promptly dispatched a jubilant telegram to Berlin, proclaiming, "Eleven great reliefs, mostly with whole figures, 30 fragments, and altar found." The finds continued, and their significance for the history of Greek art became ever more apparent. "We have found a whole epoch of art," wrote Humann, "the greatest work to have survived from antiquity is here beneath our hands."

The transport of reliefs from the acropolis at Pergamum. Humann had to construct a special road down the hillside and transport the huge slabs by buffalo-cart to the coast, a task hampered by torrential rains, inept drivers, and buffalo which insisted on wandering into the swollen streams to drink.

Battle of gods and giants, the main frieze of the Great Altar at Pergamum (c. 180–150 BC) 2·30 meters high.

All the finds from the excavations were eventually sent to Berlin. The Turks had originally claimed two-thirds, but had soon reduced this demand to one-third, and eventually sold out their interest altogether. By the end of the first season's work (December 1879) 94 slabs of the great frieze had been retrieved, in addition to those already known. With all the other sculptures, inscriptions and architectural fragments which Humann unearthed, a total of 462 cases reached the German capital.

Humann's original brief had been to concentrate on the Altar, but in the first few months of the excavation he expanded his sights to include first the Gymnasium on the lower slopes of the acropolis, then a Roman monument, the Traianeum. Conze, who acted as supervisor of the work, ensured that trained epigraphists and architects

were sent to make proper records of the inscriptions and structures found. When in 1880, following the Olympia model, an interim report was published, Conze's summary clearly envisaged a much broader and more far-sighted program of future research: "Alongside our immediate task, we soon saw before us a comprehensive final task, towards which we could take at least the preliminary steps. . . . We must gradually work out a picture of the topography and monuments of the ancient city in the different phases of its existence. . . ." Thus in further campaigns between 1880 and 1886 most of the remaining monuments of the acropolis were unearthed – the sanctuary of Athena, the terrace below the Altar, the Upper Agora, the great theater and the royal palaces. Again following the model of Olympia, the results of the work were to be incorporated in a massive multivolume publication, which duly began in 1885, but lagged on well into the 20th century.

In 1884 Humann became a full-time agent of the Berlin Museums (holding the rank of a "Director resident in Smyrna") and henceforth worked with frenetic energy mounting excavations on their behalf. The normal arrangement now was that Constantinople and Berlin shared the finds. Humann was not himself an outstanding scholar, but by brilliant organizing ability and by the force of his personality he was able to win the cooperation and coordinate the efforts of many of the greatest German archaeologists of his day. Between 1891 and 1893, with the help of the architect R. Heyne and the epigraphist O. Kern, he cleared the Agora and surrounding buildings in the Hellenistic city of Magnesia on the Maeander. Then in 1895 he began work at Priene.

The excavation at Priene, which was completed after Humann's early death by the most gifted of his henchmen, Theodor Wiegand (1864–1936), marks another landmark in the history of Greek archaeology. Thanks to the comparative shallowness of the earth and debris which overlay the ruins, it proved possible within the space of four years to lay bare the greater part of a small late Classical and Hellenistic city little affected by later structures. The result was a wonderful insight into town planning in the second half of the 4th century BC and into the types of public buildings and private houses which were fitted into the framework laid down by the planners. In the course of the work Hans Schrader carried out a definitive study of the architecture of the famous temple of Athena Polias, now sadly vandalized since the surveys of Pullan and his predecessors. The publication of the whole enterprise, though held up by various impediments, appeared within five years. Not only are the architecture and sculptures fully discussed, but, for the first time in a Classical-Hellenistic excavation report, there is also a detailed account of the pottery, plain and decorated, fragmentary and complete. Admittedly no find-spots are recorded; but the mere cataloging of the pottery represents an important step forward.

From Priene the Berlin Museums turned their attention immediately to Miletus. This was a much bigger site (the Hellenistic walls enclosed an area roughly 2 kilometers by 1 kilometer) and posed a much greater problem, in that occupation of the city had been continuous throughout antiquity and into the medieval period. Nothing daunted, Wiegand had the whole monumental city-center cleared by 1910 and, aided by an outstanding team of architectural historians, set about reconstructing the evolution of the city's plan and of its individual buildings – a task which was scarcely begun when it was interrupted by World War I.

Alongside their work at Miletus, Wiegand's team carried out excavations towards the final clearing of the gigantic temple of Apollo at nearby Didyma, an awesome undertaking, not merely because of the scale of the remains, but also because of the modern village which had grown up over them. Above the center of the temple rose a mountain of rubble crowned by a mill, and all around stood stone-built houses. Again undaunted, Wiegand bought the mill and the land; he pulled down the offending part of the village; and in 10 long campaigns he and Hubert Knackfuss had, by the outset of the war, broken the back of the task.

To catalog all the other excavations in the years leading up to the war would be a hopeless business. We need mention only some of the major projects which have particular relevance to our period. In mainland Greece, the French School uncovered the temple of Athena Alea at Tegea, finding fragments of the pedimental sculptures. In the islands, Baron Friedrich Hiller von Gärtringen excavated at his own expense the Hellenistic and Roman city on Thera, while the French School carried out a second series of campaigns on Delos. On Cos the sanctuary of Asclepius was excavated by Rudolf Herzog, and on Rhodes the sanctuary of Athena at Lindos was examined by the Danes Kinch and Blinkenberg. In Asia Minor, Austrian investigations at Ephesus were mainly concerned with the Roman city but also took in some Hellenistic monuments; while the second phase of work at Pergamum, carried out by the German Institute under Dörpfeld's direction, led to the discovery of the Lower Agora, the sanctuaries of Hera and Demeter, and other buildings on the south slopes of the acropolis. Further inland, an American team excavated the temple of Artemis at Sardis.

Outside Greece and Turkey sporadic investigations took place. At Alexandria, a private German expedition found disappointingly scanty traces of the deeply buried Hellenistic city but had more success with the cemeteries; while Evaristo Breccia, the Italian curator of the Greco-Roman Museum, excavated the necropolis of Chatby to the east of the city. In Cyrene an American team found

The acropolis at Lindos, showing the temple of Athena (after 348 BC) excavated by Kinch and Blinkenberg.

Hellenistic buildings in the winter of 1910–11. The continuing risks run by archaeologists in remoter parts are amply illustrated by the news that "the excavation was conducted under great difficulties of all sorts, especially from the natives, and was overshadowed by the murder of Mr. De Cou." The hapless De Cou would have been little consoled to learn that "this was not due to any sudden outburst of fanaticism, but murderers were deliberately hired for the purpose, and, although another explorer was intended, Mr. De Cou was the actual victim."

The interwar years (1918–1939). The excavations of the late 19th and early 20th centuries had produced a mass of material and information, particularly about Greek architecture and town planning. Indeed, the zest for discovery had far outpaced the capacity for publication. The full publication of major projects like those at Delos and Delphi was hardly begun when World War I intervened; and the results of some excavations, such as the work at Miletus, are still being published in the 1970s. So, despite the disruption and damage to antiquities which it and the ensuing Greco-Turkish troubles brought (for instance at Sardis and Miletus, where the excavation stores were ransacked or destroyed), the war had its good effects: the enforced pause which was imposed on the breakneck speed of digging provided a respite for the digestion of the new data, and in some cases hastened the process of publication without which archaeological discovery is valueless.

The theater of Dionysus in Athens, the home of Greek drama. It acquired its monumental form in the 4th century.

After the war, there was a marked tendency for excavations on Greek sites to concentrate on Archaic and prehistoric levels – partly because, in many places, the remains of the Classical and Hellenistic periods had been laid bare in the orgy of discovery between 1870 and 1914, and it was precisely the earlier phases of occupation that awaited investigation. Thus we find Dörpfeld at Olympia and the French at Delphi conducting soundings into the levels beneath those exposed in the late 19th century.

But there were still a number of sites, some old and some new, where investigations into the Classical and Hellenistic remains continued. In Athens, for instance, the Greeks worked on the Odeion of Pericles, while the Germans were active in the theater of Dionysus. The German excavations around the Dipylon gate yielded information on Classical graves and on the Pompeion. At Eleusis there was further work on the sanctuary of Demeter; at Corinth the Americans continued to glean a little information about the Greek city; and at Sicyon Greek excavations under A. K. Orlandos examined the gymnasium and other Hellenistic buildings.

More important was the new program at Olympia, where the German government celebrated the 1936 Olympic Games, held in Berlin, by launching large-scale excavations which continued into the first years of

World War II. Though the chief beneficiary was the Archaic period, the work also shed light on the Stadium in Classical and Hellenistic times and on buildings such as the South Hall, the Palaistra and the Greek baths by the river Cladeus. Taking a leaf from the book of their 19th-century predecessors, the new German team published a series of admirable interim reports, followed by a definitive publication dealing with individual buildings or building complexes and individual categories of finds.

In the Aegean, the French School continued excavating on several fronts in Delos and carried out annual work in the Greco-Roman city of Thasos; while in the Dodecannese, which had been governed by Italy since 1912, there were various excavations, notably on Rhodes and Cos. In Turkey a new phase dawned with the passing of antiquities legislation. The export of finds was now forbidden, and work assumed the purely scientific character of excavations in Greece. Nonetheless the Berlin Museums remained active, with Wiegand inaugurating another characteristically grand-scale campaign at Pergamum. Between 1927 and 1934 he excavated the Hellenistic

Arsenals, the sanctuary for the Ruler Cult, and the sanctuary of Asclepius, a great Roman monumental complex which had developed out of Hellenistic and even earlier beginnings. Meanwhile four further seasons were spent at Didyma. When the last measurements were taken in 1938, a total of 6 years and $1\frac{1}{2}$ months had been spent at the site and 178,800 man-days worked. At Ephesus the Austrians found time to examine the splendid Hellenistic Mausoleum at Belevi, 12 kilometers to the northeast.

In Egypt the cemeteries of Alexandria were further studied by the new curator of the Greco-Roman Museum, Achille Adriani; while on the Euphrates River the caravan city of Dura-Europos, which had begun life as a garrison town of the Hellenistic Seleucid dynasty, was explored by a joint expedition of Yale University and the French Académie des Inscriptions et Belles Lettres. In Libya, now an Italian colony, there were large-scale excavations in Cyrene; and in Italy the cemetery at Spina, near the mouth of the Po, yielded many Attic red-figured vases.

But the two most important and ambitious excavations of the interwar years took place back in European Greece – at Olynthus and in the Athenian Agora.

The city of Olynthus, situated in the three-pronged peninsula of Chalcidice on the north shore of the Aegean, was the object of massive excavations, directed by David M. Robinson of Johns Hopkins University (Baltimore), in

Western part of the excavations in the Athenian Agora in 1934. The American team, led by T. Leslie Shear, had to disentangle the accumulated foundations of more than 2,000 years.

1928, 1931, 1934 and 1938. Up to 400 workmen, many of them refugees from Turkey, were employed at a time, and extensive use was made of trucks and railcars to remove the spoil. Though frequently criticized for their lack of scientific method, particularly their failure to provide precise archaeological contexts for the pottery and small finds, these excavations yielded a mass of important information. Olynthus became the only city of the 5th and early 4th centuries whose town plan and development were known in detail; it provided important evidence for houses and living conditions at that time; and it produced a major series of pebble mosaics – among the earliest planned examples, and certainly the earliest with myth-ological subjects, to have survived. Above all, its de-struction by Philip of Macedon in 348 BC afforded a secure *terminus ante quem* for the veritable gold mine of small objects found in the ruins. The Olynthian material thus became an invaluable asset in studies of typology.

Whereas Olynthus was virtually a "one-period" site, the Athenian Agora had experienced continuous occu-pation from prehistoric to modern times. Its heyday, however, had fallen in the Classical and Hellenistic ages, when it was the focus of civic and commercial life in Athens. Though limited excavations had been undertaken by the Greek Archaeological Society and the German Institute in the 19th and early 20th centuries, it was not till the 1930s, when the American School obtained a con-cession for the area, that large-scale investigation began. The first step in the work was the purchase of the modern houses overlying the Agora – a lengthy and expensive business, since there were 365 properties in all. Financial support was provided by John D. Rockefeller Jr. and the expropriations were carried out in yearly blocks from 1931 to 1940. When a block was acquired, the excavators first supervised its demolition, keeping their eyes peeled for reused ancient stones (among those to turn up were fragments of the Parthenon sculptures), then cleared the underlying earth down to the level of late antiquity, and finally, during subsequent campaigns, conducted exca-vations at a deeper level. In this way they had opened up most of the area by the outbreak of the war and had established the outline of the ancient square. It was a huge project by anyone's standards. The Greco-Roman levels lay at an average depth of 15 feet, and to shift the necessary spoil, which amounted at the end of the 1939 season to 246,000 tons, a work force ranging from 145 to 300 men was employed for several months per year, and horsecarts or (in later seasons) motortrucks plied between the excavations and disused quarry-pits on the outskirts of the city. More frightening than the scale of the earth removal was the complexity of the remains, as revealed in photographs of the late 1930s; a tangled mass of foun-dations of the Archaic, Classical, Hellenistic and Roman, not to mention later periods, had to be sorted out. Added to this, huge quantities of finds accrued. By the end of 1937 there were 70,000 coins and 5,000 inscriptions. It was no small credit to the dedication and efficiency of the American team working under T. Leslie Shear that all this material could be recorded and processed, and that reports could be issued with admirable punctuality in the new periodical *Hesperia*. Perhaps the major contribution of the excavation was the light which it threw on the topo-graphy of Athens; many of the buildings mentioned by Pausanias in his itinerary of the Agora could now be identified on the ground – the Stoa of Zeus, the temple of Apollo Patroos, the Metroon, the Bouleuterion, the Tholos and so forth. The plan of the Agora, almost totally unknown in the 1920s, had begun to take shape.

The Agora excavations mark the summit of technical progress in Greek archaeology between the wars. The study of Classical and Hellenistic sites, as perfected by Wiegand and his school, was still primarily "architec-tural": in other words it was directed towards gaining the ground plans of buildings in their different phases and towards reconstructing their elevations from structural fragments – a natural approach, given the generally good state of preservation of monuments of the period, and the fact that dating was frequently provided by inscriptions or the testimony of ancient writers. But at the same time, mainly under the influence of work on prehistoric and Archaic sites, excavation techniques became more subtle. Archaeologists were increasingly ready and able to exploit stratigraphical evidence and date structures by the con-tents of the earth deposits associated with them.

The main tool in this method is pottery. The impor-tance of pottery to archaeologists interested in Classical and Hellenistic sites had been acknowledged even before 1914. Already in 1912 F. W. Hasluck could write, "Symptomatic of the prominence forced upon ceramics by the interest shewn latterly in prehistoric archaeology is the tendency to apply the same methods to the historic period and especially to recognise more fully the value of tomb-groups as chronological data." He was thinking specifically of the opening of graves by British and American archaeologists in Boeotia. Where undisturbed, these graves yielded valuable "closed groups" of pottery – groups of pots which had been buried together and were therefore roughly contemporary in date. By comparing the different groups and the different stages of develop-ment in shape or decoration which they represented, it was possible to surmise which were the earlier and which the later; and, if the groups contained the odd datable object, such as a coin, or contained pots which could be paralleled by dated pottery elsewhere, this relative chronology could be converted into an absolute chronology.

By means such as these the dating of pottery rapidly became more precise during the first decades of the present century. The most spectacular progress was achieved with red-figured wares, which had long excited the interest of art-historians, and which offered the best opportunities of studying the niceties of stylistic evolution. With the excavations of the Athenian Acropolis in the 1880s, Ross's

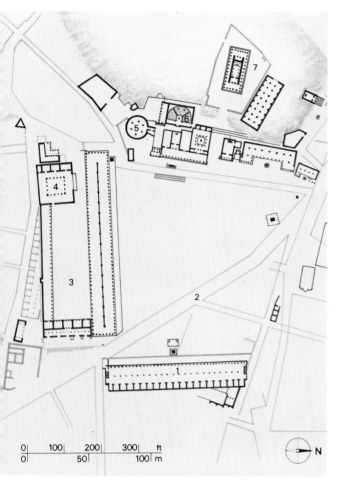

The Athenian Agora in the 2nd century BC. Note (1) Stoa of Attalus, (2) Street of the Panathenaia, (3) South Square, (4) Heliaia, (5) Tholos, (6) Bouleuterion, (7) "Theseum."

the debris left by masons. A good example of this technique in operation is provided by Thompson's discussion of the dating of the Tholos in the Agora.

"The . . . Tholos must, obviously, be dated after the final demolition of the archaic buildings beneath and around it. . . . Those buildings were reconditioned after 479 BC and continued to be used for some time, probably not for long. The limited amount of pottery found in the contemporary filling within and without the Tholos and in the broiling-pits to the north (filled in when the Tholos was built) can be little later than that from the *Perserschutt* [debris from the Persian sack]. It affords a *terminus post quem.*

"A welcome *terminus ante quem* is given by a mass of broken pottery which was found in a pit . . . 4 m. to the southeast of the Tholos. This pit had been cut down through the new ground level established when the Tholos was built. . . . [The pottery from this pit] finds a perfect parallel in a larger mass of pottery which was removed from a well beneath the Stoa of Zeus in 1935. . . . The vases from the well have been assigned to the period 480–460 BC. Additional confirmation is given by a fragment of a red-figured kantharos with the Judgment of Paris found together with the plain ware in the pit by the Tholos. It clearly belongs early in the decade 470–460 BC. . . The external evidence thus indicates that the Tholos was built shortly after 479 BC, shortly before *ca.* 460 BC."

Later destructions and reconstructions are dated in the same way by ceramic evidence. It goes without saying that this sort of study is dependent upon the precise recording of the position in which each piece of pottery (or other significant object) is discovered – and upon the ability of the student to locate it afterwards, whenever he wishes to examine it. The Agora excavations again set the highest of standards, as Shear himself made clear.

"Special attention has been paid to the development and perfection of the system of accurate recording and of careful description of the objects which are found from day to day. An archaeologist of the staff has the supervision of each area of excavation. The areas are divided into squares of one metre so that the place of finding is immediately obvious, and the depth is reckoned from a fixed point determined by the height above sea level. The scholar in charge of an area keeps a field note book in which all details of the progress of the excavation are neatly and fully recorded. The areas are designated by letters of the Greek alphabet and when an object is found it receives a serial number prefixed by the letter of the area. It is then entered in the note book with the specification of the exact place of discovery and with a description which includes its dimensions. A drawing of it is made in the book or else a space is left for the subsequent insertion of a small photograph. A tag with the date of finding and with the serial number of the area is attached to the object which is sent to the workrooms. There it is washed, its serial number is checked by the finder, and it is handed to

observation that the red-figure style was already in vogue before the Persian sack of 480 BC was fully vindicated; and during the next 20 years Furtwängler and others established the main outlines of the chronology which is still accepted today. Then from 1908 onwards came the publications of J. D. Beazley, who put the study of red-figure on a wholly new footing by isolating the style and collecting the *oeuvre* of individual painters, whether named or anonymous. By the 1930s it was possible to date almost any decorated sherd within a few years.

The study of the less exciting wares also made progress. The shapes of the ubiquitous plain black-painted pottery were classified for the 6th, 5th and 4th centuries by P. N. Ure on the basis of grave-finds in Boeotia. Then in 1934 Homer A. Thompson published his seminal article on the Hellenistic pottery of Athens, selecting for examination five sealed groups from cisterns and similar receptacles in the Agora, and thus producing a chronological framework for the period from the late 4th to the early 1st century BC.

It was with the aid of studies like these that stratigraphical archaeology developed. Buildings and building phases could now be roughly dated by the pottery found in the filling of foundation trenches, in the makeup of floors or in the cataloguing department. It then receives a final inventory number which is entered in an inventory book, and a full description of it is written on a catalogue card, which carries a small photograph of the object in its upper left corner. The color of the card indicates the type of object such as sculpture, pottery, terracottas, lamps, etc., and the position of the tab marks other specifications as, for example, the period, whether Greek, Roman or Byzantine. The object is finally placed in a drawer or on a shelf in the position designated by its serial number. By this accurate method of recording nothing from the excavations can go even temporarily astray, and any object desired can be at any time immediately located."

Here at last we have all the hallmarks of a properly conducted modern excavation. Another token of modernity was the attachment to the Agora staff in 1937 of a chemist, whose main duties were the cleaning of excavated objects, and the analysis and identification of materials. Many interesting results emerged. The colors preserved on marble coffered ceiling-blocks of the mid-5th century BC were found to have been applied with beeswax as a medium. A thin plaque of the 4th century BC turned out, on analysis, to be practically pure zinc – a mineral previously considered to be unknown to the ancient Greeks. A black substance which was used to line terracotta jars proved to be mastic from the island of Chios, and, since this substance was soluble in oil but not in alcohol, it was concluded that the jars were wine containers, lined to prevent the wine from seeping into the terracotta. All these and similar discoveries pointed the way to a fruitful collaboration between archaeologists and research chemists, not to mention other scientists.

The modern period. World War II, like World War I, seriously disrupted archaeological investigation in the Greek world. What with postwar instability and the need to repair war damage, it was not till the 1950s that programs of research achieved the scale and momentum of the 1930s. Since then excavation and other forms of fieldwork have continued apace. If anything, the study of prehistoric and Archaic remains has bulked even larger than in the prewar period, but this is partly due to a healthy desire, propagated by the prewar work in the Athenian Agora and elsewhere, to see sites in their full chronological perspective. Archaeologists are, on the whole, much more aware of flux and change within the Greco-Roman world.

Of the sites which have continued to yield Classical or Hellenistic material some are hardy perennials, like Corinth, Thasos, Delos and Pergamum, while others are new or newly come to prominence. Thus on Samothrace excavations which had been started by Karl Lehmann on behalf of the New York Institute of Fine Arts in 1939 were resumed in 1948 and have since unraveled much of the history of the sanctuary examined by Conze in the 1870s. From the early 1950s the French have been active in the

city of Argos; the Greeks in the sanctuary of Zeus at Dodona; and the Americans at Isthmia, where they have found the sanctuary of Poseidon, the site of one of the great Greek athletic festivals. Later in the 1950s began the Greek excavations at Messene in the southwestern Peloponnese and at the Macedonian capital Pella. In Turkey one of the more important among the new excavations has been that at Klaros, where Louis Robert discovered the early Hellenistic oracular shrine of Apollo; while in the west there have been massive programs in several cities and cemeteries, for instance the 5th- and 4th-century cemeteries of Posidonia (the Roman Paestum in south Italy) and the Hellenistic city of Morgantina (Sicily). Another Hellenistic city has been the object of recent excavations at Ai Khanoum in Afghanistan.

The American operations in the Athenian Agora were recommenced under the direction of Homer Thompson as early as 1946, and by the 1960s had resulted in the clearance down to the Classical levels of virtually the whole area of the original concession. During this period measures were taken for the conservation of the structures uncovered and for the landscaping of the site, while the Hellenistic Stoa of Attalus was rebuilt on its original foundations to provide accommodation for a museum, stores and workshops. More recently the area of operations has been extended north of the Piraeus railway line, exposing new buildings to the north and northwest of the ancient square.

But perhaps the most spectacular dig of the postwar years took place at Olympia, where the German excavators under Emil Kunze continued their work from 1952 to 1966. Their major achievement was to complete the total stripping of the Stadium, including its embankments, down to the natural surface, and to reconstruct it in its 4th-century form; and their most exciting discovery was the litter (clay molds, slivers of ivory, glass ornaments and tools) from the workshop in which Phidias fashioned his colossal gold-and-ivory statue of Zeus. This discovery confirmed Adler's 60-year-old theory that the workshop was the ancient structure underlying the Byzantine church to the west of the temple of Zeus. Further confirmation, almost too good to be true, was provided by the finding, in a deposit associated with the construction of the building, of an Attic black cup carrying the inscription "I belong to Phidias."

A new factor which has entered Greek archaeology since the war is the concept of rescue excavation. Instead of choosing sites at will and exploiting them purely for research purposes, archaeologists have become increasingly aware of their responsibility to salvage information from sites threatened by destruction. Their awareness has been heightened by the boom in building which has taken place over the last 20 years. Road developments, factories and housing programs have all taken their toll of the ancient remains – particularly in the cities of Greece and the Black Sea region. In Athens the Greek Archaeological

Right: the Stoa of Attalus, set up along the eastern side of the Athenian Agora by the munificent King Attalus II of Pergamum (159–138 BC), has now been reconstructed to house a museum and offices for the Agora excavations.

Below: the base of an Athenian black cup found in debris associated with the building of Phidias' workshop at Olympia. The graffito claims that the cup belongs to the great Athenian sculptor.

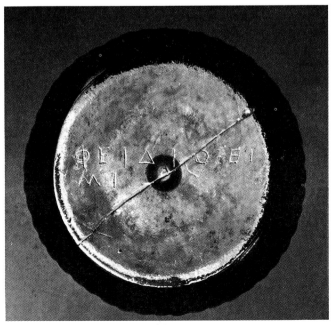

Service has been forced, in recent years, to conduct anything up to 80 rescue operations per year, some of them resulting in discoveries of major importance – though accident, as usual, has produced the more sensational finds, as when workmen digging a trench for a sewer in Piraeus uncovered a deposit of bronze statues which had been buried in the ruins of a burned warehouse in the 1st century BC.

In the valley of the Peneus River in the northwestern Peloponnese the construction of a reservoir has stimulated a large-scale rescue operation. The various foreign schools in Greece each surveyed a sector of the catchment area, then carried out trial excavations where appropriate. In this way a good deal of information about settlement patterns and individual sites, mainly farms, was retrieved before the evidence was submerged.

Technically, standards of excavation have continued to improve. The example set by the Agora project in the 1930s has led to a general consciousness of the importance of observing the stratification of a site and recording the

precise position where pottery and other objects are found. Unfortunately, the long-standing equation of Classical archaeology with art-history dies hard, and it is still believed in some quarters that a student of Classical art can run an excavation without adequate archaeological training. But in the best programs standards leave little to be desired. In the German excavations at Olympia, for instance, the history of the Stadium and that of Phidias' workshop were established by a rigorous use of stratigraphical criteria, the evidence for which has been fully presented to the public in the excavation reports.

Alongside the traditional methods of archaeological inquiry, the postwar period has seen the emergence of new techniques and new disciplines. Of supreme importance,

A vertical air photograph of the city of Rhodes. The grid plan of the city which was founded in 408–407 BC is reflected, as observed by Bradford, in modern streets, lanes and field boundaries.

though not yet fully exploited in the Greek world, are new surveying techniques, notably aerial photography. Air photographs had occasionally been used between the wars to obtain an overall view of an excavated site, for example Olynthus; but their capacity to reveal undiscovered sites or to add new information about known ones was not yet appreciated. It was only during World War II, when aerial photographs were taken during military reconnaissances, that the material was provided for archaeological researches similar to those which had been undertaken by Crawford and others in Britain.

The necessary pioneer work was undertaken by John Bradford, who combined a wartime experience of R.A.F. photographic intelligence with a firsthand knowledge of the British achievements in aerial archaeology. At Rhodes he used surface features alone. Observing that a vertical air photograph turned modern roads and field boundaries into elements of a grid pattern, he was able to reconstruct much of the street system of the Classical city. Later fieldwork, both by Bradford and by Greek archaeologists, confirmed and refined his conclusions.

But aerial photographs also enable the archaeologist to make sense of buried features. The latter can be betrayed in various ways. Where they affect the level of the surface above, they can catch the light or cast shadows; where they have been damaged by plowing, they can cause variations in the color of the soil; where crops are planted over them, they can lead to differential growth patterns. Such marks had occasionally been exploited on the ground. As early as the 1880s G. Fougères had used growth variations to determine where to dig at Mantinea; while in the 1920s G. Caton-Thompson had located a Hellenistic irrigation system in Egypt by observing bands of mesembryanthemum growing over the filling of the ditches. But only an aerial survey will provide a panoramic view. By this means Bradford was able to identify field systems, probably Classical in origin, on the hill

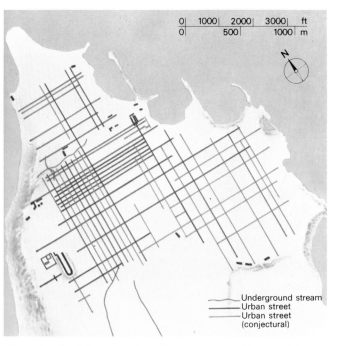

Above: details of the street-plan of Rhodes recovered from aerial photographs and subsequent surveying and excavation on the ground.

Below: a vertical air photograph used by Bradford to identify field systems on hill slopes south of Athens. The ripple-marks represent ancient field boundaries.

slopes south of Athens. The field walls and the terraces which had been erected to prevent erosion were revealed either by scatters of plowed-out stones, or, if still buried, by lines of light and shadow. Such surveys might well be expected to identify remains of field systems in other parts of the Greek world, and it is regrettable that little further work of this sort has been done. Air photography in general remains a much neglected tool. Though it has been employed to detect details of the town plans of certain Greek cities in south Italy and Sicily, and has revealed the hitherto unknown Hellenistic city at Shaikhan Dheri in Pakistan, there has been no systematic exploration of the type seen in Britain and other countries.

Another form of surveying which has been imported from archaeologically more advanced areas is geophysical prospecting by magnetic or electronic devices. This has the virtue of revealing buried structures or materials before a spade is set to the ground, and enables the archaeologist to determine in advance where excavation is likely to be most profitable. Thus at Motya in Sicily an electrical resistivity survey indicated the position and shape of buildings hidden beneath the fields; while in a house on Delos a pulse induction meter was used to locate coins and other metal objects trodden into a clay-earth floor. In both cases the data obtained meant an enormous saving of time and effort.

But geophysical surveys, like aerial surveys, have not yet bulked large in the study of the Classical and Hellenistic Greek territories. Far more important is a new field of research, the discipline of underwater archaeology. The salvaging of Greek statues from the wrecks of the Roman ships which were carrying them to Italy has been going on since the beginning of the century. As early as 1900–01 a 4th-century bronze statue of a youth with arm outstretched was recovered by sponge divers, along with many lesser works, off the island of Anticythera; and in 1928 the famous striding Zeus or Poseidon was raised from the sea near Cape Artemisium in northern Euboea. But it is only since the last war that treasure hunting has been largely superseded by the scientific study of submerged remains. This may involve the surveying and excavation of harbor works, like those of the north African port of Apollonia, or partially submerged cities, like Halieis in the eastern Peloponnese; or, more spectacularly, the examination of shipwrecks. The latter are especially valuable, not only because their timbers, where they have escaped the ravages of shipworms, can furnish detailed information about the structure and carpentry of ancient vessels, but also because their cargoes are perfect examples of "sealed deposits," providing a point of cross-reference between the chronologies of different artifacts, besides shedding light on the nature and pattern of Mediterranean trade.

The excavation of a wreck is, of course, a slow and tedious process. It has generally to be carried out by divers who can only work for short stretches at a time and whose

The mound of amphorae which betrayed the wreck of a Greek merchant-ship off Kyrenia, Cyprus.

operations may be seriously hindered by high seas or submarine currents. But, equipped with aqualungs to supply them with air, digging with special tools such as air-lifts to remove the mud, and making records with underwater cameras, plastic tape-measures and waterproof drawing materials, these aquatic archaeologists may glean a remarkable amount of information. A good example is provided by a wreck, excavated in 1968 and 1969, near Kyrenia in Cyprus. The ship in question, probably a fore-and-aft rigger, was built mainly of pinewood, the timbers of the hull being joined by mortises and tenons, while the frames within the hull were fastened by copper nails driven in from outside. The whole was sheathed with lead to protect the wood from shipworms. The cargo consisted mainly of amphorae (wine-jars) from Rhodes, Samos and elsewhere, but also included grinding stones, which may have served as ballast, and a consignment of almonds, stored in sacks in the bow area. In

Bronze statue of a youth (c. 350–330 BC) recovered from a shipwreck off the island of Anticythera. Some of the best-preserved Greek bronze statues come from wrecks, where they have been safe from the ravages of later metal-hunters. 1·94 meters high. Athens, National Museum.

addition the ship carried various items of pottery and eating utensils, thought to be the crew's equipment: the recurrent number four (oil-jars, wooden spoons, drinking cups) suggests a four-man complement. As for diet, the finding of lead weights once attached to a net hints that one of the dishes on the menu was likely to be fish.

The cargo prompts certain conjectures about the ship's ports of call. The amphorae suggest stops at Samos and Rhodes; the grinding stones may have been picked up at Cos; and the almonds could have been put aboard at Kyrenia itself, since Cyprus was famed in antiquity for this fruit.

Finally, to enhance the value of the excavation, a fairly close date could be assigned to the wreck. The amphorae, the other pottery and a couple of coins pointed to the end of the 4th or the early 3rd century BC. The almonds, moreover, when tested by the radiocarbon dating method, yielded a date of 288 ± 62 BC. That the ship had already attained a venerable age when she went down is suggested by a date of 389 ± 44 BC for the felling of the timber from which she was built.

The Kyrenia wreck excavation is almost an epitome of the modern attitude to archaeology. No longer are we content merely to salvage art treasures and other choice relics from the debris of antiquity; every aspect of a ruin or a wreck, however unexciting, must be made to yield further elements for our picture of the Greek world. Much has been achieved since the days of Cyriac of Ancona and the other early travelers and collectors. Thanks to the gradual progress of archaeology from a dilettante interest to something approaching an exact science, the picture is now beginning to acquire the nuances of color, of light and of shade which will bring it to life.

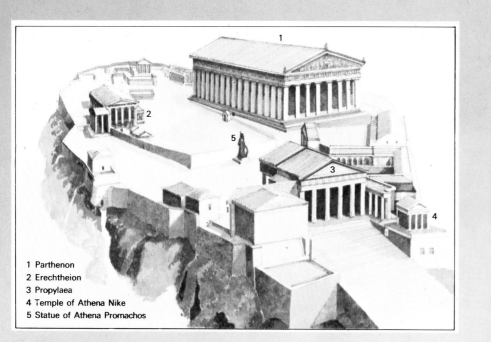

1 Parthenon
2 Erechtheion
3 Propylaea
4 Temple of Athena Nike
5 Statue of Athena Promachos

Left: an artist's impression of the Acropolis at the end of the 5th century. Dominating everything is the magnificent temple of Athena Parthenos (the Maiden), better known as the "Parthenon," completed between 447 and 432 BC. On the northern (nearer) side of the rock stands the much smaller Erechtheion, the temple of Athena and Erechtheus (a legendary ruler of Athens), built between 421 and 406 BC. The third major building is the Propylaia, the monumental entrance-structure designed by Mnesicles (437–432). Just to the right of it stands the tiny temple of Athena Nike, probably completed between 427 and 424.

The Athenian Acropolis in the time of Pericles

The Athenian Acropolis is a low rock about 150 meters wide and 300 meters long, with its main axis from east to west. It falls steeply on three sides and is relatively easy of access only at the western end. As a defensible position it early became the nucleus of a settlement and in the late Bronze Age was surmounted by a Mycenaean palace. In the 6th century BC it was used as a fortress by the dictator Pisistratus and his sons. But by the Classical period it had become purely a sanctuary of the gods, and particularly of the city's patron goddess Athena. Devastated by the Persians in 480 BC, it lay in ruins till the 440s, when, under the guiding hand of Pericles, it was rebuilt as Greece's finest architectural showpiece.

Above: a view through the columns of the Parthenon, showing part of the sculptured frieze which ran around the wall of the *cella* building. It represented the great procession which conveyed a new robe to the sacred wooden image of Athena. Now well lit by sunlight from above, it would originally have lain deep in shadow and, though colored, must have been difficult to discern. *Below*: the Parthenon's architectural refinements have long been admired. To demonstrate the convexity of the temple platform, guides used to place a hat at one corner and point out that it disappeared when a viewer looked along the steps from the next corner.

The religious focus of the Parthenon was the great gold-and-ivory statue of Athena, over 12 meters high, which stood in the *cella*. Created by the sculptor Phidias (who was also general supervisor of Pericles' building program), this statue had a majesty and richness of ornamentation which are barely hinted at in the miniature copies that have survived to our day. The "Varvakeion" statuette (*above*), a Roman trinket of the 2nd century AD, shows only the essentials. The goddess is standing, with a triple-crested helmet on her head, a figure of Victory on her right hand, and a shield and her sacred serpent by her left side.

Above: view of the Parthenon from the northwest, framed by the columns of the Propylaia. The siting and orientation of the temple are superbly chosen to present the visitor with the optimum viewpoint as he enters the sanctuary. *Right:* the sculptured metopes, of which there were 92 in all, ran around the exterior of the building. They represented episodes from legendary or mythical battles, all symbolic of the recent struggle of the Greeks and the Persians. On the main (east) side the gods were shown overcoming the giants, a subject represented on the robe which was carried in Athena's procession; on the west were Greeks and Amazons; on the south Lapiths and centaurs; and on the north probably Greeks and Trojans. Three of these themes were echoed in the decoration of Phidias' statue inside the temple: the Greeks and Amazons appeared on the outside of the goddess's shield, the gods and giants on the inside, and the Lapiths and centaurs on her sandals. Here a metope in the British Museum shows a centaur getting the better of a Lapith.

Left: an excerpt from the Parthenon frieze, showing a group of elders near the head of the procession on the north side. Taking advantage of a pause in the movement they relax and exchange conversation. Ahead of them were musicians and sacrificial animals.

Above: an artist's impression of the sculptures of the Parthenon's west pediment. Though little more than battered torsos now remains, a fair idea of the original composition can be gained from the drawings made by Jacques Carrey in 1674. The subject was the contest between Athena and Poseidon for the land of Attica – a contest which Athena won by producing an olive-tree.

Below: the east pediment represented the birth of Athena, who sprang fully armed from the head of Zeus when it was split by Hephaestus' axe. Here a majestic god, perhaps Dionysus, reclines on Olympus, as yet unaware of the cataclysmic event taking place behind him.

Above: three goddesses, wrongly known as the "Three Fates," from the Parthenon east pediment. Their identities are disputed, but, according to most experts, they are (from left to right) the hearth-goddess Hestia, the ancient sky-goddess Dione, and the goddess of love Aphrodite. Their massive forms and the rich sweep of their draperies place them among the grandest conceptions of Classical art.

Above: view from the Propylaia into the sanctuary, as it may have appeared in antiquity. Mnesicles' entrance hall was aligned on the colossal statue of Athena.

Below: the outer facade of the Propylaia. The north wing, on the far side, housed the Pinakotheke, a picture gallery which contained paintings by Polygnotus.

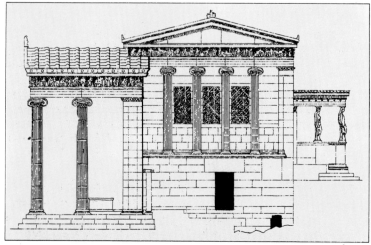

Top left: view of the Erechtheion, from the southeast. This most curious of Greek temples, with its projecting wings to north and south of the main block, is in fact a brilliant compromise between variations in ground-level (the level is much lower on the north and west sides) and between the conflicting claims of different cults. Besides housing the ancient wooden image of Athena, the Erechtheion contained altars to Poseidon (on which sacrifices were offered to Erechtheus), to the hero Butes and to the smith-god Hephaestus; it incorporated the salt-water well and trident-marks produced by Poseidon in support of his claim to Attica; and it had to leave holes in the roof and pavement of the north porch above a spot where a thunderbolt had landed, and a gap in the western foundations over the supposed grave of the ancient king Cecrops. In addition it had to provide access to, and avoid encroaching on, the precinct of Pandrosus containing Athena's sacred olive-tree to the west. *Above:* the famous caryatid porch, where the ritual dressing of Athena's image in its new robe may have taken place at the end of the Panathenaic procession. One of the sculptured maidens is a cast, the original being in the British Museum. *Center left:* the west elevation of the Erechtheion, restored. The larger proportions of the north porch, on the left, reflect the lower ground-level at this side. *Bottom left:* an excerpt from the frieze of the tiny Nike temple. Here for the first time a Greek sculptor shuns allegory and shows the actual struggle between Greeks and Persians – the struggle which was the ultimate cause of the Periclean rebuilding of the Acropolis.

4. Politics and Administration

Before considering the general aspects of life in the Greek world, it is necessary to sketch in more detail the political and administrative framework of our period – a task for which the main sources of evidence are texts and inscriptions.

The Athenian democratic constitution. The political history of the decades after the battle of Plataea was dominated by the rise of Athens. Entrusted with the direction of the follow-up campaigns against the Persians, she cynically converted a free confederacy of Aegean states into a maritime empire, and under the leadership of the arch-imperialist Pericles tried to establish a land empire as well. Though the latter project, which led in the 450s and 440s to a preliminary conflict with the Peloponnesian states under Sparta, was soon abandoned, Athens remained the strongest naval power in the Greek world for another generation.

The hallmark of Athenian civilization during this period was her democratic constitution, which served as a model for many other Greek states, notably those of the empire. The kernel of this constitution was the Assembly, a body comprising all the adult male citizens of the state, which debated and decided all matters of home and foreign policy and elected a number of the executive officers. Meetings took place three or four times a month; a quorum of 6,000 was required for major business; and

any member could speak within it and propose resolutions. Participation in the work of the Assembly was regarded not just as a privilege but also as a duty: Pericles is reported to have said of the Athenians, "We alone regard a man who takes no interest in public affairs, not as a harmless, but as a useless character."

All bills submitted to the Assembly were prepared by a smaller body, the Council, which consisted of 500 citizens over 30 years of age chosen annually by lot, 50 from each of the 10 tribes into which the citizen body was divided. Its other duties, often carried out in committee, included supervision of the magistrates, control of state expenditure, general superintendence of religious festivals, naval works and public buildings, and prosecution of charges of treason before the Assembly. The routine work was entrusted to each of the tribal units in turn, meeting in the circular building known as the Tholos.

The third main element in the constitution was the annual magistrates. The former chief magistrates, the nine Archons, were now recruited by lot and had lost all real power to the ten Generals, who were elected by the

Above: the walls of Aegosthena (late 4th or early 3rd century BC) at the east end of the Gulf of Corinth. Fortifications became more massive as siegecraft developed in the late Classical period. But, as in most Greek architecture, the functional nature of the walls did not prevent the builders from devoting great care and skill to their aesthetic effect.

Reconstruction of the interior and exterior of the Tholos in Athens (c. 465 BC). Each of the ten tribal units of the Council sat here for one-tenth of the year. After Travlos.

Assembly and could, if that body was satisfied with their performance, be reelected year after year. From Pericles onwards they were the chief executive officers of the state, being as much responsible for promoting domestic policies as directing military operations. Election was also the rule for the Treasurers who administered the tribute from the empire, but lesser officials, like the market controllers, controllers of measures and grain wardens, were selected by lot. The use of lot, both here and in the Council, meant that any Athenian citizen, however obscure or humble, might be called on to occupy one of the top administrative posts.

The popular courts (*dikasteria*) were panels of 200 or more drawn from 6,000 jurors, also chosen by lot. They tried almost every type of case, except treason, which was prosecuted before the Assembly, and homicide, which was considered by the old aristocratic council of the Areopagus. The jurisdiction of the *dikasteria* came to extend even to members of allied or subject states within the empire. There was no judge to give guidance, and litigants were obliged to conduct their own prosecution or defense, even in criminal cases. But, in non-political trials at least, judgments were probably equitable enough, great care being taken to eliminate bribery and intimidation; and there is no doubt that the average Athenian was interested in, and reasonably conversant with, the workings of the law. Comic poets like Aristophanes, indeed, poke fun at

the Athenian love of litigation. Many archaeological testimonia from the lawcourts have survived, including allotment "machines," water clocks and jurors' ballots.

One of the fundamental principles of the democracy was the state payment of public servants. Jurors, members of the Council, citizens engaged on military service, and all magistrates except the Generals and Treasurers received a small daily payment in compensation for loss of normal earnings, which ensured that rich and poor alike were enabled to play a full part in civic life. Richer citizens, however, were expected to subsidize the state by performing public services (*leitourgiai*), like the training of a chorus for dramatic performances, or the equipping and maintenance of ships of the navy.

One final aspect of Athenian government was the availability of checks upon the officials and politicians. All magistrates, even the Generals, were accountable to the Assembly for their conduct and expenditure in office; while the constitution also provided a safeguard against aspiring dictators by the device known as ostracism. Any politician could be condemned to 10 years of banishment by vote of the people. Individual votes were cut on potsherds, or *ostraka*, many hundreds of which have been

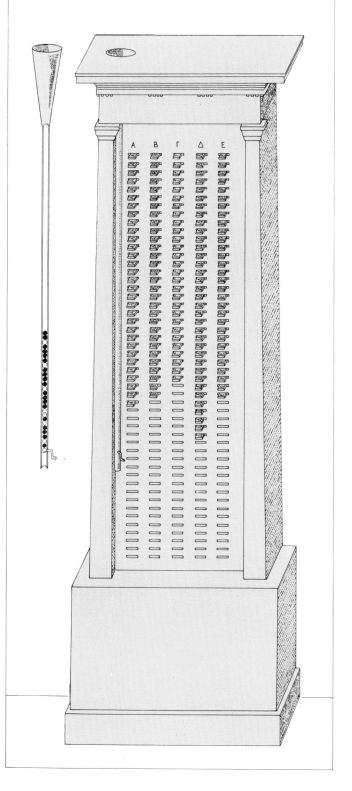

Above: fragment of an allotment "machine" or *kleroterion* (3rd century BC) found in the Athenian Agora. Black and white balls were poured down the tube at the side to determine whether jurors, represented by rows of identity cards set in the slots, should be rejected or retained for a given day or a given court. This example probably served for the allotment of presidents of the Council.

Left: reconstruction of one of a pair of *kleroteria*.

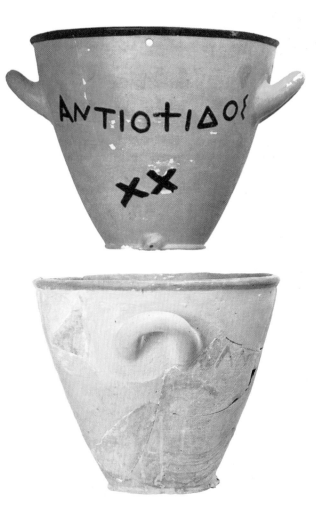

Right: model of a "water clock" from the Athenian Agora. The upper vessel was filled with water up to the hole below the rim, then allowed to empty through the lower spout (shown at the front) into a container placed at a lower level. Such devices were used to limit the time allowed to speakers in the law courts.

Ostraka from the Athenian Agora naming Aristides, Cimon and Themistocles. All three were banished from Athens for ten years by votes inscribed on such fragments of pottery.

found, including a cache of 190 carrying the name of Themistocles, many of them inscribed by the same hands – perhaps prepared in advance for the benefit of illiterate voters.

The Athenian democratic constitution was not all that its admirers have maintained. Suffrage was by no means universal. Not only did women play no part in public life, but there was a large population of resident aliens and a still larger body of slaves who had no political rights. Moreover, in 451, Pericles disfranchised men born of Athenian fathers and foreign mothers – a class which had included some of Athens' greatest leaders, such as Themistocles and Cimon. It has been estimated that, in the 430s, the voters amounted to less than one-sixth of the adult population of Attica (itself a fraction of the population of the empire as a whole). And above all, the citizen body was dangerously volatile. It was all too easy for demagogues to play upon popular emotions and sway the voters into overhasty or irrational decisions – perhaps the main contributory factor to Athens' erratic policies and eventual downfall in her great power-struggle with Sparta.

Sparta and the Peloponnesian War. Sparta was, in many ways, the antithesis of Athens: a Dorian city where Athens was Ionian; a land power where Athens was the possessor of a far-flung maritime empire; a supporter of oligarchical government where Athens favored democracy; a reactionary state with limited aims where Athens was ambitious and adventurous; a society based on a rigid concept of militaristic communism where Athens fostered a freedom of speech and thought which produced her extraordinary series of creative geniuses.

Sparta had, since the 8th century BC, ruled directly over a large territory made up of two distinct parts – Laconia and Messenia. Their inhabitants, who had no citizen rights

or political representation at Sparta, fell into two groups. The *perioikoi* ("dwellers around") enjoyed a state of vassaldom, administering their internal affairs under the supervision of a Spartan resident, but being bound to accept Sparta's foreign policy and liable to conscription in the Spartan army. The "Helots," descendants of the pre-Dorian population, were little more than serfs, kept in check by ruthless intimidation. They worked the land for their Spartan rulers.

It was the presence of a large subject population which accounted for some of the peculiarities of the Spartans' way of life. The availability of Helot labor gave them the leisure, and the perpetual risk of Helot revolt provided them with the incentive to turn themselves into a military state. In fact the whole life of a Spartan revolved around military training. From birth, when a board of inspectors ordered the exposure of weak infants, every effort was directed to producing superb fitness, great powers of endurance and unswerving patriotism. The result was a formidable army and a monumental lack of imagination.

At the age of 30, Spartans were divided by election into "Equals" and "Inferiors." Whereas the latter lacked the franchise and certain other civil rights, the former were full citizens and became members of the Assembly. The Spartan constitution was admired by many Greeks, because it struck a balance between three fundamental systems of government – monarchy, oligarchy and democracy. The monarchical element was represented by the two kings, who commanded the army in war and were the chief priests of the state; the oligarchic by the Council, a body comprising the kings and 28 elders; and the democratic by the Assembly. Within this system the main task of the Council, like that at Athens, was to prepare business for the Assembly; but here the Assembly had no right of debate and its decisions could be set aside, so that its role was essentially one of rubber-stamping – a task which it performed (much to the amusement of other Greeks) not by ballot nor by show of hands but by shouting. Yet what it lacked in deliberative power it made up for in electoral responsibilities. It elected, again by acclamation, the councillors and possibly also the chief magistrates, the five Ephors ("overseers"). The latter had come to occupy a leading position in the government; they summoned and presided over the Assembly, were entitled to attend meetings of the Council, had the power to arrest and prosecute the kings, and could decree the punishment of any citizen.

However one defines this constitution in relation to the citizen body, it is difficult to think of it in terms of the whole area ruled by Sparta as other than an oligarchy. The citizens were a small elite who controlled the destiny of a largely unprivileged population many times their number. It is, moreover, significant of Sparta's attitude that she tended to promote oligarchical governments in those states which came under her influence or entered her alliance.

Above: the river Eurotas flowing through the territory of Sparta. Sparta was the most powerful military state in Hellas during the 5th century BC, but her conservatism and economic isolationism prevented her from sharing in the great social and cultural flowering of Athens and other states.

Below: the political situation in mainland Greece and Asia Minor at the start of the Peloponnesian War. This war between the Athenian Empire and the Peloponnesian League lasted 27 years and ultimately involved virtually every state in the Greek world.

The allies collectively formed the Peloponnesian League, a confederacy of states which enjoyed internal autonomy but cooperated, under the leadership of Sparta, in matters of foreign policy. They included the powerful Dorian states of the northeast Peloponnese, with the exception of Sparta's traditional enemy Argos; the cities of Arcadia, such as Tegea and Mantinea; and some of the states of Achaea.

These cities could not but view with alarm the advancement of Athens – and none more so than Corinth, the second most powerful state in the alliance, whose interests were seriously threatened by the expansion of Athenian influence. It was the rivalry between these two states that led to the great war which broke out in 431.

The trial of strength between the Athenian Empire and the Peloponnesian League lasted for 27 years and ultimately involved virtually every state in the Greek world. Indeed, in terms of ancient communications and ancient methods of warfare, it was little short of a world war. But its importance has perhaps been magnified by the existence of Thucydides' history, which not only provides detailed information on the first 20 years of fighting but also turns the struggle into a great moral epic. In effect, though the war ended in the defeat of Athens (404), it settled nothing finally, unless perhaps it hastened the decline of the city-state as the dominant force in Greek politics.

The rise of Macedonia. The next half-century saw continued periods of warfare, frequent shifts of power, and repeated changes of alliance, the net result of which was the steady exhaustion of the resources of the states involved. First the Spartans, then the Thebans held the center of the stage. Meanwhile Athens regained much of her maritime power and sought to build a new Aegean empire; while Persia and other outside powers came to play a greater part in Greek politics, often at the behest of one or other of a pair of warring parties. It was in vain that thinkers like the Athenian Isocrates appealed to the Hellenes to sink their differences and work for peace and unity.

In the course of this half-century, warfare became a more professional business. New tactics were evolved; new types of troops, especially the light-armed "peltasts," were used alongside the traditional heavy-armed "hoplites"; and, above all, there was an increasing exploitation of mercenaries alongside the traditional citizen armies. In Sicily, Dionysius I of Syracuse built up a large empire with the aid of professional soldiery; while in central Greece in the 350s the state of Phocis financed a mercenary army by seizing funds from the religious sanctuary of Delphi. The increasing professionalism of war led to a divorce between military and political leaders, for instance at Athens, where the Generals tended to concentrate on their original task of commanding the army or fleet, while the leadership of the Assembly was exercised, more often than not, by financial officials.

The value of cavalry and of new tactical dispositions was displayed by the success of the brilliant Theban generals Epaminondas and Pelopidas at the battle of Leuctra (371), when a smaller Boeotian force overwhelmed the Spartans. They replaced a direct frontal attack all along the line by a massed attack on the left wing, where their best troops, spearheaded by the famous "Sacred Band," were concentrated in a column 50 deep. This victory established the Boeotian hoplites as the foremost in Greece and ended the military primacy which Sparta had enjoyed for nearly 200 years.

One interesting political tendency of the 360s was the formation or consolidation, under Theban influence, of federations, notably the Arcadian League. While each member state remained autonomous within its own boundaries, matters of foreign policy were determined by a federal Assembly (the "Ten Thousand") which was drawn from all citizens above a certain property census and met in the newly founded capital Megalopolis. A federal Council prepared business for the Assembly, which also elected the executive officers, as in normal democratic states; and a federal coinage existed alongside that of the individual cities. Such systems of organization, whereby citizens had voting rights not only within their own states but also in a largely democratic federal government, presaged the much more extensive and lasting leagues of Hellenistic times.

By the 350s, however, the Greek cities were in sad disarray. Sparta was crippled and the Peloponnesian

Obverse and reverse of a gold stater minted by Philip of Macedon. The head of the obverse is that of the god Apollo. Athens, National Museum, Numismatic Collection.

League broken up; the Arcadian League had crumbled; the Theban power bloc in central Greece was collapsing; and the Athenian maritime league, troubled by a revolt of some of its strongest members, was also in process of disintegration.

At this juncture a new power entered the stage of Greek politics. Macedonia was a large tribal kingdom, much troubled by the raids of its northern and western neighbors, and more often than not disunited. Its population was formed from a mixture of Greek tribes and other races; while the royal family, which was renowned for its dynastic struggles, could speak Greek and indeed claimed Argive descent. But the normal Macedonian language was unintelligible to the Greeks, and Macedonia as a whole was regarded by them as a semibarbarian state.

In 359 there came to the throne a monarch with the skill and energy to weld Macedonia into the greatest power of the Balkans. Philip II had spent two years of his youth as a hostage at Thebes, where he had developed a taste for Hellenic culture and observed the new military techniques developed by Pelopidas and Epaminondas; and, after he had secured his position by getting rid of five pretenders and defeating his troublesome neighbors to the northwest, he set about the deliberate absorption of the Greek cities into his realm. Wily and unscrupulous, he did not play the game by the rules. He was prepared (like Epaminondas) to conduct campaigns in the winter months, traditionally regarded as a close season for military action; he was prepared to temporize, to go back on agreements, to achieve his ends by bribery; and, above all, he was a past master at exploiting disunion among the Greeks – city would be played off against city, faction against faction.

By gaining control of the gold mines of Mount Pangaeus, just inside Thrace, he was able to issue the first regular gold coinage in Europe and to maintain a standing national army of professional soldiers, the finest, most complex and most efficient body of troops that the world had yet seen. The main striking arm of this force was the cavalry, notably the heavy cavalry (the "Companions"), which was recruited from the nobility and included a special corps of royal horse-guards. In the infantry the

Above: Macedonian arms, painted in the lunette of a tomb at Leukadia (3rd century BC). We see a round shield, two swords, two helmets and a pair of greaves.

Right: Demosthenes (384–322 BC), the great Athenian orator. The whole figure contributes to the characterization of the subject (here the tragedy of Demosthenes' futile efforts to halt Philip's progress). 2.52 meters high. Copenhagen, Ny Carlsberg Glyptothek.

chief unit was the "Foot Companions," who fought in a formation called the "phalanx." Enrolled from the hardy peasant classes of the country, the phalangites were more lightly armed than the Greek hoplites but carried extra-long pikes (some as long as 14 feet) with which they delivered a crushing blow to the enemy line before it could get to grips with them. At the same time they preserved an open order in action, thus achieving much greater mobility than hoplite formations. As auxiliaries to this phalanx Philip added peltasts, javelin-throwers, slingers and light-armed infantry. Like Epaminondas before him, he was an expert in the concerted use of different types of troops and in the tactical differentiation of the two wings of his battle line, one to be employed offensively, the other defensively; while he almost certainly made important advances in the art of siegecraft, hitherto little developed among the Greeks. But the main strength of his army was its loyalty and its high degree of training; inspired by the example of its leader, perfected by rigorous drilling, and seasoned by long years of service, it became an almost irresistible fighting force.

Philip's progress was steady and inexorable. Between 357 and 348 he absorbed the cities of the Macedonian and Thracian seaboard, won the leadership of the Thessalian League, gained alliances in the Thracian Chersonese and on the Propontis, reduced Chalcidice, razing Olynthus to the ground and enslaving its population, and persuaded Euboea to revolt from Athens. In 346 he put an end to the Sacred War against the Phocians, the violators of Delphi. Here he achieved a diplomatic breakthrough by taking over Phocis' place in the Amphictionic League, the venerable body which exercised guardianship over the Delphic shrine, and by being chosen to preside over the

Delphic religious festival. The "barbarian" had been officially accepted as a Hellene.

All this time Philip had been consolidating his power. In Macedonia he built roads to improve communications and fortresses to control strategic points; while campaigns against the tribes beyond its northern and western borders safeguarded the frontiers and permitted the rapid development of city life. In the territories which he conquered he allowed some cities to remain autonomous and some kings to continue ruling as his vassals; other areas he incorporated in the Macedonian state as "king's land," and parceled out to native settlers, who thus became Macedonian citizens. Meanwhile he was ever ready to win or buy friends further afield. In addition to the cities on the Propontis, Boeotia had been his ally since 354, and three Peloponnesian cities, Argos, Megalopolis and Messene, sought his friendship in 346. But Athens, which had suffered numerous losses at his hands and viewed with alarm his proximity to the vital trade route through the Bosphorus and the Hellespont, remained doggedly hostile. Inspired by her great orator Demosthenes, whose *Philippics* underlined the threat from Philip and sought to rouse the people to action against him, she won time by making peace, then prepared feverishly for war.

The final contest came in 338. Philip had now tightened his grip on Thessaly, conquered the whole of Thrace and much of Illyria, secured Epirus for his brother-in-law Alexander of Molossia, and won the alliance of Aetolia; he thus controlled an area extending from the Adriatic to the Black Sea and from the Corinthian Gulf to the Danube. But Athens had thwarted his ambitions in the Propontis and Bosphorus, and had induced the Boeotians to change sides. The Macedonian and allied armies, each more than 30,000 strong, met outside the Boeotian city of Chaeronea. While Philip's 18-year-old son Alexander, who led the Companions on the Macedonian left wing, annihilated Thebes' Sacred Band, the king himself, on the right, first feigned retreat and lured the Athenians forward till their line was extended, then struck back and destroyed them. With this defeat, the age of the independent city-state effectively came to an end.

The conquests of Alexander. The most important aspect of the subsequent settlement was the creation of a new alliance, the "League of Corinth," which brought together the states of Greece and the islands under Philip's military leadership and sought to ensure the maintenance of a permanent peace among them. Members undertook to use military sanctions against transgressors of the peace and to refer disputes to the League's Council. Philip thus imposed the kind of Panhellenic Union which Isocrates had dreamed of and which the Greeks had been unable to achieve themselves.

At a meeting of the League's Council in 337 he proposed the great mission which was to unite the League and Macedonia: a joint expedition against the Persian Empire. By 336 an advance army under the Macedonian generals Parmenion and Attalus had crossed into Asia Minor. But a few months later Philip was assassinated and the mantle of leadership fell on his son Alexander, scarcely 20 years old.

Alexander had been well groomed for his role. The philosopher Aristotle, who had been his tutor, had imbued him with a love of Hellenic culture, while Philip had vouchsafed him firsthand experience of war and government since the age of 16. Events soon showed that he had inherited not only his father's restless energy but also his military genius. When Philip's death was followed by rumblings of unrest in various parts of the conquered territories, Alexander stilled them by lightning campaigns – south into Greece, north to the Danube, and west into Illyria. Thebes, which was unwise enough to rebel twice,

The Lion of Chaeronea, set up on the battlefield as a memorial to Thebes' Sacred Band. About 8·50 meters high (including base). The battle of Chaeronea (338 BC) marked the final victory of Philip over the independent states of mainland Greece and was followed by the formation of a new Panhellenic alliance.

was stormed with frightening speed and efficiency, and condemned, in accordance with the decision of the League of Corinth, to be razed – a dire example to any other would-be troublemakers.

The great Greco-Macedonian crusade against Persia was launched in 334. The next 10 years are dominated by the triumphant progress of Alexander and his small army across the Middle East: from Asia Minor, where he defeated the forces of the Persian satraps (provincial governors) at the river Granicus and subsequently liberated the Greek cities; to Syria, where he defeated the Persians again at Issus and captured the island city of Tyre after a heroic seven-month siege; into Egypt, which capitulated without a struggle; to Mesopotamia and Assyria, where he finally crushed the Persian army at the hard-fought battle of Gaugamela; to the Persian capital Persepolis, where the royal palace was fired as a symbol of Greek vengeance for the wrongs suffered in 480 and 479; to the mountainous northeastern regions of the empire (Turkestan and Afghanistan), where he overcame stubborn guerrilla resistance; into northwestern India, where he won his most brilliant military success against King Poros and an army rendered terrifying by its columns of

Bust of Alexander the Great (the "Azara bust"). Roman copy of the head of a statue perhaps by Lysippus. 68 centimeters high. Paris, Louvre.

elephants; and finally back to Babylon across the burning wastes of the Gedrosian desert. When in 323 Alexander died after a short illness, Macedonian rule extended from the Adriatic to the Indus.

It is all too easy, in following Alexander's epic journeys, to overlook the organizational skill which lay behind the campaigns and the essential role played by his many able deputies – particularly in maintaining his lines of communication and in consolidating the conquered territories. Despite the immense distances which the king covered and the remoteness of the regions which he penetrated, reinforcements and medical supplies reached him regularly from Macedonia; and at the same time separate divisions of the army were operating in his rear. Antipater, Alexander's regent in Macedonia, quelled a rising in Thrace and a Peloponnesian revolt instigated by the Spartans; Antigonus conducted campaigns to secure Macedonian control in Asia Minor; Parmenion was left to guard Alexander's supply lines in Media; and other commanders were put in charge of sea communications.

Arrangements for peacetime administration were also set in train. Alexander himself stepped into the shoes of the Persian king, receiving the tribute which had been paid under Persian rule. Beneath him came the satraps, governing much the same areas as their predecessors, but being confined now mainly to civil duties, while military and financial powers were delegated to separate individuals. The most important aspect of this system was the extent to which Alexander was prepared to retain Orientals in high office. Though military posts were entrusted to Macedonians, many of the eastern satrapies were initially put in the hands of Persians (several of whom, however, proved unworthy of trust). Alexander even began to enroll Asiatics in his army – a policy which roused considerable discontent among the Macedonian old guard.

It was the greatest achievement of Alexander's statesmanship that, despite the opposition of his own followers, he set aside the traditional Greek contempt for barbarians and began to build a world in which all races would cooperate on equal terms. He realized that a lasting empire could be built only on a basis of toleration and multinational participation. Thus the different peoples under his sway were allowed to retain their native religions, their social customs and their legal codes; in the cities which he founded Greek, Macedonian and native were settled side by side; and by the roads which he built and the uniform silver currency which he instituted he encouraged the commerce which brought Greeks and Orientals together. He himself and many of his entourage took Persian wives.

But it was, above all, the spread of Greek culture which came, under Alexander's successors, to create a unifying element in the areas which he conquered. And the instrument by which this culture was disseminated was the city, with its Greek layout, its Greek buildings and its Greek institutions. Alexander is said to have founded more than 70 of these, all called Alexandria or Alexandropolis, in areas as far apart as Thrace and the Punjab, Egypt and Afghanistan. The most successful was Alexandria in Egypt, but an eloquent testimony to the spread of Hellenization has been provided also by recent discoveries in the eastern parts of the empire, where Greek-style cities have been found north and south of the Hindu Kush, complete with all the trappings of Hellenic life. The reign of Alexander, in fact, marks a turning-point in the history of Greek civilization; under his guidance it was transformed from a Mediterranean phenomenon into the common heritage of much of the civilized world.

The Hellenistic kingdoms. It was too much to hope that such a vast and heterogeneous empire could long remain under the rule of one man. The next half-century is one of the most confused periods in Greek history. First one general, then another made a bid for supreme power, only to be thwarted by alliances of convenience between the other contenders. Fortunes and frontiers changed with bewildering rapidity.

Amidst this chaos the subject peoples of Egypt and Asia, cowed by the armies of their Greco-Macedonian rulers, but also governed, on the whole, with tact and skill, remained quiet. Though the constant wars doubtless hindered economic development, they were largely

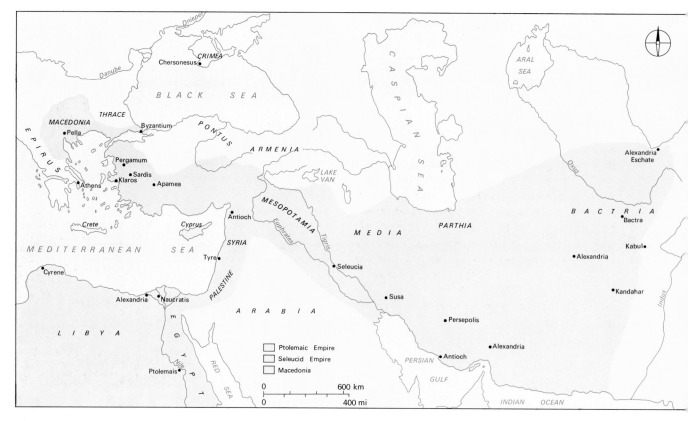

The Hellenistic empires about 275 BC.

fought with professional armies and to some extent financed with the treasures captured by Alexander from the Persian king; the results were neither so bloody nor so ruinous as the old internecine struggles of the Greeks. Under these circumstances the process of Hellenization begun by Alexander was able to develop. And, eventually, the new "Hellenistic" world acquired a more stable political shape.

In this world there were three main kingdoms, one in each continent. Egypt had, from the first, been taken by the astute Ptolemy, who strengthened his claim to power by snatching the body of Alexander for burial in his new capital of Alexandria. He assumed the title of king in 305, and, when he died in 283, his kingdom passed smoothly to his son Ptolemy Philadelphus and a dynasty (the "Ptolemies") was thus created which endured for a further two and a half centuries. In Asia the dominant figure to emerge from the turmoil was Seleucus. Though forced to cede Alexander's Indian territories to the native king Chandragupta, he managed to unite the rest of the empire east of the Aegean under one rule and to hand it on to his son Antiochus in 280. The "Seleucid" dynasty lasted till 83 BC. The third and final kingdom was that of Macedonia, including Thessaly, which came under the control of a settled line of kings in 275, when Antigonus Gonatas, the grandson of Alexander's general Antigonus, won the throne. Alongside these kingdoms many of the cities of southern and central Greece retained or regained their freedom, but they now lived very much under the shadow, if not under the direct influence, of the Anti-

gonids in Macedonia.

Within this basic framework fluctuations naturally continued to take place. The eastern portions of the Seleucid Empire began to melt away, though Antiochus III ("the Great") reasserted his authority over them for a brief time in the late 3rd century. The Seleucids and Ptolemies indulged in a series of contests (the "Syrian Wars") for possession of the seaboard of Asia Minor and, more particularly, for the strategically and economically important region of southern Syria, which passed into the hands of now one side, now the other. But the major developments in the Hellenistic world were the emergence of the new kingdoms of Bactria and Pergamum.

Bactria, the area north of the Hindu Kush, made itself independent soon after 250 and, under a line of energetic Greek rulers, eventually extended its conquests over Afghanistan and much of northern India. The kings of Bactria and India continued Alexander's policy of cooperation with their subject peoples and of promoting Greek city life. It is to them that we must attribute the main impetus to the building of the Hellenistic cities which have been found south of the Hindu Kush and in the Indus valley – Begram, Shaikhan Dheri and Taxila. Their territories were gradually attenuated by waves of nomadic invaders and they themselves were ultimately eliminated during the 1st century BC, but the cities continued to be occupied under new rulers, buildings containing Greek elements continued to be put up, and echoes of the Greek tradition can still be discerned in the 2nd to 5th centuries AD in the so-called "Gandharan" Buddhist art of north-west India.

The Pergamene kingdom came into being in the second quarter of the 3rd century when a eunuch named Philetaerus, who had been entrusted with the stewardship of a treasure deposited at Pergamum in western Asia Minor, used the funds to hire mercenaries and to make himself semi-independent. Under his successors Eumenes I and Attalus I Pergamum acquired a considerable realm at the expense of the Seleucids and, by virtue of a spectacular victory over the marauding Galatians, an amalgam of Gaulish tribes based in the mountainous hinterland, won a reputation as a champion of Hellenism. This reputation was assiduously cultivated by the Pergamene monarchs, who turned their city into a great center of scholarship and the arts and were conspicuous in their munificence to Athens and other centers in the Greek homeland. In the 2nd century, with Roman help, Eumenes II became master of much of Asia Minor. The kingdom of Pergamum retained its preeminence till it passed into Roman hands in 133 BC.

For the administration of the Hellenistic kingdoms our knowledge is uneven. Certain features they shared in common. In reaction to Alexander's tendency to adopt Persian dress and court ceremonial, his successors on the whole observed a comparative simplicity in their manners; and, though they often took two or three wives, they did not practice polygamy in the Oriental sense, since the rule was only one wife at a time. The succession passed

A papyrus from Ptolemaic Egypt (1st century BC) carrying a letter of a workman to his wife. Such papyri shed fascinating light on social life in the Hellenistic kingdom and preserve the language of everyday conversation. Toronto, University Library.

Silver coin of Demetrius I, king of Bactria (c. 200–185 BC). Demetrius, who perhaps campaigned into India, wears an elephant's scalp helmet, like Alexander on some Hellenistic coins, to symbolize his eastern conquests. British Museum.

through the male line according to the law of primogeniture, and the appointment of a new king was effected, in theory at least, by the acclamation of the army – just as it had always been in Macedonia.

The power of the king was paramount. Though his subjects had the right of petition, they had no constitutional means of exercising influence on his policy or government: he made the laws, deliberated with men of his own choosing, and appointed all executive and judicial officers. Within his realm the Greek and Hellenized cities enjoyed a degree of local autonomy, but they were generally obliged to pay taxes and to acknowledge the overriding authority of the crown.

Despite the aid of secretarial staffs and other administrative assistants, the king found himself confronted with an enormous volume of work, from answering his subjects' petitions and issuing ordinances to undertaking tours of inspection and commanding the army in the field. Seleucus is supposed to have said that no one who knew his burden of correspondence would want to pick up a crown, even if he found it on a scrap heap. Nonetheless, there was always the risk of usurpation, and to give their supreme power some form of special sanction many kings connived at or actively encouraged the practice of ruler worship among their subjects.

With regard to details of administration, we are best informed about Egypt, thanks to the survival of large numbers of documents, official and semiofficial, written on papyrus – documents which record matters as diverse as royal edicts and private lawsuits. We get a glimpse of an immensely complicated bureaucratic machine in which every activity was supervised or regulated by the government – perhaps the most complete experiment in nationalization attempted before the present century.

In opposition to the evident intentions of Alexander, the Ptolemies gave little part in their administrative system to the native Egyptians; the government was largely run by a Greco-Macedonian minority. Even in the 2nd century and later, when there is increasing evidence for intermarriage between Greeks and Egyptians, and a decline in immigration compelled the Ptolemies to make more use of Egyptians both in the army and in the administration, it is clear that the ruling classes remained Hellenic in culture if not in blood. Greek remained the language of official business, and the cumbersome Macedonian calendar, which involved a varying number of months per year, was for a long time preferred to the scientific solar calendar of the Egyptians – much to the distress of those who had to compute dates from one into the other. In short, the partnership of races which Alexander seems to have envisaged fell by the wayside; a Greek elite maintained a vast mass of natives in a state of subjection.

In view of the density of population along the Nile valley and the close-knit organization which had been handed on by the Pharaohs, the Ptolemies found it both impracticable and unnecessary to plant a series of Greek-style cities in Egypt. Apart from small colonies of military reservists and a Greek enclave in the ancient capital Memphis, the only Greek settlements of any size were the new capital Alexandria, the long-standing Delta city of Naucratis, and a new foundation in Upper Egypt called Ptolemais. These had their own territories and a certain measure of self-government, though supervised by royal officials. The rest of the country, however, was the property of the king. The basic units of division, inherited from the Pharaohs, were the counties ("nomes"), about 40 in all, each of them governed by a Greek or Macedonian General, who was in charge of maintaining order, and also developed certain judicial powers. The nomes were subdivided into smaller areas called *topoi*, which were in turn divided into villages (*komai*); both units were under the control of native officials.

The dichotomy between Greek and Egyptian was well illustrated by the apparatus for civil jurisdiction. While disputes between Egyptians were settled by native judges, the *laokritai*, those between Greeks were adjudged by panels of itinerant judges called *chrematistai*. Each race had its own form of law, so that problems arose when the suitors were of different nationalities. Such cases were at first submitted to special mixed tribunals; but there was a tendency for the *chrematistai* to usurp the functions of the *laokritai* and for Greek law to grow at the expense of Egyptian. At the same time, there was a tendency to short-cut the system altogether: suitors anxious for a speedy verdict would resort to the informal arbitration of administrative officers such as the Generals.

All disputes of a fiscal nature and all those involving the king's dependants were placed under the jurisdiction of the financial officials. The treasury was, in fact, the most complex branch of the administration. The assessment and collection of land rents, in money and in kind; the supervision of the various industries and businesses in which Ptolemy had a monopoly or at least a share; the dispensing of the licences which were necessary for activities as diverse as beekeeping and selling cooked lentils; the collection of all the manifold taxes and duties, such as death duties, customs dues, sales tax, poll tax, transit dues, taxes to maintain police and doctors, and taxes in respect of exemption from forced labor – all these entailed the employment of a veritable army of officials. Even to go fishing in the Nile required the purchase of a licence and the attendance of an official who would assess Ptolemy's share of the catch.

At the head of the financial machine stood the finance minister, the second most powerful man in the kingdom. Ptolemy II's minister Apollonius, whose correspondence with Zenon, the steward of one of his estates, has survived, maintained his own court in Alexandria, owned thousands of acres of land, engaged in overseas trade on his own account, and wielded considerable political influence. He controlled, above all, the two great centers to which taxes came – the King's Barn, for the royal quota of grain and other produce, and the State Bank for all revenues in money. These centers were fed by subsidiary barns and banks in the nomes and villages, all with their appropriate officials.

The whole purpose of this elaborate system was to swell the coffers of the state – an aim in which it succeeded admirably. Though committed to the maintenance of the largest fleet in the eastern Mediterranean and to the cost of running their vast bureaucracy, the Ptolemies managed to amass a fortune which was the envy of the Romans in the 1st century BC. But there was no serious attempt to put money back into improving the lot of the native Egyptians. Indeed, when weaker men were at the helm, serious abuses crept in, as shown by Ptolemy VIII's decrees to curb extortion and other malpractice by officials. At the same

Opposite: scene of the river Nile, showing a Ptolemaic warship (bottom left) and merchantman (middle left), as well as scenes from religious ritual and everyday life. Detail of the Nile mosaic from the sanctuary of Fortune at Praeneste (Palestrina) in Italy (c. 80 BC).

time, price-rises added to the difficulties of the population. Not surprisingly, increasing signs of unrest appeared – especially after 217, when the use of Egyptian troops in the Fourth Syrian War revealed to the people their power and their indispensability to the government.

Of the other kingdoms the most interesting is that of the Seleucids. But here our information is much sparser. The vast size and heterogeneous nature of the realm obviously made for a looser organization than in Egypt; the Seleucids were, in some more remote areas, content to entrust the government to client kings, and, even where they ruled directly, they relied on the Persian system of large provinces (satrapies) which were often ethnically and geographically very different from one another and could easily break away to form independent states. In an effort to hold the system together, the royal roads and couriers of the old Persian Empire were maintained and in some respects improved; and a collegiate system was adopted, whereby the ruling king concentrated his attention on the western provinces with his capital at Antioch in Syria, while his heir looked after the east from Seleucia-on-the-Tigris. These measures were not sufficient, however, to prevent the progressive shrinkage of the empire.

Internally the satrapies, at least those east of the Euphrates, were subdivided into smaller territorial units called eparchies and hyparchies, but the details of their administration are notoriously uncertain. The most important aspect of Seleucid rule in Asia was the spread of Greek city life. Clusters of Seleucid cities, many of them called by the dynastic names Seleucia, Antioch, Laodicea and Apamea, developed in Asia Minor, in Syria, along the Euphrates and the Tigris and in Iran. From these, Greek influences, and especially the use of the Greek language, traveled to surrounding areas, often quite remote ones. The process of urbanization and Hellenization continued under Roman rule in Asia Minor and Syria, while, even in the further east, Greek cities survived long after the Seleucid possessions had reverted to Asiatic overlords: Seleucia-on-the-Tigris retained its Greek form and identity as late as the 2nd century AD.

The Greek homeland and the coming of the Romans. One of the striking developments of Hellenistic times is the increasing spirit of cooperation between the old Greek cities. To a large extent, especially in western Asia Minor, this was the result of supervision by the kings; but, even where the cities had greater freedom of action, an improvement in relations can be discerned. Exchanges of consuls became more frequent; states were more ready to invite each other's burghers to their festivals; states in dispute were increasingly willing to have recourse to the arbitration of a third party; and grants of citizenship were made by one city to individuals or indeed to the whole citizen body of another. A variant on this process was the formation of truly federal leagues, of which the Aetolian and Achaean were the most important.

Unlike earlier federations, these two transcended narrow tribal areas to include states which had diverse traditions. The Aetolian League, formed in the 4th century, expanded during the 3rd to embrace virtually all the states of central Greece; while the Achaean League between 255 and 191 grew into a union of the whole Peloponnese. Both followed the example of the older, more limited Arcadian League in offering their citizens a federal, as well as a local, franchise. The constituent cities remained sovereign in the domestic field, those of the Achaean League even continuing to mint their own coins alongside the federal coinage; but all questions of military and foreign policy were settled by the federal parliament, ostensibly democratic in form. In the Aetolian League it consisted of the Assembly of all the citizens and a deliberative Council composed of deputies from the constituent units. Since the Council eventually became too large and unwieldy for effective discussion, much of its work was delegated to a committee of about 100 *apokletoi*, who kept in close touch with the chief executive, the General, who was elected annually and could not hold office for successive terms. In the Achaean League the Council and Assembly were merged in the *synodos*, which comprised all citizens over 30 years of age, a certain quorum from each city perhaps being obliged to attend the meetings and being paid for their trouble. The chief executive was again a General, annually elected and ineligible for consecutive terms of office.

Gold stater of the Aetolian League. The emblem, showing a seated woman (Aetolia) holding a figure of Victory on her outstretched hand, is probably based on a statue dedicated at Delphi in honor of a victory over Gaulish invaders in 278 BC.

The two leagues embody the most successful attempts at unification between Greek republican states. On the one hand the principle of local self-government was respected; the federal meetings were too infrequent to have constituted a serious threat of encroachment on the member cities' private interests. On the other hand, all the constituent states had a fair say in federal decisions, and the Achaean quorum system for meetings of the *synodos* approximated very closely to representative government. In practice, neither federation was fully democratic. The Aetolian *apokletoi* tended to usurp the functions of the Council, becoming to all intents and purposes the government of the federation; while the Achaean *synodos* seems to have been dominated by the better-off classes and by the power and influence of the Generals, notably Aratus and Philopoemen, who were elected to office with monotonous frequency. But, whatever the true nature of their government, both leagues were remarkably successful in holding together and stabilizing large areas of the Greek homeland.

It is ironic that this last and most significant experiment in cooperation belongs to the twilight years of the independent Greek world. A new power had loomed in the west and was destined, during the last two centuries BC, to absorb Hellenistic republics and kingdoms alike, incorporating them in the most durable multiracial empire that has ever existed.

The Romans had conquered the Greeks of Italy and Sicily by the third quarter of the 3rd century but were at first reluctant to become embroiled in lasting commitments east of the Adriatic. They were drawn into Greek politics primarily by the aggressive movements or mutual hostilities of the Hellenic powers themselves, and, though content for many years with *ad hoc* interventions, were eventually forced to adopt a more long-term policy by the failure of the Greeks to set their own house in order. From being the arbiter of Greek affairs Rome passed into the role of conqueror. In 148 she turned Macedonia into a Roman province; in 146 a challenge to her authority by the Achaean League led to the destruction of Corinth and the annexation of southern Greece, now constituted as a Roman protectorate. Roman rule was shortly extended beyond the Aegean: in 133 the last monarch of Pergamum died childless and bequeathed his kingdom to the new masters of Greece, who created from it the province of Asia. The remaining Hellenistic kingdoms followed during the next 100 years. In 65–63 Syria, the last remnant of the Seleucid Empire, succumbed to Roman arms; and finally in 31 BC the defeat of Antony and Cleopatra added Egypt to the empire.

Thus eventually the whole of the Greek world was conquered by a foreign race. But Greek civilization lived on. The Romans learned quickly from their new dependants; they studied Greek literature, collected Greek art, imitated Greek architecture, borrowed Greek social institutions. "Captive Greece captured her wild captor,"

Reconstruction of the monument of Aemilius Paullus at Delphi. A memorial set up by the Roman general after his victory over the Macedonians at the battle of Pydna (168 BC). The frieze at the top of the pedestal illustrates scenes from the actual battle. Roman rule was soon extended beyond the Aegean and by 31 BC, with the fall of Egypt, all the Hellenistic kingdoms had been conquered. After Homolle.

wrote a Roman poet. In the eastern Mediterranean, particularly, the Hellenic way of life, expressed most forcibly by the use of the Greek language, continued under the Romans. In the west the tradition was adapted to new purposes, modified by new influences, and in many respects transformed; but nonetheless it survived – to be rediscovered by the Italian Renaissance. It was through the medium of the Romans that Greek culture was handed down to the modern world.

Everyday Life in the Greek World

For daily life in the Greek world our most important source is Greek literature, especially informative about Athens in the 5th and 4th centuries BC. Writers like the orator Lysias, the philosopher Plato and the comic playwrights Aristophanes and Menander all contribute to the picture. But this picture is confirmed, and to some extent elaborated, by the evidence of material remains, whether actual objects of daily use or artistic representations of everyday scenes. These enable us to observe almost every aspect of Greek life from the cradle to the grave. The illustrations on the following pages show a few facets of the story.

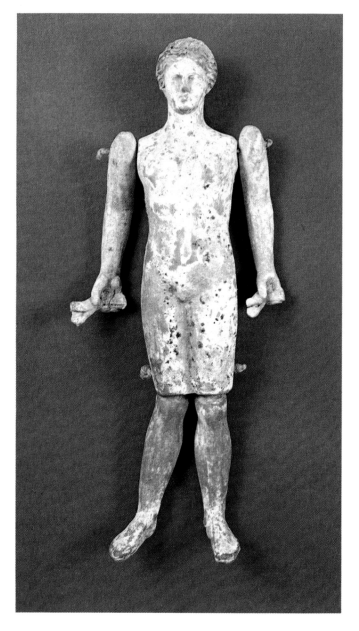

Many of the paraphernalia of childhood would be readily recognized by parents and children today. *Above:* a baby's bottle made of black-painted terracotta, the ancient Athenian equivalent of glass. *Right:* a child's plaything, a terracotta doll with jointed arms.

Below: a child seated in a "potty-chair." An early example of such a commode was found in the excavation of the Athenian Agora. The actual "potty" would be placed in the lower part of the stand.

Left: children's games, painted on one of the little jugs given to children at the Athenian spring festival, the Anthesteria. Two boys play with an improvised chariot-cum-"go-cart."

Above: school-scene. One teacher instructs a boy in the lyre, the most popular instrument of antiquity, while another gets his pupil to read a passage of verse.

Above: wooden school-tablet from Ptolemaic Egypt. Schoolchildren used various methods of writing – for instance, incising with pointed styli on waxed tablets, or writing with ink on wooden tablets, as here. Their exercises shed fascinating light on the methods (often quite artificial) used in schools. For example, the names of letters were learned before the characters were seen; syllables were taught in a list embracing every possible combination of letters; rare and difficult words were juxtaposed with common ones. In fact it seems to have been thought that the scholar should be presented with difficulties as early as possible, so that everyday language should seem simple by comparison.

Right: the second of the two instruments taught by the music-teacher was the *aulos,* a pipe or double-pipe made from reeds (or bone, or wood, or ivory), and frequently misnamed a "flute." We know much less about music than about the other arts (and what we do know suggests a very different taste from our own), but it was clearly an important element in Greek life. It was inseparable from poetry, most of which was meant to be sung, or recited to an instrumental accompaniment; and it played a vital part in religious festivals, particularly those involving dramatic performances or displays of choral singing and dancing.

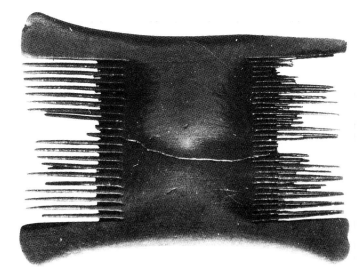

Left: women's dress. The basic garment is the long tunic of linen with short sleeves (*chiton*) over which is wrapped a heavier mantle of wool (*himation*). This was traditionally the Ionian style of dress; Dorian women wore a woolen *peplos*, which was sleeveless and fastened by brooches at the shoulders.

Right: combs were normally of wood (as here) or ivory. In Classical times women wore their hair piled on top of their heads in various fashions; men wore their hair shortish but generally sported beards. Shaving only became normal from the time of Alexander.

Below: sole of a sandal, studded with hobnails. Similar hobnails were found in a shoe-shop excavated near the southwest corner of the Athenian Agora.

Below: footwear was expensive, and Greeks often went barefoot, especially indoors. But many figures are shown in vase-paintings wearing boots and sandals, for instance when traveling. Here a girl carries a pair of "winkle-picker" boots.

Above: scene of women fetching water from a fountain. Given the absence of piped water-supplies, householders were dependent on wells, cisterns or the public fountains. Several of the latter have been excavated in Athens and other cities.

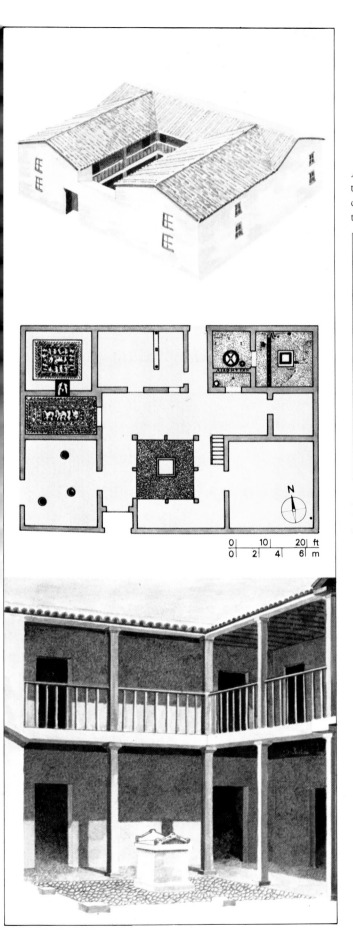

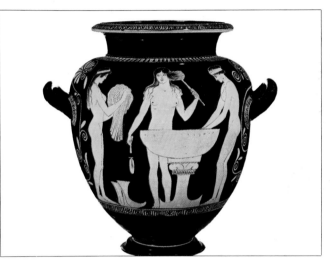

Above: women washing at a basin. The central figure is washing herself with a type of mop, presumably a sponge on a stick, while she holds a perfume jar in her right hand.

Above: bakers rolling dough. Bread was the staple item in the Greek diet, along with cheese, vegetables, eggs and fruit. Meat was rarely eaten, except at the time of festivals; the commonest flesh-dish was fish.

Left: plan and artist's impressions of a Greek house (exterior and interior). The rooms are arranged around a south-facing colonnaded court, with the main reception room (the *andron*), paved with an elaborate pebble mosaic, at the northwest corner.

Above: cooking pots on stands and a Hellenistic tripod pot. Cooking was carried out in terracotta pots placed over a charcoal fire or brazier. Roasting and baking were done in portable clay ovens, also set over a fire.

Right: a wedding procession. Engagement took the form of a pledge between the suitor and the bride's father or guardian, and the actual handing over of the bride (*ekdosis*) took place soon afterwards, preferably at full moon and in winter. The central feature was the procession, portrayed here. The bride and groom are escorted to their house by friends and relatives; music is provided by a flute-girl, and light by torch-bearers.

Left: doctor treating a boy with a distended stomach. Medicine became more scientific as a result of the work of the schools of Cos and Cnidos in the 5th and 4th centuries BC. Though they sometimes practiced surgery, doctors normally allowed nature to take its course, aided by diet, purges and emetics.

Below left: lying-in-state represented on an Attic *loutrophoros,* a vessel used to mark the tombs of those who had died unmarried. The body was laid out in the home and mourned by the family before the funeral. Here the deceased is a girl, crowned as if for her marriage, while one mourner is a relative tearing her hair in the standard gesture of mourning, and the other is a slave (as revealed by her short hair).

Below: the dead were sometimes cremated, sometimes interred. In Athens the most important cemetery lay outside the Dipylon gate; among the many different types of monument set up was a series of sculptured reliefs (5th and 4th centuries BC) showing members of the family bidding the dead person farewell. Here the dead woman, Hegeso, seated in an easy chair, is being handed a jewel-box by her maidservant.

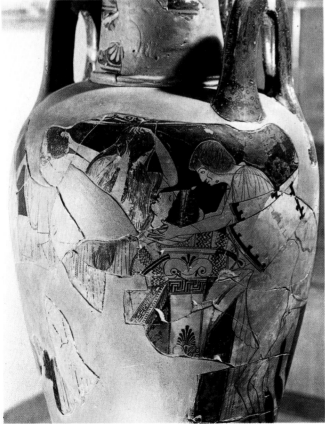

5. Economics and Society

Agriculture. The staple economic activity of the Greek world was, as in all ancient societies, agriculture. It was traditional among the Hellenic states that the bulk of the citizens should own land: social systems and military organization alike were originally based on assessments of landholdings and agricultural wealth. It was the pressure for land, always at a premium in the narrow valleys and coastal plains in which most Greek settlements lay, that provided the major impetus to the waves of colonization in Archaic and early Hellenistic times.

Different regions naturally favored different types of farming. Grain crops were a vital need, but the dry summers and thin soil of the Greek homeland were generally unfavorable to their being cultivated in bulk. Apart from Euboea, the main sources of corn were overseas: south Russia, Cyprus, Egypt, south Italy and Sicily. Thus Athens was always dependent for about two-thirds of her grain upon importation, notably from the Black Sea region. Olives and grapes, however, flourished

Opposite: woman grinding corn in a handmill: 5th-century terracotta figurine in Athens, National Museum.

Below: a reconstruction of a farm near Vari in Attica, showing beekeepers in the foreground. The hives are terracotta tubes laid on their sides in racks.

in most parts of the Greek world. Olive oil, used for cooking and burning in lamps, was one of the main Athenian exports, while the most famous wines were those of the Aegean islands, such as Chios and Thasos. Other general, though less important, items of produce included fruits (especially figs), vegetables (peas, onions, cabbages, lentils and garlic), flowers, necessary for the wreaths worn or displayed at festivals, and honey, which was the only source of sweetening in ancient times. Mount Hymettus in Attica was particularly renowned for its honey, and a farm recently excavated on its southeast slopes has yielded fragments of terracotta beehives with traces of beeswax.

Fishing and stockbreeding were also, of course, widely practiced. The most important fisheries were those of the Bosphorus and Black Sea; while the chief horse- and cattle-raising area was the plain of Thessaly; and the most famous sheep were those of western Asia Minor and of Taras in south Italy. Outside Thessaly good grazing land for cattle was in short supply, but all the Greek states pastured a fair number of sheep and goats in their upland regions, while donkeys and mules were bred for transport purposes, and pigs for their meat.

The conquests of Alexander both took traditional Greek forms of agricultural production to new regions and brought new plants and animals into the Greek world. On the one hand, viticulture became much more common in Egypt and the Near East; and, on the other, the Greeks became acquainted with exotic fruits and vegetables, and with unfamiliar breeds of sheep and poultry. Among animals, the most striking novelty was the camel, used in Ptolemaic Egypt as a beast of burden. Egypt, with the alluvial silt deposited by the annual floods of the Nile, was a particularly fertile addition to the Greek world. Besides grain and vegetables, it yielded flax, papyrus (the basic source of paper in ancient times), sesame and many other plants.

Methods of cultivation, especially before Hellenistic times, remained rather primitive. The plow was a simple wooden implement consisting of three parts: the stock, which broke the ground; the tail, by which the plowman directed the plow and pressed the stock into the ground; and the pole, to which the draught animals were attached. There were no wheels. This contraption merely produced a furrow, without turning the earth over, so that a further plowing might be necessary before the sowing took place. Harvesting was carried out with sickles, and threshing was performed in a manner still seen in the Greek countryside: that is, by allowing the sheaves to be trampled by a team of horses or mules driven round a circular threshing floor. Such threshing floors have been found on several ancient

farms, often in exposed positions, where the wind would have blown away the chaff. The corn, after being dehusked with a mortar and pestle, was finally reduced to flour with the aid of hand-worked grindstones.

In the 5th century there was little idea of how to get the best out of the soil. The shortage of cattle meant a lack of manure, and crops were grown on a simple biennial system, the land being cultivated one year and left fallow the next. In the 4th century more careful exploitation began to appear, with a possible use of the "three-fields" system, in which a field was sown with different crops in the first and second years and left fallow in the third. But it was only in Hellenistic times that agriculture achieved something of the status of a science. Aided by learned treatises and practical manuals, landowners explored various new methods. Among the most avid experimenters were the Ptolemies, who missed no opportunity of increasing Egypt's production, whether by carrying out irrigation schemes, by selecting the best available seed corn (including some foreign strains), or by ensuring regular crop rotations.

On the cultivation of vines and olives we have a fair amount of information; for instance, planting-pits excavated in fields outside the city of Chersonesus in the Crimea show the former spaced rather less than two meters apart. Vines were generally layered along the soil to protect them from the summer winds, and bunches of grapes were dusted to protect them from the heat of the sun. The grapes were picked to the sound of flutes and trodden in vats equipped with handrails by which the workers could steady themselves; the must was led by channels in the floor of the vat to a spout which drained into a jar placed ready at the side. Olives could be picked by hand or shaken down with long sticks. They were pressed, after a preliminary pulping in a handmill, by being heaped in flat envelopes or cakes beneath a beam on which pressure was exerted either with weights or (later) by the tightening of a screw. The same device was also used to extract further juice from grapes after the treading.

Systems of landholding naturally varied from place to place and period to period. The land of the Greek cities, in both Classical and Hellenistic times, was normally in private hands. Fifth- and 4th-century Attica was a country of small farms, some of them worked by the farmer himself with the aid of a few slaves or farmhands, others run by a bailiff on behalf of an owner who spent much of his time in Athens. Many Athenians had both a town house and a farm; indeed, the close relation between town and country in the Classical city-states in general is well shown by finds of agricultural implements, oil presses and wine-treading floors in towns, for instance at Olynthus. In Laconia and Messenia most of the land was divided into lots held by Spartan citizens and farmed on their behalf by the Helots; each citizen received a fixed amount of the produce of his lot as a living allowance. Owing, however, to the breakdown of the property system and the

Above: olives, one of the staple items in the economy of the Greek world.

Right: a stone press-bed from an olive-press, found on Delos. The bed would have been laid horizontally and cakes of olives heaped on top of it.

diminution of the citizen body, more and more lots came to be concentrated in the hands of a few families, who thus accumulated large estates. In other parts of the Greek world, such as the Thessalian plain with its stockbreeding farms owned by the ruling aristocracy and worked by a serf population, large estates had presumably existed from the start.

In the Hellenistic kingdoms, virtually all land except city land belonged to the monarch, who either granted it in estates to large landowners and in lots to soldiers, or farmed it through serfs, who were obliged to pay rents in money or in produce. As usual, we know most about Egypt, where the royal peasants were subject to strict controls. Ptolemy supplied their seed corn, prescribed how much acreage should be given to each kind of crop, and bound them to the land from sowing to harvest. He also charged a fee for the use of all pasture-land and imposed a tax on farm animals. His permission was needed even to fell a tree. The old Egyptian temple lands, too, became the property of the king, who allocated a certain proportion of the produce to the priests and took the rest.

Industry. The largest-scale industries in the Greek world were usually the extractive ones: the mining of metals and the quarrying of stone. Among the metals the most valuable were gold and silver, the former mined at Mount Pangaeus in Thrace, on the island of Thasos, and, in Hellenistic times, in Nubia (the modern Sudan), and the

latter obtained from mines at Mount Pangaeus again and at Laureion in southeast Attica. Copper, important as a constituent of bronze, came from Cyprus and from various parts of the territories conquered by Alexander, notably Phoenicia and areas further east; lead was gained as a by-product from the silver mines at Laureion; and iron was mined in numerous places throughout the Greek world, but especially in the Black Sea region. Of stones the finest were the marbles – those of Mount Pentelicus near Athens; those of Paros and Naxos, in the Cyclades; and those of Asia Minor. But much commoner as a building-material was limestone, which was quarried far and wide. The huge quarries worked by Athenian prisoners-of-war at Syracuse in 413 still exist as an eloquent testimony to the scale of operations which could be achieved.

So far as we can judge from the available evidence, mines and quarries were often under the control, direct or indirect, of the state, and were often worked, as at Syracuse, by unfree labor. At Laureion the Athenian government leased pits to private citizens who might dig there with their own hands but more often than not hired gangs of slaves for the purpose. The rich capitalist Nicias had 1,000 slaves who were let out to mine-masters during the first part of the Peloponnesian War; and there were perhaps as many as 20,000 slaves altogether in the Laureion mines at this time. In Ptolemaic Egypt the kings worked their mines and quarries directly, using the labor of criminals and prisoners-of-war. A horrifying description

of conditions in the gold mines of Nubia has been preserved by the Roman historian Diodorus.

For methods of work in the mines we are best informed about Laureion. Here vertical shafts less than two meters wide, equipped with wooden ladders, led down to the contact zones, where galleries radiated outwards along the veins of silver-bearing galena. These galleries were so tight that the miners, who perhaps operated in 10-hour shifts, actually digging for two hours at a time, were obliged to work on all fours or on their backs. They used hammers, chisels and different types of picks for hacking at the rock or scraping up loose material, while further workers carried off the ore and debris in baskets. Light was provided by oil lamps set in niches, and ventilation by air shafts; and the danger of roof collapses was obviated by leaving standing pillars of rock as "pit-props" – though a law of 339 makes it clear that these were often removed by unscrupulous concessionnaires anxious to tap their potential ore content. Once the ore had been hauled to the surface, it was pounded in mortars and crushed with handmills, then washed in basins to remove alien material, then smelted in furnaces to isolate the lead from the ore. The silver was finally extracted from the lead by the process of cupellation.

The evidence from Laureion relates mainly to the 4th century, but methods and tools seem to have been much the same at other times and in other mining centers. An interesting detail of work in the Ptolemaic gold mines of Nubia, if we can trust our literary sources, is that the men there had lamps attached to their foreheads, as on modern pit-helmets. Otherwise the Hellenistic period saw few changes, although a few mechanical aids may have been introduced for drainage and surveying – viz. the screw pump invented by Archimedes and certain types of optical levels.

The manufacturing and service industries were normally carried out privately and on a smaller scale, especially during the Classical period. In the better-off households some processes, like spinning, weaving and baking, continued to be done at home, either by the womenfolk or by domestic slaves; but the typical industry was that of the small specialist house-workshop, in which a family of craftsmen, helped perhaps by a few slaves, passed down the expertise of its trade from generation to generation. Several such units have been recognized in excavations southwest of the Agora in Athens: for example, the house whose courtyard contained the workshop of Simon the shoemaker, and the house of Micion, which was occupied by a family of marble-workers from about 475 to the end of the 4th century. Even the flourishing Athenian red-figure pottery production, which may have involved a total of 150 potters and painters at a time, was probably shared by small five- or six-man shops. Few industries attained the size of Cephalus' shield factory, which at the end of the Peloponnesian War employed most of its owner's 120 slaves.

Even in the Hellenistic age small-scale production remained the rule. But the cities of continental Greece now declined in importance and their place was taken by the great industrial centers of Asia Minor, Egypt and Syria, in some of which larger factorylike undertakings seem to have been conducted. The production of transport- and storage-jars in Cnidos and Rhodes perhaps fell into this category, for tens of thousands of examples have turned up in various parts of the Hellenistic world. In Pergamum the royal textile and parchment factories, where slave labor was extensively used, were certainly large-scale enterprises; and the same applies to the royal textile and papyrus factories in Ptolemaic Egypt. The Ptolemies, in addition, extended state control or state interest to virtually all the lesser businesses of Egypt. For instance linen-weavers throughout the country, including those of the temple estates, were obliged each year to deliver a certain quantity of cloth and garments to the government and to make good in money any deficiency. Oil manufacturers were fully in the service of the state, all mills being registered, and all the produce bought by the king. Other forms of production, like brewing, could only be exercised under licence. It should be stressed, however, that industries in Hellenistic times, whatever their size, and whether government-directed or private, progressed little from the methods practiced in the workshops of the Classical period. Inherent conservatism and, to some extent, the availability of slaves or, as in Egypt, of cheap free labor militated against the general development of labor-saving devices. Only in architecture and military engineering were technological discoveries widely applied – for example in the construction of artillery and siege engines.

Every state had its builders, its potters, its metalworkers, its weavers, its shoemakers and so forth; but obviously some places became renowned for particular forms of production. In the 5th and 4th centuries Athens was the center of the painted pottery industry; while Corinth and Chalcis (in Euboea) were celebrated for their metalwork, Miletus and Taras for their woolen textiles, Miletus again for its furniture, and Megara for its cloaks. After Alexander the most popular types of fine pottery were the glossy black or red wares and those decorated in relief; Athens remained an important production center at first, but Pergamum and other places later took the lead. Pergamum also joined Miletus and Taras as a leading manufacturer of woolens, and her kings promoted the large-scale production of parchment as a counterweight to the Egyptian papyrus industry. The island of Cos spun thread from the wild silkworm of Asia Minor. Egypt was celebrated for linen, silver plate and glassware, in addition to papyrus. Silver plate and glass were specialities of Syria too.

The technical skills of the Greek craftsman, despite his often primitive tools and methods, were highly developed. As an example we may take the manufacture of Attic red-figure vases. The potters, whose workshops were focused in the area of Athens known as the Kerameikos, used an exceptionally fine clay whose iron content gave it a rich red color. After purifying this clay in large settling-basins, they shaped their vessels on a wheel operated by hand by a boy assistant, then kept them in a damp room till ready to be painted. The painter, often a different man from the potter, first coated the surface with an ocher wash to heighten the color of the clay, then carried out the actual ornamental and figure decoration, generally with the aid of preliminary sketch lines. Finally the pot was submitted to firing in a kiln. The painting and the firing were the most characteristic and sophisticated features of the production process. The paint, used for filling in the background and supplying linear detail within the figures, was in fact made from the same clay as the body of the pot and, when first applied, was barely distinguishable in color from it; but a complex three-step firing at carefully regulated temperatures produced the familiar color scheme of red and black. This required great technical expertise; but many Attic potters and painters went further. Though creating essentially functional objects, they endowed their pots with a beauty of form and an elegance of decoration which elevate them to the realm of art.

The relief wares popular in Hellenistic times were more mechanically produced, being wheel-made in molds which carried stamped impressions of the decorative motifs; but their workmanship still generally conformed to high standards of technical and artistic accomplishment. In other fields craftsmen displayed similar virtuosity. Workers in the finer metals were conversant with all the techniques employed today: repoussé, chasing, hammering, casting, filigree. Bronze-casters had mastered the art of creating large-scale hollow statues by the *cire perdue* ("lost-wax") method – that is, by melting out a layer of wax enclosed between a mold and a core, and replacing it with molten bronze. Glassmakers, though not yet familiar with blowing, were able in Hellenistic Egypt to mold and cut their vessels, and to decorate them with threads of color.

For techniques in the humbler crafts we have evidence from artistic representations, notably in Attic vase painting. Blacksmiths, naked for the heat, soften iron in a tall, pillarlike forge, whose fire is fanned with bellows made from goatskin; then one holds the red-hot metal with tongs while another hammers it over the anvil. A cobbler works leather into shape, his tools and patterns hanging on the wall behind him; or he cuts a sole around the foot of a boy standing on his work bench. Carpenters are shown squaring off a beam with a long-handled, hammerlike instrument, or drilling a hole in a chest with a bow-operated auger. A woodcarver lightly chisels a herm; an armorer lovingly polishes a helmet.

We also see women spinning and weaving. The tufts of wool were drawn out over the extended leg, a process

Scene from a pottery workshop. The painter seated at the left is decorating a mixing-vessel very similar to the vessel which carries the scene (5th century BC). Attic red-figure pottery dominated the market for fine tableware for much of the Classical period. Oxford, Ashmolean Museum.

which was sometimes facilitated by the use of a semi-cylindrical pottery thigh-shield, the *epinetron*, of which numerous examples remain. Then the strands were spun into thread on a spindle in the manner still employed by peasant women; and finally the cloth was woven upon the loom. The latter was of the primitive vertical type, with the warp held taut by pyramidal loom weights and the weft thrown across, starting from the top and proceeding downwards, by means of an oval shuttle pointed at the ends. Although hardly any Greek textiles have survived, representations and reflections in the visual arts demonstrate the skill achieved by weavers (many of them, of course, professionals) in patterned work as well as plain.

Transport and trade. In a mountainous land divided into fiercely independent city-states, as continental Greece was before the time of Philip and Alexander, overland transport was naturally difficult. Wars and bandits hin-

dered communications; roads were often no more than tracks, passable only by foot or on donkey or muleback. The great religious sanctuaries, whose festivals attracted large crowds, were admittedly served by better roads, some of them provided with artificial ruts along which the wheels of carts could run, but there was rarely space for two vehicles to pass. Under these circumstances the Greeks naturally tended to do a lot of their traveling by sea. Merchandise in particular was best conveyed in boats: a single vessel could be loaded with goods which on land would require a small army of pack animals or oxcarts. After Alexander the situation changed. In the newly conquered areas the Greeks inherited the developed road system of the Persian Empire, where overland travelers, whether the horsemen of the government dispatch service or the merchants of the camel caravans, could pass with relative ease and security. But seafaring still remained the most important means of communication, especially in

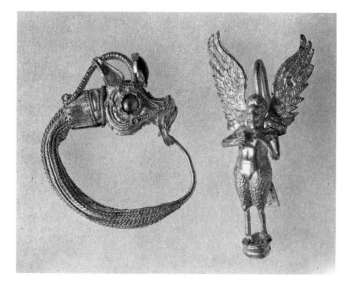

Earrings of the Hellenistic period. Greek jewelers were masters of techniques like filigree and granulation. British Museum.

those parts of the Hellenistic world which lay around the Mediterranean.

Greek ships, like all ancient seagoing vessels, fell into two main types: those that carried oarsmen and those that relied on sail power. The former were frequently used for merchandise, e.g. for carrying grain down the Nile in Ptolemaic Egypt, but were more characteristically ships of the line – the triple-banked triremes, or more properly *triereis*, on which Athens based her sea power; the heavier *tetrereis* and *pentereis* which began to appear alongside them in the 4th century; and the gigantic galleys with which Alexander's successors tried to outdo each other. Sailing ships, however, served exclusively as merchantmen. Their normal rig was a large square mainsail lying athwartship, sometimes supplemented by small fore and mizzen sails; but the fore and aft rig, in which the sail is set parallel to the keel, was also known. As for size, they varied in capacity from 70 to over 400 tons burden, while wrecks which have been excavated (generally carriers of heavy loads) ranged in length from 19 to 40 meters. At least one vessel, however, belonged to the super-freighter class: the *Syrakosia*, built under the supervision of Archimedes about 240 BC, had three decks and carried a cargo weighing nearly 2,000 tons.

Seaborne commerce was not, of course, without its disadvantages. There was the ever-present danger of storms or shipwreck on treacherous headlands like Cape Artemisium and those of the southern Peloponnese. Sailing was, in fact, generally suspended during the winter months. Even in summer the first thing which the merchant did on arrival in port was to offer grateful thanks to Poseidon for a safe voyage. At the same time travel was slow. With favorable winds an ancient ship could achieve $4\frac{1}{2}$ to 6 knots, but it might be becalmed for long periods or held up by adverse winds. Added to the natural hazards were the risks afforded by frequent warfare and by

marauding pirate ships. Although Athens in the 5th and Rhodes in the early 2nd century policed the Aegean and virtually suppressed piracy, at other periods the threat from privateers always retarded trade to a greater or lesser extent.

Given the predominance of maritime commerce, the most prosperous cities were almost invariably those with flourishing ports. In the 5th and 4th centuries the principal trading center of the Greek world was Athens, with its port of Piraeus. But other cities were not far behind. Corinth, commanding ports on both the Corinthian and Saronic gulfs, as well as the overland route across the Isthmus, retained a good deal of its earlier wealth, while in Asia Minor, south Italy and Sicily the leading states were respectively the harbor cities of Miletus, Taras and Syracuse. In Hellenistic times the great Levantine ports came into prominence. Alexandria, which received in its newly built harbors the traffic of the Nile and the Red Sea as well as the Mediterranean, overshadowed the rest, but Tyre, Sidon and Seleucia (the port of Antioch) all benefited as entrepots between the Mediterranean and the overland trade routes from the east. Meanwhile Rhodes, standing at the entrance to the Aegean, enjoyed a heyday as the focus of seaborne commerce between that sea and the Levant. Only in the 2nd century did the Rhodians lose ground to Delos, which Roman policy elevated to an artificial supremacy by the conferment of trading advantages.

The conduct of this maritime trade was very largely left to private enterprise. Merchants, often the actual owners of the ships, would pass through several ports during a voyage, buying or selling freight wherever appropriate. States confined themselves to exacting customs dues, usually at 2%, and to ensuring the supply of certain basic commodities, notably grain. Thus Athens made it a capital crime for her merchants to carry corn to a foreign port and instituted a board of grain wardens to supervise the sale of the ship loads which arrived at Piraeus. Only after Alexander did state interference become more extensive, particularly in Ptolemaic Egypt, where the kings exercised their usual close management – among other things claiming the ownership of all imported spices and imposing protectionist tariffs of up to 50% to keep out foreign wool, wines and olive oil.

The normal medium of exchange in the Greek world was coinage. The Spartans perversely continued to use the primitive currency of iron spits till the end of the 4th century, but then even they decided to move with the times and issue coins. With the conquests of Alexander coinage was also brought into common use throughout the Middle East. The traditional method of exchange by barter lingered on, for example in Egypt, where the government received rents and paid some of its salaries in kind; but a money economy gradually came to predominate. Greek money was based on a system of weights. The staple unit was the drachma, which weighed between

4 and 7 grams (depending on the standard used) and was divided into 6 obols (the "spits" retained in Sparta). Higher units were the stater (2 drachmae), the mina (100 drachmae) and the talent (60 minae). These weights varied from state to state, so that the coins based on them varied in value; but the money of the great trading states, particularly Athens in the 5th century, tended to acquire the standing of international currency. Although the cities of the Asiatic coast struck electrum, and gold coinages began to appear in the 4th century, the normal metal used by the mints was silver. In early Hellenistic times a great boost was given to world commerce by Alexander's policy of establishing a uniform currency, based on the Attic standard, for his empire; but, as the empire broke up, unity gave way once more to diversity, though less pronounced than in the Classical period. The Seleucids, the Antigonids and the kings of Pergamum retained the Attic standard; the Ptolemies adopted their own standard, derived from that of Phoenicia; the Greek cities, whenever free, issued coins according to their old local standards, whether Attic, Phoenician, Asiatic or another.

It is impossible to give modern monetary equivalents for Greek coins. Attention is often drawn to the building inscriptions of late 5th-century Athens, which record that skilled craftsmen were paid one drachma per day; but it is possible that this was merely a conventional payment and was normally supplemented by other earnings. In any

Above: a Boeotian black-figure cup showing a parody of the story of Odysseus and Circe. At the right is a typical Greek vertical loom with a shuttle in position. 4th century BC. Oxford, Ashmolean Museum.

Below: a stretch of the tramway (*diolkos*) by which ships were hauled across the Isthmus of Corinth. This route enabled merchants to avoid the hazardous voyage around the promontories of the southern Peloponnese, and presumably provided the state of Corinth with a valuable source of revenue. The modern canal is visible at the right.

case, values fluctuated greatly from period to period and from place to place. For example, the vast amount of bullion released by Alexander's capture of the Persian hoards made money more plentiful and pushed prices up sharply for a generation or so, while in the late Hellenistic period prices rose again, particularly in Egypt, where a shortage of silver led to rapid inflation in terms of the copper coins which served for small change.

A natural concomitant of the growth of a money economy was the development of banking. The first bankers were money changers, called into being by the needs of the traveler in a world of multifarious currencies. They sat behind tables in the streets and marketplaces and thus became known as *trapezitai* ("table-men"), a term which has passed into modern Greek. From money-changing they expanded their business to looking after clients' money, paying interest on deposits, and advancing loans on various forms of security. A favorite form of investment was the loan on bottomry, the means whereby most merchants were able to finance their shipping operations. Alongside the private bankers, there grew up city banks and temple banks: the temples, in particular, aided on the one hand by their sanctity and on the other by their ample bullion reserves, were in a good position both to attract deposits and to undertake investments. Banking flourished in the Hellenistic age, when Rhodes replaced Athens as the financial capital of the Greek world. Although the use of cheques and bills of exchange was unknown, payment by book entry began to take the place of cash transfers; and the increasing demand for such services is attested by a papyrus of the 2nd century BC which records the transactions of an Egyptian country bank. This bank, a department of the Egyptian State Treasury, handled the private accounts of people as diverse as wholesale dealers, government officials, small shopkeepers and artisans.

It would be a formidable task to survey the objects of trade which traveled between the various regions of the Greek world. Many items, like Attic oil and Milesian woolens, have already been mentioned. Generally speaking an export trade developed where an area had a surplus of some crop, as the Black Sea had of corn; where it possessed particular agricultural or mineral resources which were difficult to obtain elsewhere, like Egyptian papyrus or Cypriot copper; and where it produced a celebrated brand of manufactured article, such as Attic red-figure pottery. Imports, conversely, were required by regions which had shortages of basic commodities or a taste for certain foreign goods. Fifth- and 4th-century Athens offers an example of the volume and complexity of inter-state trade. In addition to grain and to timber, vital for the construction of ships and public buildings, she imported iron and copper, salt fish, hides, slaves, fine wines, drugs, paints and dyes, papyrus, linen and innumerable other items; at the same time she exported her pots (full of wine and oil), marble and silver, honey, arms, cutlery, furniture and books.

There was also a good deal of trade with countries beyond the Greek world. In Classical times commerce with parts of the Persian Empire, such as Egypt, naturally falls into this category. But the sources of some imports remained outside Greek control, even in the Hellenistic age. The tin which was essential for the manufacture of bronze must have been obtained (partly perhaps via Carthaginian middlemen) chiefly from the west, from Spain, France and Britain; ivory and elephants (the latter used in Hellenistic warfare) came from Africa and India; and many luxuries were imported from the east – frankincense from Arabia, gems from Arabia and India, ebony and spices from India, silks from China.

Both the Seleucids and the Ptolemies took measures to foster and safeguard their trade with the east. The Seleucids planted settlements on the Persian Gulf to receive boats from India and south Arabia, and their river port of Seleucia-on-the-Tigris became the focal point of the caravan trade; converging there by land and by water, goods continued their journey overland to Antioch and Ephesus. The Ptolemies, when they finally lost southern Syria to their rivals, were dependent on the maritime route around Arabia and into the Red Sea. To secure its final stages they built ports on the Egyptian coast of the Red Sea and ensured that the road from there to the Nile was provided with wells and protected by a chain of block-houses.

The quest for trade engendered a number of notable voyages of discovery. Seleucid generals explored southern Russia, searching in vain for a northern sea route from Afghanistan to the Black Sea; Ptolemaic fleets ranged down the east coast of Africa as far as Somaliland in pursuit of elephants; and about 120 BC, guided by a Hindu sailor who had been rescued from a wreck in the Red Sea, a captain named Eudoxus made the first Greek voyage to India, learning in the process the secret of the monsoon winds which had enabled Arabian and Indian crews to monopolize the maritime trade route. Between May and September, steady winds carry boats directly east to India; between November and March, winds from the reverse quarter blow them back again. But the most spectacular journey of all was that accomplished soon before 300 BC by Pytheas, a Greek from Massilia. Motivated no doubt by an interest in the sources of Atlantic tin, he sailed through the Straits of Gibraltar; reached and circumnavigated Britain, where he visited the stannaries of Cornwall; voyaged northwards nearly to the Arctic Circle; then returned to the north coast of Europe and traveled east as far as an island with an abundance of amber (Heligoland?). His stories were received with the incredulity which has greeted countless explorers before and since.

Social classes. For social divisions in the Classical Greek states we are, as usual, best informed about Athens. Here, in the earlier part of the 5th century, the citizen body contained a small minority of nobles (the *eupatridai*), who

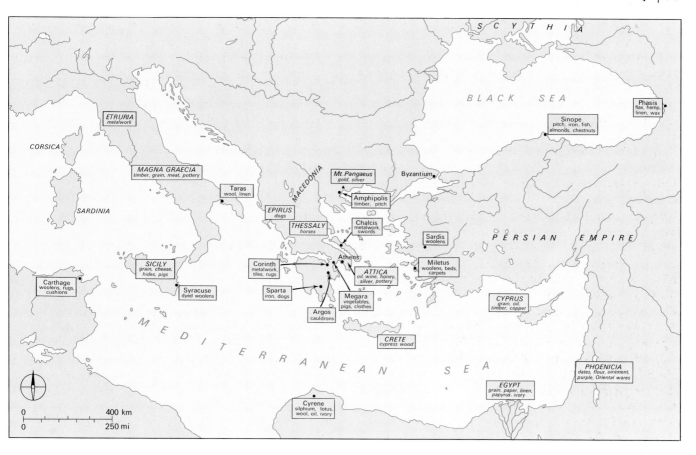

The produce and natural resources of the different parts of the Classical Greek world.

generally owned large country estates; alongside them were the much more numerous smaller landholders, who formed a conservative middle class; and at the bottom of the scale stood the commercial and industrial classes, many of them concentrated in the city itself – craftsmen, shopkeepers, laborers, sailors and suchlike. The formal census divisions, reflecting the traditional importance of farming in Athenian life, had originally been based on annual income in terms of agricultural produce, though in practice the assessment was by now largely monetary. The top class, the *pentakosiomedimnoi*, were those whose farms yielded over 500 *medimnoi* (some 700 bushels) of grain, or the equivalent in other produce or money. Beneath them, the *hippeis*, who served as cavalry in the army, started at 300 *medimnoi*, and the *zeugitai*, who served as infantry, at 200. The *thetes* (less than 200 *medimnoi*) were mainly craftsmen and laborers who owned no land. From them were recruited the rowers of the fleet.

The tendency during the 5th century, as Athens became the greatest commercial and industrial center of the Greek world, was for the landowning nobility to lose ground and to give way to an aristocracy which owed its wealth to trade and manufacturing. Partly as a result of the practice of dividing property between heirs, the larger country estates seem to have become less common, while small-holdings proliferated. The landowning classes were further hit by the devastation of their estates during the

Peloponnesian War, and it was precisely at this time that rich industrialists, like Cleon the tanner and Cleophon the lyre maker, came to the forefront of Athenian politics.

At the same time the lower classes had acquired considerable importance. The vital role of the *thetes* in manning the navy which secured Athens' grip on her empire, and the strength of their numbers in the city, where the meetings of the Assembly were held, enabled them to exert a strong influence on the government and its policies. Some of them eventually rose to high positions of state. Along with political influence came social benefits. Grants were made to poor citizens to enable them to attend the dramatic festivals, and in the late 5th century a system of two-obol doles was instituted. Soon afterwards the government began to pay the citizens for attending meetings of the Assembly. Meanwhile the wealthier citizens, nobility and *nouveaux riches* alike, were subjected to increasing demands from the state, in the form of war-time taxes and of the naval and dramatic *leitourgiai*.

Alongside the citizens there existed a much more numerous population which lacked the franchise. This was divided into three main elements: resident aliens, slaves, and women. The resident aliens, or "metics" (*metoikoi*), comprised immigrants from other Greek states who had come to practice their crafts in Athens; the descendants of such immigrants; the children of unions between citizens and non-citizens (after 451); and freed slaves and their descendants. They had to be registered, they needed to find citizens to represent them in lawsuits, and they paid a small annual tax; in addition, they were forbidden to own houses or land, and were liable to military service and, if sufficiently wealthy, to *leitourgiai*. Against the obligations and disadvantages, however, must be set considerable benefits. The aliens were socially accepted, were allowed liberty to worship their native gods, and were free to follow whatever trade or profession they chose. In fact, they came to play a major part in the industrial and commercial life of the city. Many of Athens' leading merchants and manufacturers belonged to the metic class, for instance the Syracusan shield manufacturer Cephalus who owned 120 slaves and enabled his sons to be educated among the foremost intellectuals of the late 5th century. It was only in exceptional cases that metics were elevated to full citizenship, but the more prominent among their number were sometimes honored with grants of *isoteleia*, a status of equality with the citizens in all matters but the right to vote and eligibility for public office.

Slaves were essential to the Athenian way of life. They carried out much of the labor which left the citizens, or at least the better-off ones, free to devote their time to civic responsibilities. Obtained by capture in war or purchase in the slave markets, these slaves, who were chiefly of non-Hellenic origin, from the interior of Thrace, south Russia and Asia Minor, were owned by private individuals (both citizens and metics), by temples or by the state itself. They were generally employed directly by their owners, or hired out to other employers; but some of them, particularly those who were skilled in some craft, were set up in businesses of their own, on condition that they guaranteed their masters a percentage of the profits. The majority worked in industry, but a fair number were engaged on the land, and a large proportion were in domestic service. Their conditions were often quite tolerable. Domestic slaves became virtual members of their owner's family, sharing the same religion and being buried in the family plot; they were allowed to contract a form of marriage and produce children (who became the property of the master); and they were able to save money for their old age. Even if they experienced cruel treatment, they had the right of asylum in religious sanctuaries, though they could not appeal to the law against their masters. Finally, they were not infrequently rewarded by being given their liberty – though they remained tied to their former master and his family by the religious and social obligations of clientship. Some slaves, in fact, rose to extraordinary heights. The moneylender and banker Pasion began his career as a slave in a banking firm in the late 5th century, won his freedom, set up his own business, acquired a fortune and eventually became an Athenian citizen. When he died in 370, he left his business to another freedman.

The third underprivileged group was women. The wives and daughters of citizens had no more legal and political rights than slaves, and, in middle-class homes at least, spent most of their time indoors in the women's quarters, emerging only to do their personal shopping, to take part in special family events like weddings and funerals, or to attend religious festivals, notably the Thesmophoria, which was reserved for married women. Even their choice of marriage partners was severely circumscribed. A husband was generally selected by the girl's father, who also fixed the date of the wedding and gave the suitor a solemn pledge of engagement before witnesses. In the event of a breakdown of the marriage, the husband could repudiate his wife at will, whereas the wife, having no legal standing, was dependent on persuading an archon to take up her cause. A further source of inequality was society's attitude to adultery, which was tolerated in men but regarded as an automatic ground for divorce in women. The only realm, in fact, where the wife held unchallenged sway was the household: here she was responsible for the management of domestic slaves, the handling of finance, and the supervision of all domestic crafts like spinning, weaving and breadmaking.

The numerical proportions of the classes in 5th-century Attica cannot be determined with any exactitude. It has been estimated that, in 431, when the population was at its height, there were from 40,000 to 45,000 male citizens and, adding women and children, some 170,000 people altogether in the citizen classes. Estimates for the metics range from 20,000 to 35,000, and for the slaves from 80,000 to 200,000 or more – in each case including women and children. The total population would thus have been between 270,000 and half a million. Of this figure perhaps one half lived in Athens, Piraeus and their environs – one-third of the citizens, nearly all of the metics, and two-thirds of the slaves.

Athens was, with the possible exception of Syracuse, the most populous of the Greek *poleis*. For the population of other states we can only found guesses upon the numbers of their armed forces at various periods; but Taras in the 4th century may have come near to Athens, while Corinth may have numbered over 80,000, and three or four others about 50,000. Within these populations the proportions of the classes varied from case to case. Slaves were commonest in the industrial and commercial centers, rarest in agricultural states. In some rural societies, like those of Laconia, Messenia, Crete and Thessaly, their place was largely taken by serfs, the descendants of early inhabitants who had been reduced to bondage by the Dorians and other invaders. In Sparta a citizen elite of a few thousand lorded it over a Helot population several times as large. Oligarchical states, moreover, maintained sharper class divisions within the free population. The Spartans themselves were divided, as we have seen, into Equals and Inferiors; and between them and the Helots stood the non-citizen *perioikoi*, that is the free peasants, artisans and traders. No oligarchy extended full citizen rights to the artisan classes. As for metics, these existed in many Greek states, but little is known about their position and privileges. Xenophobic Sparta prohibited immigration altogether.

During the 4th century the Greek states suffered increasingly from social problems. Exhaustion from incessant wars, depletion of financial resources, population pressures, the difficulty of obtaining a livelihood from the land – all these contributed in different measure to the breakdown of the social systems in different *poleis*. An obvious effect was the growth of mercenary armies. Many Greeks, particularly from backward areas like Arcadia, left their homes to seek more remunerative employment as soldiers of fortune, notably with the Persian king. The Greek states themselves came to rely more and more on mercenary forces, which aggravated their economic difficulties. By the end of the 4th century some of them had even resorted to the sale of citizenship to raise funds. Under these circumstances the conquests of Alexander had a cataclysmic effect on the old Greek world. Huge numbers of Greeks and Macedonians were absorbed in the mercenary armies of the Hellenistic rulers and in the colonies which they planted throughout the Middle East; as a consequence, the population of Greece proper in the 3rd and 2nd centuries seems to have shrunk well below its level during the Classical period.

In most respects, social life in the old Greek cities remained little altered in Hellenistic times. One or two women aspired to fame in philosophy and the arts, and some concessions were made to slaves, but generally speaking these two classes saw no radical change in their condition. The main development concerned the free citizens and non-citizens. Here there was an increasing polarization between the wealthy (citizens and metics alike) and the poor – a situation exacerbated by fluctuating prices and a shortage of work for the laboring class. The plight of the poor no doubt contributed to the ever more common practice of limiting the size of families by exposing unwanted children, especially girls; but its chief result was social unrest on a scale not seen in the Greek world since the 6th century. In numerous states, notably at Sparta, more or less violent attempts were made to abolish debts and to redistribute land and other property among the poor. Partly in fear of proletarian risings, several cities took the first steps towards municipal socialism, especially with regard to the corn supply. The difficulties caused by shortages of corn and the resulting price rises were now regularly solved by the liberality of the richer citizens, including sometimes the grain commissioners and corn merchants themselves, who provided subsidies to keep the price down. In one or two places, for instance Samos, the government even instituted free distributions at fixed intervals. Other social services subsidized by the state or its wealthier citizens included medicine and education: public doctors and teachers became a feature of many cities during the Hellenistic age.

In the Hellenistic kingdoms, or at least those of Egypt and Asia, a new factor in the social life of the Greek world

Hellenistic bronze statuette of a Negro musician (2nd century BC). 19·1 centimeters high. Paris, Bibliothèque Nationale.

Votive relief (a relief offered in fulfillment of a vow) dedicated to Artemis. The goddess, shown conventionally on a larger scale, is greeted by a line of her worshipers. From the sanctuary of Artemis at Brauron (in Attica). 4th century BC.

was introduced by the dichotomy between Greek and native. As time went on, there was some blurring of the original distinction, owing to intermarriage and to the adoption by some of the leading natives of a Hellenic education, but there remained a social and cultural contrast between a more or less privileged ruling minority, essentially Greek in its way of life, and the mass of peasants, laborers and artisans who were native in language, religion and outlook. This latter class (the *laoi*) suffered considerable restraints on its liberty. Peasants were obliged to pay rent in money or kind and to carry out compulsory labor; artisans were trammeled, at least in Egypt, by a network of taxes and regulations. In the later Hellenistic period, as political and economic difficulties set in, social unrest developed. In Seleucid Syria this took the form of antagonism between country and town – i.e. between the *laoi* of the villages and the Hellenized bourgeoisie of the cities. In Egypt it was spread more generally among the working classes and led not only to organized revolts but also to "strikes," wherein peasants or other workers deserted their employment and sought asylum in temples, hoping vainly for some slight amelioration of their conditions. In the Pergamene realm the death of the last king was followed by a serious uprising in which the rural serfs threw in their lot with discontented slaves.

Even within the "Greek" stratum there were, of course, social divisions. The majority consisted of the thousands of ordinary soldiers and civilians who had been settled in the new colonies and cities or had come of their own accord in search of a better living. Above them were the royal officials, especially numerous and distinct in Egypt, where the bureaucracy enjoyed immunity from accusation and arrest. And at the top stood the court aristocracy, personal favorites of the king, who were divided into a hierarchy of grades – "Kinsmen," "Friends," "Bodyguards" etc. Some of these were men of great power, not to mention great wealth: Ptolemy II's minister Apollonius and Antiochus III's minister Hermias were clearly the ancient equivalent of millionaires.

Finally, reference must be made to those who were neither "Greeks" nor "natives." The most famous of these groups were the Jews of Alexandria, who were permitted to form their own corporation (*politeuma*) and perhaps had their own senate and jurisdiction. The tendency of aliens to form such groupings within urban centers is exemplified not only in the great kingdoms, where native elements themselves might be organized into *politeumata*, but also in the free Greek cities, where the rash of religious and social clubs which emerged in Hellenistic times included many associations of foreigners.

Religion. Perhaps the most bewildering aspect of the religious life of the Greeks is the multitude of gods that they worshiped. Each god had his particular role or roles; each must be appeased by the faithful on particular occasions and often in particular places or particular ways. Traditionally the most important were the twelve Olym-

pians – Zeus, king of the gods and lord of the sky;
Poseidon, god of the sea; Hera, goddess of womankind
and consort of Zeus; Athena, the most warlike of
goddesses but also the mistress of crafts and wisdom;
Aphrodite, goddess of love, beauty and marriage; Demeter, goddess of the earth and crops; Artemis, goddess of
wild life and hunting; Apollo, god of archery, music,
medicine and prophecy; Hermes, patron of merchants and
travelers, god of fertility, divine herald, and guide of the
souls of the dead; Hestia, goddess of the hearth (replaced
on the Parthenon frieze by Dionysus, god of wine and the
forces of nature); Ares, god of war; and Hephaestus,
patron of smiths and craftsmen. These gods formed the
focus of the public religion of the city-states, the worship
of here one, here another being singled out for emphasis;
thus Athena was the patron deity of Athens, Artemis of
Ephesus, and so forth. At the same time, there were
countless minor deities. Some were heroes – that is,
mortals or legendary mortals whose exploits had earned
them divine status, like Heracles and (in Athens) Theseus.
Some were spirits of the countryside, like Pan and the
nymphs (the nymphs of the springs and the river-gods
were of especial concern to farmers and shepherds in a land
of irregular rainfall). Others were personifications of
abstract ideas, like Eros (Love), Plutus (Wealth) and
Nemesis (Retribution). Childbirth was the province of
Eileithyia, culture of the Muses, and so on. All this vast
pantheon had been woven together in an intricate web of
family relationships, and embellished with the fantastic
embroidery of colorful stories (many of them mutually
contradictory) which has subsequently become such a
powerful source of inspiration in European art and
literature.

It was a fundamental characteristic of the Greek gods
that they were conceived as human in form and human in
mind. They were pleased, therefore, by the same things
that pleased humans: food, drink, flowers and plants, works
of art, music and dancing, sporting competitions. Offering
such pleasures to the deity was the basis of all Greek
worship. Plates of fruit and cereals, vegetables and cakes
were laid on his altar; libations of milk, wine or honey
were poured over it; garlands were hung from it. Statues,
vases or other ornaments were set up in his sacred precinct.
New altars were dedicated to him. Musical concerts,
displays of dancing, athletic games, horse and chariot
racing formed the centerpiece of the festivals held in his
honor. Buildings, too, might be constructed for him. The
temple itself was, in a sense, an offering, since it was purely
and simply the house of the deity: all acts of homage were
performed at the altar, which stood outside.

The most important gift was the blood offering, formed
by the sacrifice of an animal (sheep, ox, pig, goat, deer).
The species, sex and color of the victim varied according
to the deity honored. Poseidon and Athena preferred
oxen, while Artemis and Aphrodite liked goats; gods
normally received sacrifices of male animals, goddesses

Eirene and Plutus, by Cephisodotus of Athens (c. 375–370 BC). Roman
copy of a statue which illustrates the tendency to divine
personification in sculpture during the 4th century. 1·99 meters high.
Munich, Glyptothek.

of female; and the Olympians were honored with white beasts, while the gods of the earth and of the underworld preferred black or dark-colored ones. The immolation was performed with due ritual. The altar was garlanded, the worshipers were dressed in white and wore wreaths, even the victim was wreathed and decked with woolen fillets. After the altar and hands of the priests had been purified with water poured from a holy vessel, a fire was lit on the altar, there was a formal sprinkling of barley, the beast was stunned with an axe, and finally its throat was cut in such a way that the altar should be spattered with its blood. A special offering of the entrails and other portions wrapped in fat was burned on the altar fire, but the bulk of the animal was consumed by the worshipers at a communal sacrificial feast. Only in sacrifices to the underworld deities was the whole victim given to the god.

These offerings were, of course, not made in a purely altruistic spirit. Though the gods' freedom of action was hampered by forces such as Necessity and by the Fates, their will was still thought to influence the course of human events. So one of the main objects of the faithful was to win their favor, either in the negative sense of keeping in their good books by providing a regular quota of gifts and sacrifices, or in the positive sense of persuading them to grant particular requests. The latter was done by prayer. The sailor would pray to Poseidon for a safe voyage, the farmer to Demeter for a good harvest, the trader to Hermes for the success of a business transaction. The prayer would be accompanied by an offering, or more commonly, on the principle of cash on delivery, by the promise of an offering to be rendered when the wish was granted. There survive many examples of sculptures or altars dedicated to a deity in fulfillment of such a vow.

Another prime concern of the faithful was to learn the will of the gods in advance. Divination could be practiced in numerous ways, for example by interpreting portents of various forms (monstrous births, eclipses, claps of thunder, dreams or even sneezes), by studying the flight of birds, or by examining the liver of a freshly slaughtered animal. The main centers of divination were the great oracular shrines, to which both individuals and governments went to find out what the gods had in store for their undertakings. At Dodona, Zeus's sanctuary in Epirus, the priest-diviners foretold the future from the way the wind rustled the leaves of oak trees. But in the sanctuaries of Apollo inquirers were provided with oracular responses by a prophetess who received direct inspiration from the god. The most famous oracle was that of Delphi, where an old woman known as the "Pythia," seated on the prophetic tripod in a state of ecstasy, would utter unintelligible words which the temple clergy, listening from an anteroom, would translate into a written reply in hexameter verse. The priests were past masters in the art of producing equivocal answers and in wriggling out of apparent errors. After advising the Athenians to send their expedition to Sicily in 415, the priests at Dodona sought to explain its disastrous outcome by claiming that the "Sicily" of which Zeus had been thinking was a small hill of that name near Athens.

The national gods were, as can be seen, a self-interested tribe – and a jealous one too, since they grew angry when denied their proper dues. The government had to maintain the public rites to ensure the collective well-being of the state; the paterfamilias had to keep up the household cults to safeguard the interests of the family. In all this there was little real comfort or satisfaction for the individual. Though he might win support for his enterprises by prayer, he had no sense that a god felt an interest in him, still less a love for him. Similarly, the gods demanded no standard of moral behavior from the worshiper: the performance of the necessary ritual was all that was required. Worst of all, they offered little hope of happiness beyond the grave. Their follower faced the prospect of an indefinite term in the underworld, which was a grim place; though his material needs might be met by burying some of his clothes and possessions with him, and by nourishing him with offerings of food and drink made at the grave, he was given no reassurance as to his spiritual welfare in the hereafter.

This is where the numerous "mystery religions" had an advantage. They promised their adherents immortal bliss, provided that they underwent initiation and carried out the prescribed ritual. As the name implies, the "mysteries" often involved an element of secrecy, and such cults were generally fostered by private groups rather than governments. But one of them, that of Eleusis (near Athens), was officially recognized by the Athenian state and attracted votaries from all parts of the Hellenic world. Based on the worship of Demeter and her daughter Persephone, who were at once goddesses of the corn and powers in charge of the dead, the Eleusinian Mysteries combined a traditional fertility cult with the idea that initiation was a passport to a better life after death. The ceremonies, which were preceded by the declaration of a holy truce to enable observers to come from different states, took place in September and lasted eight or nine days. The first days were occupied with preliminaries in Athens: a proclamation to the assembled participants; a purification ceremony in which they went down to the coast and bathed in the sea, each dragging a piglet which he had to sacrifice to Demeter; and a great sacrifice conducted by the king archon, the traditional guardian of Athenian religion. On the fifth day everyone – priests and priestesses, state officials, foreign observers and the mystics themselves – took part in a splendid procession along the 14-mile road from Athens to Eleusis, escorting the sacred cult objects, which were carried in round baskets known as *kistai*. Finally came the secret part of the festival, the initiation proper, which was held at night, by torchlight, in the Hall of the Mysteries. Although the veil of secrecy remains drawn over much of the ceremonial, we know one or two details. A fundamental part was played by the

Attic red-figure plaque dedicated by one Ninnion to the deities of Eleusis. Two processions, one led by Persephone and the other by the mystic deity Iacchus, advance towards Demeter, seated at the top right. The lower seated figure is perhaps Ninnion herself. Athens, National Museum.

revelation of the sacred objects, perhaps fertility symbols in the form of sexual organs. There was also probably some kind of liturgical drama in which the myth of Persephone's abduction by the underworld god Hades was acted out. And at the climax of the proceedings the initiates were shown, amid silence, an ear of reaped corn. To judge from later writers, the initiation was clearly an uplifting experience; it brought the mystic a glimpse of the true joy which he would find in the afterlife.

The history of Greek religion during the Classical and Hellenistic periods is one of growing disenchantment with the traditional gods. The majority of Greeks, including many of the well-to-do classes, remained true to their ancestral cults, whether from genuine feeling or simply as a matter of form. But more and more people, especially thinking people, were prepared to look elsewhere for spiritual or intellectual satisfaction – to philosophy or to more personal religions like the mysteries.

We can see this happening in 5th- and 4th-century Athens. In the years following the Persian Wars a small number of philosophers began to preach various forms of rationalism which called into question the accepted beliefs; and they gained sufficient notoriety to rouse outbursts of popular hostility, like those which led to the indictments of Anaxagoras, Socrates and others for impiety. In the 420s, after the great epidemic which had decimated the population of Athens, a group including the playwright Sophocles introduced the cult of the healing god Asclepius. This deity, whose chief sanctuary was at Epidaurus, dispensed miraculous cures to the sick while they slept in a special portico; they dreamed that they were visited by the god, who either restored them immediately or prescribed some remedy which they could put into effect when they awoke. Many of them, in gratitude, set up inscriptions or votive models recording the details of their cures and representing the parts of the body treated. The cult of Asclepius exercised considerable appeal because it recognized the needs of the individual and established a close personal contact between him and the divine; it spread from Epidaurus not only to Athens but to several other cities during the last decades of the 5th century.

At the same time Athens saw an influx of foreign gods, many of whom were worshiped with orgiastic rites. Such were the Thracian goddesses Bendis and Kotytto and the Anatolian deities Cybele and Attis. All of these new-comers, presumably brought by metics and slaves, seem to have shared certain features with the cult of Eleusis, such as a process of initiation and a belief in immortality; and Bendis at least received official recognition, her festival being celebrated at Piraeus.

Alongside the new cults, some older established re-ligions, such as the worship of Dionysus in his orgiastic aspect, may have won increased support in the late 5th and 4th centuries. The votaries of Dionysus, grouped in companies known as *thiasoi*, traditionally indulged in the

Coin showing Alexander in the guise of a god. He has the horn of Zeus Ammon, his reputed father. The coin was minted by Lysimachus, king of Thrace from 306 to 281 BC. British Museum.

rite of *omophagia*, tearing an animal to pieces and eating the flesh raw – an act whereby they attained communion with the divinity, who was incarnated in the animal. Closely related to Dionysiac mysticism were the doctrines of Orphism. The Orphic movement, which also took Dionysus as its god, propounded a sophisticated theology which included the doctrines of original sin, soul-migration and salvation; man was created with a mixture of good and evil, and must strive, by initiation and by a life of purity and asceticism, to escape from the cycle of births to a realm of eternal bliss; the uninitiated and the morally unclean would descend to the underworld, now con-ceived as a kind of hell. In a debased form these ideas enjoyed some popularity in Classical times, but in their pure form they were probably too demanding for all save a high-minded few, and it was only in the Hellenistic and Roman periods that they emerged to a position of greater importance.

In the Hellenistic age all manner of new concepts and new religions entered the Greek experience. The Olym-pian pantheon was carried eastwards to the new Greek cities and colonies, where the due rites were zealously observed, and no doubt those natives who aped the ways of the conquerors became converted. But the old Greek gods were unequal to any major work of proselytization, particularly when confronted by more vigorous local cults; and many of the Greeks themselves found the lure of the native gods too strong to resist.

Of the new elements in the religious picture, two were Greek in origin. The first was the worship of Tyche (Fortune), a force which dictated the ups and downs of human existence but was beyond man's control and understanding. This religion, or anti-religion, somehow answered to the sense of disorientation felt by Greeks in the late 4th and 3rd centuries, and gained wide currency in the Hellenistic world. Cities and individuals alike acquired each a personal Tyche; a community's Tyche was often represented on its coins and became something like the city goddess.

The second Greek contribution was ruler worship. This idea, which developed out of the practice of according great men hero cults after their deaths, received its first major boost from Alexander, who believed himself to be descended from Heracles and Achilles, and in 324 asked the Greek states to pay him "godlike honors." When it came to Alexander's successors, the cities needed no bidding but fell over themselves to set up municipal cults to whichever king had protected them or shown them favor. Much of this was doubtless time-serving or conventional homage, but there was at the same time much genuine gratitude and veneration for the rulers, and the hero-cult tradition made deification a natural way of expressing these feelings. Official, as opposed to unofficial, ruler worship flourished in Egypt, whose people had customarily regarded their monarchs as incarnations of the sun god. Ptolemy I set the pattern by establishing a cult of

Alexander; Ptolemy II then deified his father; and the same ruler took the final step by deifying himself and his sister-consort Arsinoe II. Henceforth not only dead but also reigning monarchs automatically became gods – a policy which was soon copied by the Seleucids in Asia.

Towards native religions both Ptolemies and Seleucids adopted a policy of toleration. The result was that deities like the Syrian Hadad and Atargatis and the Anatolian Men Askaenos flourished and eventually made headway even among people of Hellenic blood. Their worship was also carried to the cities of old Greece and the Aegean, where Asiatic and Egyptian residents would form religious clubs, and Greeks might join them. By far the most successful Oriental cults were those of the Egyptian deities Sarapis and Isis. Sarapis was a hybrid created by Ptolemy I by grafting Greek elements on to the native underworld god Osiris; he achieved great popularity as a god of healing and protector of seamen, and by the 2nd century was worshiped as far afield as India, Sicily and the Bosphorus. His consort Isis, an all-powerful goddess who offered a new life of salvation to her initiates after they had gone through a ceremony involving the simulation of death, was even more popular and became one of the leading deities of the Mediterranean world.

The spread of the Isis cult and the new importance of other mystery religions, including that of the "Great Gods" on the island of Samothrace, are further testimonies to the failure of the Olympian cults to satisfy the

A *symposion* scene. The drinkers recline on couches, as for all banquets and drinking-parties, and the right-hand figure prepares to cast his dregs in the game of *kottabos*. A flute girl provides musical entertainment. Attic red-figure cup in Corpus Christi College, Cambridge. About 490–470 BC.

individual's needs. The feeling of dissatisfaction also opened the door to magic and astrology. Both were well-established Near Eastern practices; and both seem to have taken the Hellenistic world by storm in the 2nd century.

But perhaps the most striking aspect of religious development in Hellenistic times was the trend towards monotheism. This phenomenon, which had much to do with the mixing of races and cultures that followed Alexander's conquests, manifested itself in various ways. It appeared in the Stoic philosophy, which, with its ideas of a brotherhood of man and of a universe ruled by a Supreme Power, was tantamount to a religion – though appealing to intellectuals rather than to a broad segment of society. More characteristically, it took the form of syncretism, the fusion of one deity with another. Zeus, for example, was identified with Hadad and many other eastern gods; Dionysus with Sarapis and the Phrygian Sabazios. Sarapis was equated, at times, not only with Zeus and Dionysus, but also with Hades, Asclepius, the sun god Helios and others. Isis gobbled up goddesses with astonishing voracity. All this was perhaps an inevitable consequence of the mixing of races and cultures that followed Alexander's conquests. As the inhabitants of the Hellenistic world grew accustomed to the idea of multinational states, they began to think in terms of multinational religions. Might not, then, all local gods, Greek or non-Greek, be merely aspects of one universal deity?

Entertainments. The ways in which a Greek could divert himself during his leisure time were legion. He might go to the public baths, take exercise in the *gymnasion*, stroll in the *stoai*, visit the barber's shop – all favorite places for the exchange of conversation, elevated or otherwise. He might watch musicians, jugglers, acrobats etc. performing in the street or in the *agora*. He might play board games like draughts; games with dice or knucklebones; or, if sufficiently young and energetic, games with balls or hoops.

In the evening a favorite amusement was the dinner party with its essential sequel, the *symposion* (drinking party), at which the men reclined on couches and sipped their wine to the accompaniment of good talk, parlor games and cabaret – the last frequently provided by girl dancers and girl musicians who were as ready for flirtation as for flute playing. Many vase paintings show the aftereffects of such revels. Among the games played in the course of the evening the most popular was *kottabos*, which involved tossing the dregs of one's wine on to an agreed mark; this could be an empty bowl, or a series of floating saucers which had to be sunk, or a scale which had to be brought down on the head of a small figure.

But the most important entertainments were the public ones – the poetry recitals, singing and dancing displays, dramatic performances and sports which formed part of the religious festivals. Though never divorced from their religious contexts, these activities were obviously apprec-

A rhapsode reciting epic poetry (perhaps Homer) in a musical contest. Detail of an Attic red-figure amphora by the Cleophrades Painter (c. 490–480 BC). British Museum.

iated in their own right and attracted crowds whose sole aim was enjoyment.

Every state had its calendar full of festivals, both minor ones confined to parishes and major ones shared by the whole *polis*. Athens was particularly well endowed; Pericles himself commented on the number and regularity of her contests and sacrifices. Most of these celebrations were of purely internal interest, such as two of the festivals in honor of Dionysus – the Anthesteria, whose chief attractions were a drinking competition and a carnival procession, and the Lenaia, whose junketings offered one of the opportunities for new theatrical productions. But, as Athens' political and commercial influence expanded in the 5th century, two state festivals, the Panathenaia and the Greater Dionysia, achieved a wider renown and lured concourses of foreign visitors to the city.

The Panathenaia, which took place in the month of Hekatombaion (July–August), was the national festival of Athens' patron goddess, Athena. Though held annually, it was celebrated with special pomp every fourth year, when a great procession moved through the center of the city and up to the Acropolis, carrying a new robe for the cult statue of the goddess. Other elements in the festivities included a torch race on the eve of the procession, athletic games of the Olympian type, a boat race, and musical contests held in the Odeion of Pericles. In the latter there were recitals by lyre players and flute players, performances by solo singers to a lyre or flute accompaniment and recitations from the epic poems of Homer. Whereas athletic victors were given special jars (the characteristic Panathenaic amphorae) full of oil from the sacred olives of Athena, musical victors received prizes of money.

The Greater Dionysia, which took place in March, was the dramatic festival *par excellence*; here many of the most famous plays of Aeschylus, Sophocles, Euripides and Aristophanes saw the light of day. The performances took place in the theater of Dionysus on the south slopes of the Acropolis, where the bill of fare provided for the holiday crowds consisted of five solid days of music and drama. On the first day there was a contest of "dithyrambs," choral songs in honor of Dionysus, performed by choruses of 50, a men's and a boys' chorus being sent by each of Attica's ten tribes. The producers (*choregoi*) nominated by the tribes were rich men who had to shoulder the cost as well as the organization and presentation of the 20 entries; in the event of victory, they and their choruses were awarded a bronze tripod, which was frequently dedicated to Dionysus and incorporated in a permanent triumphal monument. One street near the theater became so full of such monuments that it was named the Street of the Tripods. The actual songs were specially composed for the occasion, and the writers were awarded prizes of their own – a bull for the first, a jar of wine for the second and a goat for the third.

The remainder of the festival was devoted to drama. The contest of comedies, in which there were five plays, each written by a different author, was completed in one day; but the tragedy competition extended over three days, the whole of each being allotted to one author; he had to present three tragedies and a light-hearted "satyr-play." In both comedy and tragedy the dialogue was in verse and was punctuated at regular intervals by choral songs; the effect, indeed, must have been closer to opera than to modern drama. The singers of the chorus, who in comedy were often represented in outrageously improbable guises, as birds, as clouds or as frogs, were again equipped and trained by wealthy *choregoi*, one of whom was assigned by lot to each playwright. In addition to the chorus there were normally three male actors. These wore grotesque masks, with laughing expressions for comedy and weeping for tragedy; they could act more than one part; and they performed both male and female roles. One or two extra actors could appear bur rarely spoke. As for their costume, tragic actors were conventionally dressed, but those of comedy wore padding and, at least in the 5th century, giant phalli. When one reflects that the dramatis personae in a comedy included not only fictitious characters but also gods, mythological heroes and prominent living Athenians, it is clear that the effect must have been devastating.

Scenery and props were very simple. In the Classical age the chorus and actors performed alternately on the circular dancing floor (*orchestra*) which formed the focus of the curving bank of seating. There were obviously no curtains, and the background scenery, which consisted of painted wooden panels, remained unchanged throughout each play. At first there were only temporary structures behind the *orchestra*, but later the theater was given a monumental form by the addition of a permanent stage building. This provided a facade to which the scenery could be attached, while its interior housed dressing rooms and spare scenery, as well as some of the crude mechanical devices exploited by dramatists – the wheeled platform which could be rolled out to display the interior of a house or temple, and the crane which could be used for the midair epiphany of a *deus ex machina*. Ultimately, in Hellenistic times, a raised stage was built along the front of the stage building to bring the actors into greater prominence.

The prizes were purely honorific. In each category, comedy and tragedy, a panel of judges decided on the winning entry, and its author, *choregos* and leading actor were awarded ivy wreaths. There was, however, some consolation for the losers, in that the authors and leading actors of all the productions received fees.

Athens was the birthplace of drama, but the new art form rapidly spread, first to the smaller centers of Attica, where theatrical productions formed part of the rural Dionysia, and then to other states. By the second half of the 4th century dramatic festivals and theaters existed throughout the Greek world. As the Greeks traveled eastwards in the wake of Alexander's conquests, they carried the art with them, and theaters became an essential

Red-figure vase painting showing the meeting of Orestes and Electra at the grave of their father Agamemnon, a scene from a surviving Greek tragedy, the *Choephoroi* of Aeschylus, produced in 458 BC. The vase, which is south Italian, belongs to the mid-4th century. Paris, Louvre.

Above: the starting-gate in the stadium at Isthmia. The starter stood in the pit at the bottom left and controlled cords which ran along the grooves to a series of wooden gates, one for each runner. The runners started from a standing rather than a crouching position.

Opposite: Myron's discus thrower, a Roman copy of a statue of c. 460–450 BC. Throwing the discus formed a part of the ancient pentathlon. 1·25 meters high. Rome, Terme Museum.

ingredient in the new cities which they founded. At the same time drama became a more professional business. This is well shown by the growth, in the 3rd century, of the associations of Dionysiac *technitai*, that is of artists and craftsmen connected with the theater; these attained considerable size and influence, were patronized by kings and were granted privileges (for instance inviolability) normally accorded to independent states.

If Athens' major festivals leapt into international prominence during the 5th century, some festivals were already well established as Panhellenic events. Such were the four great jamborees for which Pindar was commissioned to write victory odes. Two of these – the Isthmian Games in honor of Poseidon, and the Nemean Games in honor of Zeus – were celebrated every second year and included both musical and athletic contests, with the emphasis on the latter. The Pythian Games, which were dedicated to Apollo and held near his oracle at Delphi, took place every fourth year and put the emphasis, appropriately enough for a musical god, upon song and dance. But the greatest of all were Zeus's games at Olympia, where everything was subordinate to athletics.

The ancient Olympics, like their modern counterparts, were held every four years and brought together the world's (the Greek world's) finest athletes and sportsmen. Here contestants from Sicily and the south of Italy, mainland Greece, the islands, Asia Minor, the Black Sea and any other outpost of Hellenedom could meet to pit their skills against one another. Not only the athletes and their retinues but thousands of visitors, attracted by the excitement of the games and by the atmosphere of the festive occasion, took advantage of the specially declared sacred truce to make the journey to Olympia. Writers came to recite their latest works, philosophers to win converts, traders to sell their wares. So important did the festival become that it was made the basis of the only chronological system common to all Greeks: instead of measuring dates from the birth of Christ or, as the Romans did, from the foundation of a city, they expressed them in terms of "Olympiads," taking the first Olympiad as 776–773 BC.

After a day of preliminary formalities, the games proper lasted for three days. The program of events was restricted to running-races, wrestling, boxing, the *pankration*, the pentathlon and races for chariots and mounted horses. There were also boys' classes in running, wrestling, boxing, and (after 200) the *pankration*.

Prizes in the Olympics were wreaths of olive, while at the other three Panhellenic festivals they were wreaths of laurel, pine or wild celery. Athletes competed not for material gain but for kudos. And indeed the prestige accruing from an Olympic victory was tremendous; it led to privileges in one's home state, the composition of celebratory poems, the erection of commemorative statues at Olympia itself. Athletes like the wrestler Milon and the runner Ladas passed almost into the realms of legend. In view of all this, it is not surprising that the competitors in the Olympics of Classical times were mainly rich young aristocrats who could afford the time and expense required for traveling to the different festivals. Many of them made a show of their wealth, like the Athenian politician Alcibiades, who in 416 entered nine teams in the chariot race and scooped first, second and fourth places.

But, as time went on, the professionalism which entered dramatic festivals crept into athletics too. Money prizes became more common, especially in the new festivals which proliferated after the time of Alexander; amateurs found themselves gradually driven out of top-flight competition by full-time, highly trained professionals. At the same time the more brutal and spectacular sports, boxing and wrestling, gained popularity at the expense of running and field events. By the end of the 1st century BC, the prize for the pentathlon was only a quarter of that awarded for combat events. But the most striking trend in the latter part of our period was the spread of athletics to the east. As the Greek colonists built theaters throughout the Hellenistic world, so they constructed stadia and *gymnasia* and instituted athletic games, some of which (like the Ptolemaieia at Alexandria) were ranked with the four great Panhellenic festivals. The lists of victors at Olympia reflect the new situation. Names from Italy, Sicily, Athens and Sparta give way to names from Alexandria and newly Hellenized parts of Asia Minor, not to mention Macedonia and Thrace. Athletics, like drama, were contributing to the bond of cultural unity which linked the far-flung cities of the new kingdoms.

Delos

Delos, a barren rocky islet in the middle of the Aegean Sea, owed its importance largely to accidental factors. The mythical birthplace of the god Apollo, it became in Archaic times the leading religious center of the Ionians and the home of splendid festivals held in his honor. Because of this religious importance it was chosen as the center of the naval confederacy led by Athens after the Persian invasion of Greece in 480–479 BC. In Hellenistic times it reached a peak of importance as a great trading emporium, especially after 166 BC, when the Romans declared it a free port in order to undermine the economy of Rhodes. From the mid-2nd to the early 1st century Delos was something of a boom-city, with a rapidly expanding cosmopolitan population. Much of the residential quarter and many of the public buildings date to this period. But such prosperity was short-lived. Sacked twice during the wars between Rome and Mithridates of Pontus (88 and 69 BC), and ruined by the economic competition of Italian ports like Puteoli, Delos declined almost overnight from a flourishing city to little more than a village. Today the island is uninhabited for most of the year.

Plan of the sanctuary of Apollo, the religious center of the island. The three temples are successive foundations of the 6th and 5th centuries BC, while many of the outlying buildings were donated or subsidized by Hellenistic monarchs.

Stone lion, one of a series overlooking the "Sacred Lake." There were perhaps 16 of them, carved in marble from Naxos at some date in the late 7th century BC. One of them now stands in front of the Arsenal in Venice.

0 100 200 ft
0 20 40 60 m

N

1   1 2 3

1 Great Temple
2 Temple of the Athenians
3 Tufa Temple

Above: a pedestal surmounted by the stump of a gigantic phallus, from one side of the shrine of Dionysus, outside the northeast corner of the sanctuary of Apollo. The phallus, symbol of fertility, played an important part in the mystic rites of Dionysus, god of the forces of nature.

Above right: view of one of the streets in the residential quarter near the theater. This quarter grew up spontaneously in the period of Delos' expansion after 166 BC. Unlike planned cities such as Priene or Alexandria, it developed haphazardly with twisting, narrow streets and close-packed, irregular houses. The walls, which often survive to a considerable height, were constructed from pieces of stone quarried on the island and were covered originally with a thick layer of stucco.

Right: plan of the settlement on Delos. The island is long and narrow, about 5 km from north to south, but never more than 1,300 meters from east to west; the city was concentrated in a saddle of land near the northern end, taking advantage of two of the only three good harbors on the island – the bay of Ghourna (top right) and the main port (center left), where visitors are still landed. At the bottom right is Mount Cynthus, 112 meters high, the highest hill on the island, site of several venerable religious shrines.

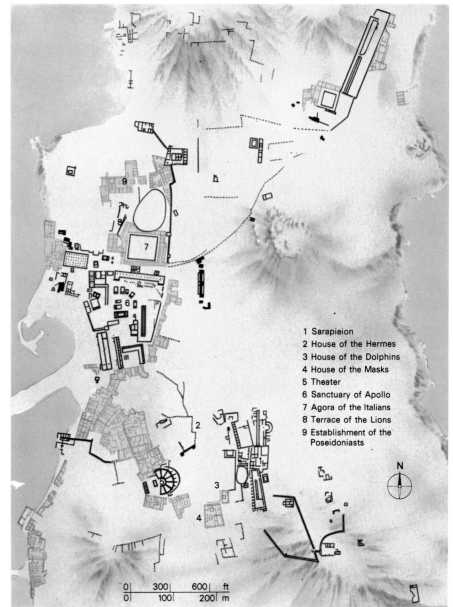

1 Sarapieion
2 House of the Hermes
3 House of the Dolphins
4 House of the Masks
5 Theater
6 Sanctuary of Apollo
7 Agora of the Italians
8 Terrace of the Lions
9 Establishment of the Poseidoniasts

N

Above: arches over a water cistern near the theater. As Delos had only one stream, most of the city was dependent on wells and cisterns for its water-supply. The paving which rested on the arches has now disappeared.

Above left: remains of the House of the Hermes, one of the best preserved of all Delian houses. Terraced up a hillside, it originally had four stories, of which three are partly preserved. The central courtyard was framed by a colonnade in two tiers.

Left: the courtyard of the House of the Hermes. An artist's impression of how it might have looked in its original state.

Right: remains of the Establishment of the Poseidoniasts of Berytus. The many foreign merchants who came to Delos when it became a great trading center in the 2nd century BC tended to form national and professional associations, sometimes under the patronage of a national deity. These premises belonged to the national association of merchants from Berytus (Beirut), under the tutelage of the god Poseidon of Berytus. They included chapels, living rooms, stores, and an assembly hall which may have been used as a kind of stock market. Four columns from the courtyard at the northeast corner have been reerected.

Left: mosaic of Dionysus riding a leopard from the House of the Masks. The mosaic floors which adorn rooms in some of the better-appointed houses of the city form one of the main attractions of the archaeological site and are among the best examples of the art form to have survived from Hellenistic times. The technique used is *opus vermiculatum*, in which the stones are cut to minute proportions to produce subtle detail and gradings of color which approximate to those of painting.

Left: an example of a wall decoration from a Delian house of the late 2nd century BC (the House of the Dionysus). This type of decoration, used in the "state" rooms of better-class houses, is sometimes referred to as the "Masonry Style": it consists of plaster raised in relief to imitate ashlar masonry and richly painted.

Right: the remains of Sarapieion C, the largest of the three sanctuaries of the Egyptian gods established on Delos during the Hellenistic period. The columns standing in the background are the facade of a temple dedicated to Sarapis' consort Isis.

Right: statues of a certain Cleopatra and her husband from the House of Cleopatra. The base of the two statues carries the inscription: "Cleopatra, daughter of Adrastus of Myrrhinus, [has set up the statue of] her husband Dioscurides, son of Theodorus of Myrrhinus, who dedicated the two Delphian tripods in silver which are in the temple of Apollo, on either side of the entrance." Cleopatra was a common name in the late Hellenistic period. The statues show the fashionable style of drapery carving in which the folds of the lower garment show through the upper.

Right: Pan and Aphrodite. This statue group, set up by one Dionysius in the Establishment of the Poseidoniasts of Berytus, is a good example of the more playful side of Hellenistic sculpture. The grotesque goat-god Pan is making advances to the goddess, Aphrodite, who rather half-heartedly seeks to fend him off with a slipper, while a chubby cupid flies between them, symbolizing the power of love. The sculpture is now in the National Museum in Athens.

Left: reconstruction of part of the entablature of the Stoa of Antigonus. Built along the north side of the sanctuary of Apollo, this portico was financed by the Macedonian king Antigonus Gonatas in the third quarter of the 3rd century – a good example of the conspicuous munificence of Hellenistic kings towards international centers. The application of bulls' heads to triglyphs is an unusual feature.

Above: dolphins, detail of a mosaic floor in the House of the Dolphins (called after this mosaic). The dolphins, who are ridden by a tiny cupid, come from one of the corners of a mosaic whose central part consists of a medallion containing a floral motif and framed by concentric borders with various decorative motifs. One of the borders carries the signature of the artist, Asclepiades of Aradus (in Phoenicia). This pavement and the other decorations in the house form an eloquent statement of the refined taste of the bourgeoisie of Delos during its heyday in the late 2nd and early 1st centuries BC.

6. Architecture and Art

Striding bronze Zeus or Poseidon, found in the sea off Cape Artemisium. The god, represented over life-size (2·09 meters high), is throwing a projectile (presumably either a thunderbolt or a trident). 460–450 BC. Athens, National Museum.

Architecture. One of the distinctive features of the architecture of the Classical and Hellenistic Greeks is the emphasis placed on planning. Though old cities like Athens were the product of gradual and haphazard growth, those cities and sanctuaries which were laid out during the 5th century and later show a conscious effort to relate the parts in an integrated whole. Among sanctuaries, the Athenian Acropolis, replanned under Pericles after its devastation by the Persians, provides an excellent example, with its subtle variation of axes, its oblique views, and its careful arrangement of buildings to reflect and enhance the contours of the hill. In the planning of towns the normal Classical mode, first applied in Archaic colonies, was the rectangular grid. Its most famous exponent was Hippodamus of Miletus, who may have been involved in the reconstruction of his native city on orthogonal lines soon after 479, and was certainly called in by Pericles to design the new town of Piraeus a few years later. The "Hippodamian" system was employed on flat and hilly sites alike. At Priene, a small city in Ionia, rebuilt in the mid-4th century, it was ingeniously adapted to a steep hillside, with the main streets running east–west along the contours, and the cross-streets taking the form of steep flights of steps. Here, as elsewhere, groups of one or more blocks created by the grid were merged to accommodate large religious and public complexes, notably the *agora*; while the stadium, for which a long level area had to be found, was set obliquely to the formal layout. The city walls bore no organic relationship to the street system but followed the best defensive line, though this meant including much uninhabited space.

In the Hellenistic age, while the new cities of Egypt and the Seleucid Empire took over the orthogonal system of planning, generally using units twice as long as they were wide, certain cities in Asia Minor developed a brilliant new style of landscaped architecture, similar to that of the Athenian Acropolis but applied on a much larger scale and in a much more thoroughgoing way. The prime example is the upper city at Pergamum. Here, on a westward-facing hillside, two or three generations of architects created a series of terraced buildings which, for all their variety and the asymmetry of their arrangement, achieved a remarkable degree of architectural unity. This was due partly to the careful disposition of the elements, with the fanlike theater acting as a focal point and the long theater terrace providing a solid baseline below, and partly to the use of recurrent themes like the Doric order and of linking devices like the two- or three-story porticoes which opened at front and back on to different levels.

Despite the care lavished on public buildings and town planning, Greek cities fell short in many amenities that we take for granted. Apart from the main thoroughfare in Alexandria, which was reputedly 100 feet wide, and an avenue in Rhodes which measured over 50 feet, streets were relatively narrow, the important ones ranging from 24 to 36 feet, the remainder from 12 to 18. Paved surfaces or raised sidewalks were rarely provided. Drains, both open and covered, became more common from the 5th century on, but were far from universal. Aqueducts brought water to fountain houses and public buildings, but were not used to supply private houses; many householders sank wells or collected rainwater in cisterns. The one public service on which no expense was stinted was defense: as siegecraft improved in the 4th century and Hellenistic times, fortification walls became ever more massive and were equipped with ever larger towers to carry artillery weapons.

For the construction of public buildings like temples, the Greeks were limited to certain basic materials and methods. Their standard material was stone – usually limestone or marble, but in some of the western colonies sandstone. Marble seems to have been the ideal, but, since it was not quarried in many places and was slow and difficult to work, it was normally used sparingly; only a few particularly lavish buildings were wholly or largely constructed of marble before Hellenistic times. Where inferior stones were employed, however, they were often made to look like marble by being given a thin coat of stucco. Apart from stone, the only materials incorporated in a building were timber, used for the roof frame and internal ceilings, and terracotta, used for the tiles (except in one or two sumptuous monuments which had tiles of marble). The method of construction was essentially megalithic. The stone was cut into large blocks of the appropriate shape, which were lifted into position with simple tackle and then held together, not by mortar, but by the force of gravity. Care was taken to obtain close joints, and in the best work the fitting shows extraordinary precision. There were also precautions against shifting: courses of blocks were secured with metal clamps and dowels, and the drums of columns with wooden pins. Openings were spanned by flat lintels: the arch and vault, though known by the 4th century, were used diffidently and in minor roles, for example in gateways and underground chamber tombs.

One of the most characteristic features of Greek architecture was the colonnaded facade. This could be treated in two main ways. In mainland Greece and the western colonies builders favored the Doric order, whose columns had simple cushion capitals, fluted shafts and no bases, and whose upper members contained a frieze of alternating vertical elements called "triglyphs" and square elements, often sculptured, called "metopes." In the islands and east Greece the normal order was the Ionic, which had taller columns with elaborate bases, more finely fluted shafts and volute capitals. Its entablature was lower than Doric, with the most noteworthy feature being a series of toothlike projections called "dentils" hanging beneath the cornice. In Attica, where Ionic buildings were constructed alongside Doric, the dentils were normally replaced by a continuous frieze, which frequently carried sculptures; and by the Hellenistic period, in the mainland

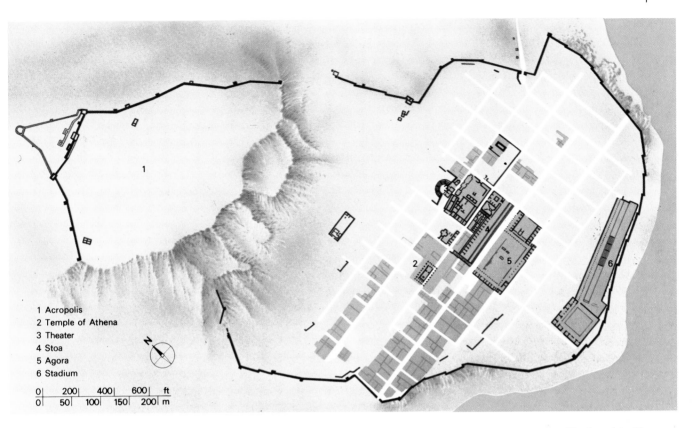

1 Acropolis
2 Temple of Athena
3 Theater
4 Stoa
5 Agora
6 Stadium

| 0 | 200 | 400 | 600 | ft |
| 0 | 50 | 100 | 150 | 200 | m |

Above: plan of Priene (laid out mid-4th century BC) on the coast of Asia Minor. A fine example of the grid system of planning, applied even on a steep hillside.

Below: comparative drawings of the Doric and Ionic orders. Note the tall slim dimensions of the Ionic columns as compared with the Doric.

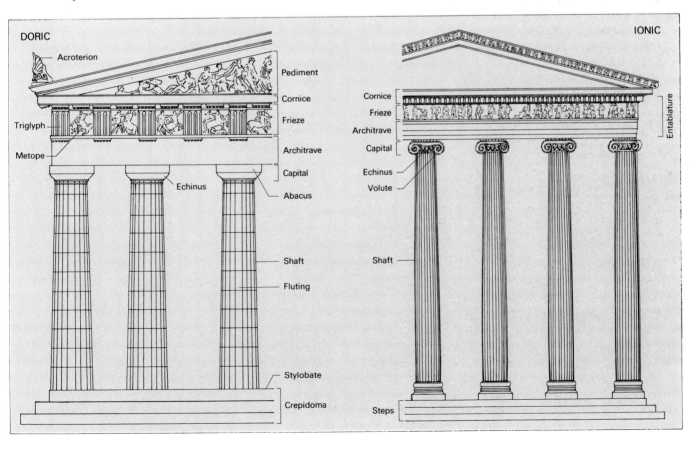

DORIC

Acroterion
Triglyph
Metope
Echinus
Pediment
Cornice
Frieze
Architrave
Capital
Abacus
Shaft
Fluting
Stylobate
Crepidoma

IONIC

Cornice
Frieze
Architrave
Capital
Echinus
Volute
Shaft
Steps
Entablature

and the east alike, there was a general tendency to use the frieze and dentils together. All in all, the Ionic order was more elegant and contained more subsidiary decoration than the austere, sturdy Doric; it has frequently been compared to the female of the species, and the Doric to the male. In either case much attention was bestowed on the proportions of the various elements and (particularly in Doric architecture) on subtleties of line and design; Doric columns of the Classical period, for example, had an almost imperceptible convexity of outline (*entasis*), designed to give them a vibrancy which would have been lacking with a straight profile. In both cases, too, there was a role for color: selected details of the elevation were picked out in red, blue and occasionally gold.

The best examples of columnar buildings are, of course, the temples. These normally consisted of a rectangular central hall (the *cella*) with a porch at the front and a false porch at the back, and an encircling ring of columns (the peristyle), sometimes doubled in the Ionic temples of the east. The finest examples were the Classical shrines of the mainland. The temple of Zeus at Olympia, constructed in the generation after the Persian Wars, set a new standard for the Doric order with its massive columns and carefully balanced proportions. The Parthenon in Athens, begun in 447 and completed in 438, was outwardly Doric but showed a strong debt to Ionic, notably in the slenderness of its columns, in the width of its facade (eight columns instead of the usual six) and in the application of a continuous carved frieze to the upper wall of its *cella* building. Built entirely of marble, this was the most perfect of all Greek temples. Though the largest Doric structure of the mainland, its scale did not exclude a multitude of aesthetic refinements – not only the *entasis* of the columns, but also their slight inward lean, the subtle thickening and closer spacing of those at the angles, the slight outward lean of the entablature, and the way in which the temple platform fell gently away to the corners.

A perfect foil to the Parthenon was provided by the neighboring Ionic temple, the Erechtheion. Here the architect was hampered by religious demands and by the configuration of the terrain, but his response – a unique plan with projecting porches to north and south rising from different levels – was a brilliant success. Small in scale and richly decorated with floral carving, the Erechtheion was a jewel among Classical buildings.

The influence of Ionic upon Doric temples continued in the late 5th and 4th centuries. The temple of Apollo at Bassae, designed by Ictinus, one of the architects of the Parthenon, contained in its *cella* a range of engaged Ionic columns and a continuous sculptured frieze, not to mention the earliest known example of a "Corinthian" capital. This bell-shaped variant of the Ionic capital, carved with acanthus leaves and volutes at each corner, lent itself, unlike the Ionic, to all-round viewing, and was to enjoy a triumphant career in Roman times. Two further Peloponnesian temples, those of Athena Alea at Tegea and

Zeus at Nemea, had peristyles of Doric columns whose slender proportions were even closer to Ionic than those of the Parthenon; and one of them, the Tegean temple, was also provided with 14 Corinthian half-columns in the interior of the *cella*.

In Asia Minor, after a barren period in the 5th century, the 4th saw several important Ionic temples erected or begun. In 356 the Archaic temple of Artemis at Ephesus was largely destroyed by fire, and the Ephesians set to work on a replacement, more or less identical in form, though raised on a higher platform. This gigantic structure, one of the Wonders of the World, incorporated no fewer than 117 columns, each almost 58 feet high. At nearby Priene the small temple of Athena Polias, built by the architect Pythius between 350 and 330, was regarded in antiquity as the Ionic temple *par excellence*, partly, no doubt, because of the thoroughness with which simple numerical ratios were applied to the design. Further south, at Didyma near Miletus, another outsize temple was that of Apollo, started about 300 and still unfinished 500 years later. Scarcely smaller than the Ephesian temple, it adopted several exceptional features, the most noteworthy of which was an open court in lieu of a *cella*. The forest of enclosing columns and the *cella* walls were, in fact, merely a screen; the real shrine, containing the cult statue, was a miniature temple set in the back half of the court.

In the Hellenistic period the orders, now less geographically distinct, were used with greater flexibility, and details from each were mingled freely. The Doric order, in particular, was transformed: its entablature was lightened, its columns were made ever thinner, and Ionic details, such as column bases, were often incorporated. But many architects lost sympathy for Doric altogether. One such was Hermogenes, who invented a new system of ideal proportions for Ionic. His temple of Artemis at Magnesia on the Maeander, much admired for its beauty in Roman times, was the last big Greek temple of Asia Minor. It was probably built in the second or third quarter of the 2nd century – about the same time as work was resumed, after a gap of over 300 years, on the temple of Olympian Zeus in Athens, now converted from a strictly Ionic temple into one of the first with a Corinthian peristyle.

Buildings other than temples fall into certain clearly defined types. The *propylon*, for example, was the gateway of a sanctuary, given monumental form by the addition of columnar porches at front and back. The finest surviving example, the Propylaia on the Athenian Acropolis, built between 437 and 432, had Doric porches, a central passageway flanked by Ionic columns and projecting wings whose asymmetry was cunningly masked by the treatment of the facade and by the neighboring temple of Athena Nike.

The *tholos* was a round building with a conical roof. It

Opposite: the Tholos at Delphi (early 4th century BC). The architect, Theodorus, wrote a book about the building.

served various purposes, primarily religious, and was frequently equipped with an external colonnade. Fourth-century examples at Delphi and Epidaurus had Doric columns outside and Corinthian columns (in one case engaged to the wall, in the other free-standing) inside; the Epidaurian building is notable also for the profusion of its carved ornament – flowers in its ceiling panels, rosettes on its metopes and acanthus spirals along its gutter.

The theater, originally an informal arrangement with wooden seats and temporary pavilions, began to assume permanent shape in the late 5th and 4th centuries. A bank of stone seating describing a curve little longer than a semicircle was cut into a hillside overlooking the dancing floor (*orchestra*) and stage building; while the stage building itself and the side entrances to the *orchestra* were given elaborate architectural treatment. One of the best-preserved examples, which also happens to have been Pausanias' favorite, is the theater at Epidaurus, probably datable to the early 3rd century. Its auditorium, capable of holding 14,000 spectators, is beautifully proportioned, with the arc opening out slightly towards the ends, and the upper third of the seating rising more steeply than the lower part; its excellent acoustics are still exploited by the National Theater of Athens and by would-be Thespians among the crowds of tourists who throng there.

The hall, whether designed for concerts, religious ceremonies or council meetings, was generally a square or near-square building with rows of internal supports. In 5th-century structures, like the Hall of the Mysteries at Eleusis, the supports were equally spaced; but in the Thersilion at Megalopolis, built soon after 371 for meetings of the Assembly of the Arcadian League, this scheme was modified in the interest of the users. The speaker's platform was set short of center, and the supporting columns were ranged in lines radiating from it so as to cause the minimum of obstruction to the view of the audience, which apparently sat on tiered benches around three sides of the chamber. In some smaller halls, like the Bouleuterion at Miletus, the auditorium adopted the curved plan of a theater – an awkward arrangement within a rectangular building.

The *stoa* was essentially a colonnade with a solid back wall. Providing shade from the sun and shelter from the rain, it became an indispensable adjunct of sanctuaries and public squares. Where greater depth was required, there was one, if not two rows of inner columns, usually twice as widely spaced as the outer; often there were also shops and offices in the back part. Further elaboration could occur in various ways. The *stoa* might be L-shaped or have short projections at either end; it might be extended to enormous length; or it might run round three sides of an agora. In Hellenistic times two- or three-storied *stoai* were added to the repertory, and some specimens had colonnades at both back and front – for example the Middle Stoa in the Athenian Agora.

Other structures occasionally received monumental

The theater at Epidaurus (4th or early 3rd century BC). This finely proportioned structure, 118 meters in diameter, was attributed by Pausanias to Polyclitus the Younger, the architect of the Tholos in the same sanctuary.

treatment. Certain Hellenistic altars, notably the Great Altar at Pergamum, were raised on a colonnaded platform approached by a broad flight of steps. In Asia Minor a series of tombs dating from the late 5th century onwards took the form of a temple set on a high podium; the outstanding example was the magnificent Mausoleum at Halicarnassus, built around 350. Residential buildings too – houses and hotels – began to acquire architectural importance in the 5th and 4th centuries. The normal type involved the introspective grouping of rooms round a court or courts. In hotels like the 4th-century Leonidaion at Olympia the rooms were regularly spaced around all four sides of the court and gave on to a continuous portico; but in houses the principal rooms and the portico were usually situated on the north side, where, facing south, they could be warmed by the winter sunshine and provide shade from the high sun of summer. As time went on, houses tended to become more elaborate. Courts with colonnades on all four sides, found occasionally in the 4th and 3rd centuries at Olynthus and Pella, became common in the 2nd-century residential quarter of Delos; walls largely composed of mud brick gave way to walls of stone; and more expense was lavished on interior decorations and furnishing. The change is partly a reflection of the increased wealth of the bourgeoisie in certain cities; but it also corresponds to the general trend in Greek art and architecture to give the secular and the private the sort of attention that was once reserved for religious subjects.

Sculpture. Of the major art forms of the Greek world, sculpture is the best known. Even so, there are tremendous gaps in our knowledge, particularly regarding free-standing statues. For all the scores of great sculptors of the Classical period whose names are mentioned by ancient writers, especially by Pliny, and for all the lists of their works which are recorded, pitifully few original statues survive. The favorite material for free-standing statuary from the 5th century onwards was bronze, which proved too attractive to the metal-hunters of the Dark Ages for many works to escape the melting-pot; of the few large-scale originals known today virtually all were lost at sea or already buried in antiquity. The outlook would be bleak indeed, were it not for the fact that we have many marble copies made in Roman times by the pointing process: though merely mechanical reproductions, they give us at least the general appearance of lost masterpieces. In the 4th century and later some sculptors showed a renewed interest in the carving of stone – with a resulting increase in the survival rate of originals. It is significant that the only statue which can be attributed with any degree of confidence to the hand of one of the great masters (and even this has been disputed) is by Praxiteles, who did not disdain to work in marble. For architectural sculptures, however, we are rather more fortunate: fragments and, in many cases, considerable remains of the reliefs and statues carved to adorn major public buildings have survived from almost every period of Greek history.

By the time of the Persian Wars, Greek sculptors had more or less mastered the representation of human anatomy. In not much more than a century, concentrating on a few basic types (primarily the standing nude male, the standing draped female and the seated draped figure of either sex), they had progressed from patternlike statues, mere symbols of the human form, to figures which actually lived and breathed. In their more elaborate projects, the groups of statues which filled the pediments (gables) of temples, they had achieved some success in rendering figures in action and uniting them in large yet coherent compositions. And in reliefs, notably those of metopes and Ionic friezes, they had begun to master foreshortening and the trick of grading the height of relief to suggest recession in depth.

The first generation after the Persian invasion saw the consolidation and perfection of these achievements. Free-standing male statues, for example, show a new relaxation, with the weight thrown on to one leg, and a consequent loosening about the hips and shoulders. Some, indeed, go much further by exploiting the versatility of bronze to produce strong movement. A good example is the majestic bearded Zeus or Poseidon, found in the wreck off Artemisium, who strides forward imperiously with one arm extended and the other drawn back to hurl his thunderbolt or trident. The outstanding sculptor of the age, Myron of Athens, certainly experimented with action

postures: his Diskobolos (discus-thrower), though anatomically imperfect and squashed into an unnaturally shallow plane, was a bold and aesthetically pleasing composition. Among architectural sculptures, the finest works are the metope reliefs and pedimental statues of the temple of Zeus at Olympia, with their studied use of variety, expression, and (in the west pediment) complex interlocking poses. They illustrate well the new austerity of mood which characterizes the sculpture of the period and has won for it the label "Severe Style." The drapery of standing female figures adopts the plain, heavy folds of the Doric dress in reaction to the fussy zigzags of Ionic garments portrayed in late Archaic times; and faces are heavy-jowled and brooding, with the nose prolonging the line of the forehead in the idealizing "classic profile."

The second half of the 5th century, the "High Classical" period, represents something of a reaction against the trends of the preceding years. Mood, expression and movement are toned down, to be replaced by dignity, restraint and grandeur. This may be one of the cases in the history of western art where the pattern of stylistic

The Bouleuterion (council chamber) at Miletus, subsidized by the Seleucid King Antiochus IV (175–164 BC), as an inscription reveals. The roof of the auditorium was supported by four Ionic columns.

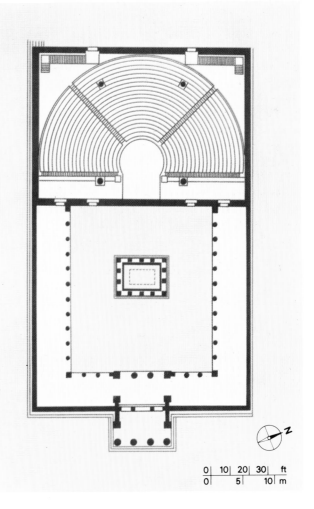

development has been shaped by the genius of one or two great artists. Both Phidias of Athens and Polyclitus of Argos were best known in antiquity for their colossal gold-and-ivory cult statues – Phidias for his Athena Parthenos for the Parthenon in Athens, and his Olympian Zeus (one of the Wonders of the World) for the temple at Olympia; and Polyclitus for his Hera for the sanctuary of that goddess near Argos. But all three works are now lost, and little conception of them can be gained from the miniature copies and coin representations with which we must eke out the literary descriptions. So we have to judge their style by other means.

For Phidias there is a beautiful head in Bologna which is perhaps a Roman copy from his famous "Lemnian" Athena. There are also the sculptures of the Parthenon, over which he exercised a general supervision. Though he himself, in view of his other commitments and the sheer volume of work entailed in the carving, could have executed very few, if any, of these sculptures, they were certainly designed by him and certainly bear his stylistic imprint. The metopes, which represent mythological struggles, are sometimes majestic, sometimes stiff in execution; but the internal frieze and pedimental figures are consistently masterful. The 520-foot-long frieze, showing the great Athenian procession in honor of Athena, handles the relief technique with consummate skill and manages, by its rhythmic alternation of vigorous and stately movement, and by its subtle variation of glance and gesture, never to be dull. Of the pedimental groups, one of which portrayed the birth of Athena, and the other the contest between Athena and Poseidon for possession of Attica, the remains are scanty. But the overall compositions were clearly characterized by the same manifold variety as the frieze, and individual statues remain to testify to the grandeur of the conception. Outstanding are the superbly relaxed reclining Dionysus from the east pediment and the three goddesses popularly known as the "Three Fates," whose exquisite drapery, now falling over the breasts in delicate crinkles, now swept over the knees in broad masses, is truly Olympian in its quality.

While Phidias excelled in gods, Polyclitus seems to have been more at home with athletes. He perfected an ideal system of proportions which he embodied in a statue called the "Kanon," perhaps to be identified with his Doryphoros (spear-bearer), known from Roman copies. This was a squarely built statue shown in a walking attitude, with the right leg bearing the weight, the left leg relaxed and bent at the knee, and the head slightly inclined to the figure's right. The same posture appears in other copies of Polyclitan statues – the Diadoumenos (athlete binding a fillet of victory around his head) and the wounded Amazon, with which he allegedly won a sculptural competition at Ephesus. For all his formal perfection, Polyclitus cannot escape the charges of monotony (hinted at by one ancient writer) and, more especially, artificiality: the walking attitude is ill suited to

The "Hestia Giustiniani," a good example of the "Severe Style" in Greek sculpture. Roman copy of a bronze statue of c. 460–450 BC. The figure is probably a goddess, though not certainly Hestia. 1·93 meters high. Rome, Torlonia Museum.

the action of the Diadoumenos, while the Amazon's raised arm, though revealing the wound beneath the armpit and the sculptor's knowledge of the shoulder muscles, must have caused her untold pain.

In the 4th century new currents affected Greek sculpture. With the gradual impoverishment of the city-states, artists were obliged to travel more in search of commissions, sometimes even to work for non-Greek patrons, such as Mausolus, the prince of Caria, who engaged a team of leading Greek sculptors to decorate his tomb, the Mausoleum at Halicarnassus. The result of this mobility was a decline in the old ideals of patriotism and religious reverence which had inspired artists like Phidias. Art grew less aloof – gods tended to become more human; emotion, often depicted with great subtlety, became a dominant theme; and there was a heightened interest in the individual.

The great figures of the century are Scopas, Praxiteles and Lysippus. Scopas, from the island of Paros, seems to have been a sculptor of passion. A frenzied maenad (worshiper of Dionysus) in Dresden may be a copy of his work, and various heads from the pediments of the temple of Athena Alea at Tegea, of which he is said to have been the architect, may also reflect his style. Their twisted brows and deep-set eyes give them an expression of haunting intensity. The Athenian Praxiteles, on the other hand, produced figures with delicate features and gentle, almost wistful expressions. His most famous work in ancient times was the Aphrodite at Cnidos, described by Pliny as the finest statue in the world. Supposedly modeled on the courtesan Phryne, the goddess was represented leaving her bath, a theme which enabled the sculptor to introduce the genre of the female nude to Greek statuary. The Aphrodite is now lost, and it is difficult, from the indifferent Roman copies, to appreciate her sensuous beauty, which provoked extravagant praise and at least one indecent assault. In the case of the Hermes at Olympia, however, we almost certainly have a Praxitelean original. The young god, who is holding the baby Dionysus in his left arm and teasing him with a bunch of grapes held in the right hand, is carved with a grace and softness which are a far cry from the lofty detachment of Phidias' immortals. His flesh has a soapy smoothness, his eyes are indistinct and dreamy, and there is a suggestion of a smile on his lips. As in other Praxitelean statues, the body has a languid S-curvature, with the weight so strongly displaced to one side as to require a support (a treetrunk) under the left arm. Such supports were less necessary for bronzes, and had rarely been used in free-standing statuary; but Praxiteles, working in marble, now frankly admitted them as an integral part of his compositions.

Lysippus of Sicyon straddles the boundary between Classical and Hellenistic art. He had a long career, extending from about 360 to near the end of the century, and is said to have produced 1,500 works. Though exclusively a bronze caster, his versatility is shown by the range of themes and types which he tackled – athletic statues, portraits, statues of gods and heroes (including both colossal and miniature works), multifigure compositions, animal sculptures, allegorical and genre subjects, even vases. Of this vast output only copies and echoes remain. The exaggeratedly realistic Heracles of the Farnese type, for instance, which shows the mighty hero, with bulging muscles and swollen veins, leaning wearily on his club after the completion of his labors, may be based on a Lysippan statue. And a relief of a lion hunt on the "Alexander" sarcophagus, dating to the late 4th century,

may reflect a bronze group at Delphi on which Lysippus collaborated. As court sculptor for Alexander, he also created idealizing portrait statues of the king, one of which may have been the prototype from which the "Azara bust" in Paris is derived. The emergence of portraiture is one of the phenomena of the age; it evidently received an important fillip from the work of Lysippus and his brother, who is supposed to have developed a process for taking plaster impressions from the human form. In the field of athletic sculpture, Lysippus' most notable statue was the Apoxyomenos (athlete scraping oil from himself). A Roman copy in the Vatican confirms the statement of Pliny that the sculptor modified the Polyclitan canon of

Hermes and the child Dionysus, by Praxiteles. This masterpiece of the mid-4th century BC was found in 1877 in the temple of Hera at Olympia. 2·15 meters high. Olympia Museum.

proportions "by making the head smaller than old artists did, and the body more slender and firmly knit, to give his statues the appearance of greater height." More important, the figure shows a new sense of movement. This is achieved partly by the turn of the neck, partly by the way in which both legs are tensed, as if the weight is being transferred from one to the other, but mainly by the projection of the arms in front of the body. For the first time a Greek sculptor has exploited the third dimension and thus broken away from the tradition that a statue should be seen from one main viewpoint only.

The achievements of Lysippus and the conquests of Alexander opened a new era in the history of sculpture. Artists had now virtually attained technical mastery in the representation of the human figure, whether nude or draped, at rest or in motion, alone or in groups. There was little room for further progress, except in the direction of greater elaboration or greater exaggeration. Many sculptors tended, therefore, to look back to earlier styles, or to apply their technical expertise to different subjects and different aims. At the same time the changed political and social situation had its own effects. Artists now found themselves working less for the state and more for kings and rich private individuals, so that personal taste, often favoring the trivial or the vulgar, came to exercise influence on the choice of subject-matter and the manner of its treatment. All in all, the Hellenistic world presents a bewildering diversity of styles. To make matters more complicated, the freedom with which sculptors traveled and the distances which they covered (for example, pupils

Detail of the "Alexander" sarcophagus from the royal tomb at Sidon. Alexander is riding to the rescue of his client king Abdalonymus, whose horse has been attacked by a lion. Late 4th century BC. Istanbul, Archaeological Museum.

of Lysippus were active as far afield as Rhodes and Antioch) meant a constant movement and interchange of ideas; although certain cities – Athens, Alexandria, Antioch, Pergamum and Rhodes – were celebrated as centers of sculptural activity, it is impossible to associate particular regional styles with any of them. We shall do better to pick out just a few aspects of the Hellenistic achievement.

Among single figures the female nude and the draped figure were favorite motifs. The many descendants of the Cnidian Aphrodite include the beautiful Aphrodite from Cyrene and the Aphrodite from Melos (Venus de Milo), whose spiral twist and jutting knee create a restless note characteristic of innumerable post-Lysippan works. An interesting variant on the standing type was the crouching Aphrodite by Doidalsas, preserved in several Roman copies. The first of the great Hellenistic draped statues was the Tyche of Antioch, made by Lysippus' pupil Eutychides. Seated on a rock, with a bunch of palm leaves in her hand and a personification of the River Orontes swimming beneath her feet, she wore an all-enveloping cloak, pulled by her crossed legs and weight-supporting left arm into a pattern of contrasting folds – taut and loose, straight and curved, vertical and diagonal. Later sculptors made great play of drapery effects. A popular theme was the semitransparent wrap through which the folds of a lower garment could be seen; in a statue from Asia Minor in the British Museum there is a double transparency, the folds of the skirt showing through the cloak, which in turn shines through its own overfold. But the finest of Hellenistic draped statues is the Nike (Victory) of Samothrace, dated to the early 2nd century. The winged goddess is shown landing on the prow of a ship, and her drapery is used to suggest the force of the wind in her face; the cloth is pressed flat against her upper body and left leg, but swirls in deep and tumultuous folds, giving a fine sense of movement, across her right leg.

Virtuosity, as shown by some of the more precious tricks in the rendering of drapery, is one aspect of Hellenistic sculpture; triviality is another. Many of the themes which were tackled would have been rejected as quite unworthy by sculptors of the Classical age. A drunken satyr sprawls backwards clutching a wineskin; an old hag sits crooning with a wine jar in her lap; the god of love, formerly a handsome youth, now a chubby cupid,

Right: Nike (Victory) from Samothrace, perhaps by the Rhodian sculptor Pythocritus, who would have carved it in honor of a naval victory in the early 2nd century BC. Fragments of the right hand have turned up in recent years. 2·45 meters high. Paris, Louvre.

Left: reconstruction of the Apoxyomenos by Lysippus (c. 320 BC). An athlete is using a strigil (bronze scraper) to remove the oil from his forearm after exercise. The forward projecting right arm creates a strong three-dimensional effect. 2·05 meters high. Warsaw, National Museum.

lies asleep on a rocky couch. The sleeping hermaphrodite known from several Roman copies is typically Hellenistic for two reasons: because it is sleeping and because it is a hermaphrodite. Such frivolity is totally alien to the high moral and religious tone of Classical art. Hellenistic sculptors excelled particularly in the representation of the very young and very old. A study of a boy sitting with a goose shows a close sympathy for the gestures and expression of a small child; while the Louvre fisherman, with his shriveled flesh and stooping shoulders, conveys well the ravages of age. Yet another type is furnished by the seated bronze boxer in the Terme Museum in Rome: his massive shoulders, scarred face, flattened nose and cauliflower ears make him the personification of brutish ugliness.

The influence of Lysippus was possibly strongest in the spheres of portraiture and group sculpture. His portraits of

Right: reconstructed facade of the Great Altar at Pergamum, erected by Eumenes II (197–159 BC). The reliefs of the gigantomachy frieze originally blotted out the background wall, so that the colonnade above seemed suspended in midair above a mass of struggling figures. Total width 36·44 meters.

Left: copy of the Gaulish group which formed the centerpiece of a victory monument set up in Pergamum in the late 3rd century BC. Though the poses are a little theatrical, the nobility of the Gauls, who will commit suicide rather than surrender, is brought out by the detachment of their facial expressions. 2·11 meters high. Rome, Terme Museum.

Alexander stand at the head of a long line of Hellenistic ruler portraits, individual in appearance but displaying a measure of idealism. In the portraits of lesser mortals, too, the Hellenistic age shows a considerable advance on efforts of the 4th century; the poignant statue of Demosthenes and the heads of merchants from Delos are finely observed character studies. Group sculpture almost certainly benefited from the lost multifigure compositions of Lysippus and from his exploration of the third dimension, which permitted artists to establish much more coherent and realistic relationships between different figures. The pair of wrestlers in Florence not merely invites but positively demands inspection from different angles; only thus can the action of the arms and legs be properly understood. Other groups, while using depth to the full, put the emphasis on physical and psychological contrasts: young and old, beautiful and ugly, taut and slack, suffering and sadistic. The shaggy Marsyas, bound to a tree, waits in terror while a tough, balding slave sharpens a knife to flay him, watched by the youthful god Apollo. In a famous assemblage of dying Gauls, set up in Pergamum to commemorate Attalus I's victory over the Galatians, the centerpiece showed a chieftain driving a sword into his chest after having already killed his wife – a theme which enabled vigorous action to be contrasted with the limpness of death. Copies of this centerpiece and another statue from the group illustrate the cosmopolitan outlook of the new world: though barbarians, the Gauls are depicted with profound sympathy.

In architectural sculpture the age is dominated by the Great Altar at Pergamum. Its external frieze, carved along the edge of the podium, is a massive achievement, 2.28 meters high and 120 meters long, for which the term "baroque," so often misused in discussions of Hellenistic art, is for once not inappropriate. The subject, the battle of gods and giants (gigantomachy), has given the opportunity for a *tour de force* of virtuosity and erudition. Represented now in human form, now with serpent legs or with wings on their backs, and sometimes even with animals' heads, the giants reel this way and that before the onslaught of the rampant gods, who include not only the twelve Olympians but also about 75 lesser deities, dug up from the mythological archives with a typically Hellenistic zeal for scholarship. The composition weaves bodies, wings and snakes together to form a writhing mass which virtually blots out the background and in places seems to come right out of the architectural framework (as where a giant crawls up the steps to the altar). But more impressive still is the feeling for texture: snake scales, animal fur, feathers, flesh, hair, drapery – all are carved with such loving care that it is possible, for example, to distinguish the inside and outside of cloth. In terms of sheer technical brilliance, the gigantomachy frieze marks the climax of Greek sculpture. But the Pergamum altar also looks to the future. Its smaller, internal frieze, portraying the life story of Telephus, the city's legendary founder, makes much greater use of landscape than previous reliefs, toys with perspective, and employs a narrative technique, episode

succeeding episode in the manner of a cartoon strip. These are all features which were to bulk large in the sculpture of the Romans.

The "Alexander mosaic" from Pompeii reproduces a painting of the late 4th century BC of the confrontation between Alexander the Great and Darius at the battle of Issus. Height 2·71 meters; width 5·12 meters. Naples, National Museum.

Painting and mosaic. An important feature of Greek sculpture, at least of stone sculpture, is that it was colored; figures and drapery were, by the Classical period, given a fairly natural hue, while the backgrounds of reliefs were painted red or blue. Surprisingly, the man who colored a statue was esteemed as highly as the sculptor and could even be one of the leading picture painters of the day. Only in a very few cases have appreciable remains of this coloring survived – for example on the Alexander sarcophagus. And with picture painting we are even worse off: apart from one or two painted tomb-chambers in southern Italy, Macedonia, Thrace and south Russia, and items like painted gravestones, all of minor importance and mostly from areas remote from the mainstream of art, we have no firsthand evidence. For an awareness of the achievements of Greek painters we are forced back on the testimony of ancient writers and, to some extent, on reproductions or adaptations of the Roman period.

Both these sources show that wall and panel painting was an art form on a par with sculpture. Working generally on a wooden surface (even murals were commonly executed on paneling attached to the wall), to which colors were applied by tempera or encaustic, great artists like Polygnotus, Apollodorus, Zeuxis, Parrhasius and Apelles gradually evolved the techniques of illusionism. Before the Persian Wars, foreshortening and three-

quarters views of the human figure had been mastered, but painting was still a linear technique, like vase painting, and colors were applied in flat washes. Over the next hundred years or so modeling by the use of shadow and highlights was introduced, first for drapery and inanimate objects, then for the bodies of men, and finally for the bodies of women, which were normally much paler than men's. At the same time a better understanding of linear perspective was attained; 4th-century vase painters, reflecting monumental painters, occasionally depict buildings with receding sides. Coloring, too, became more subtle and naturalistic. Though we may doubt the truth of anecdotes like the one about the painted grapes by Zeuxis at which birds flew, they bear witness to the *trompe l'oeil* effects which Classical painters accomplished. The greatest master of this illusionistic ideal was Apelles of Ephesus, whose works included numerous celebrated portraits of Alexander, as well as the Aphrodite Anadyomene (Aphrodite rising from the sea), painted, according to one story, after the same redoubtable Phryne who had acted as a model for Praxiteles' Cnidian Aphrodite. The Alexander mosaic in Pompeii, which is apparently a copy of a picture by Apelles or someone of his age, affords a precious glimpse of the skills of which he must have been capable.

Painted pottery, in view of the vast quantities in which

it has survived, assumes a significance out of all proportion to its true standing. Ancient writers barely mention vase painting, let alone the names of vase painters. Modern research, however, tends to place as much emphasis on vase painting as on architecture and sculpture, and has devoted inordinate energy to the stylistic study of individual artists, who, if their work is unsigned, are known by such whimsical sobriquets as "the Painter of the Woolly Satyrs," "the Chicago Painter" or "the Painter of London F64."

In the 5th century the figured pottery market of the Greek world was dominated by Athens; other centers had local styles but still imported the bulk of their decorated ware from Attica. Here the normal fashion was for red figures on a black ground (though one traditional class of vessels, the Panathenaic amphorae, retained the old black-figured style). Shapes ranged from small oil bottles and low-stemmed cups with shallow, spreading bowls to large amphorae and mixing-vessels up to 75 centimeters high. Each painter tended to concentrate on a specific series of shapes, preferring for instance cups and other smaller vessels to large pots, or vice versa. As for subject-matter, mythological episodes of various sorts were always the most popular, but scenes from everyday life were also common. In either case the subject chosen might be relevant to the function: thus vessels used in marriage ritual were decorated with wedding scenes; funerary vases generally carried funerary subjects; and wine jars and cups often showed drunken revels, whether those of the gilded youth of Athens or those of Dionysus and his mythical followers, the satyrs and maenads.

Styles obviously varied from artist to artist or school to school; but there was a general trend, at least among the more creative painters, towards richer effects. In the generation after the Persian invasion the Pan Painter worked in a mannered, archaizing style with elegant, long-limbed figures; while the Niobid Painter, inspired by the murals of Polygnotus, experimented with pictorial devices which other vase painters of the time spurned as unsuitable – faces in three-quarters view; items of landscape, like rocks and the occasional tree; and the setting of figures at different levels to suggest space and depth. The third quarter of the century saw the Achilles Painter and others cultivate a calm, reflective style appropriate to the age of the Parthenon. Then, in the last decades of the century, while a conservative tradition continued, artists like the Meidias Painter developed an ornate, sugary manner in which the pictorial tricks explored by the Niobid Painter were revived but now applied to erotic rather than heroic scenes. Theirs is the world of the boudoir, in which elegant women wearing golden bracelets and filmy drapery tilt their heads in poses of languid affectation.

In the 4th century Attic red-figure remained divided into two principal streams – one preserving a "Phidian" restraint and the other favoring greater elaboration. The

Attic white-ground *lekythos* (oil flask) by the Achilles Painter. The subject, a soldier's leave-taking from his wife, doubtless symbolizes death, since these *lekythoi* were generally intended as offerings to the dead. 42·5 centimeters high. About 440 BC. Athens, National Museum.

latter produced the more interesting work, finely if sketchily drawn; but the overall decoration is frequently rather indigestible. The simple black and red scheme is disturbed by a free use of white and an occasional use of gilt; and cupids flit about unnervingly in almost every space. Even more florid are many of the pots now produced in south Italy, where local red-figure styles had ousted Attic imports from the market. The main surface is peppered with figures set at different levels and picked out in white and yellow; while masses of plant ornament, often sprawling in three-dimensional confusion, fill the subsidiary spaces. Eventually, almost as if artists felt that they had no tricks left to play, the finer styles of vase painting were quietly dropped: Attic red-figure finished during the 320s, South Italian in the early 3rd century. Such painting as occurred on later pottery was usually coarse and unambitious.

After red-figure the most important style of painted pottery in our period was white-ground, made in Athens in the middle and second half of the 5th century. At first employed on a range of shapes, including the interiors of cups, it was soon confined to the slender oil flasks (*lekythoi*) which were dedicated at graves as offerings to the dead. Since these vessels did not have to withstand daily handling, the painters felt able to decorate them with friable colors, applied after firing. The surface was treated with a white or whitish slip, figures were drawn in outline, and drapery and other details were filled in with flat washes of purple, brown, yellow, red, blue and, later, green. The supreme exponent of this technique was the

Pebble mosaic from Pella, the Macedonian capital, showing a stag hunt. The signature of the artist Gnosis is preserved at the top. About 300 BC.

Achilles Painter, whose two-figure scenes, showing such themes as a mistress and her maid or a soldier's farewell to his wife, have a simplicity and serenity hardly rivaled in Classical art. Though much of the coloring has perished, they give us a fair idea of the effect which the less pretentious panel paintings of the period must have presented.

Another medium which came to reflect contemporary panel painting was mosaic. The first mosaics, laid towards the end of the 5th century, were formed by black and white pebbles inserted into the floors of houses so as to provide a more durable surface than the traditional beaten earth or plaster. Examples at Olynthus show simple figure scenes and geometric or vegetable patterns carried out in white on a dark ground; they are perhaps indebted to textiles. Later, however, smaller pebbles and a greater range of colors were introduced, so that more pictorial effects could be achieved. Mosaics of a stag hunt and lion hunt from Pella, dating to the late 4th or early 3rd century, employ brown, yellow and blue as well as black and white, and give an illusion of depth by devices such as

foreshortening, overlapping, shading and the use of a ground line. The next step was to replace pebbles by specially cut cubes of stone (and later glass) called *tesserae*. This change was accomplished in the second half of the 3rd century, and from now on mosaic pictures, which were generally set in the middle of the floor, surrounded by borders of pattern, became ever more sophisticated. *Tesserae* were cut to minute sizes (1 or 2 millimeters across), and different colors were juxtaposed to simulate the painter's mixing of pigments. The end result could often pass, at first sight, for a painting, and indeed a bust of Alexandria from the Nile Delta and of course the Alexander mosaic are clearly copies of famous paintings. But many mosaics, for all their pictorial manner, were original creations. One mosaicist, Sosus of Pergamum, even won a mention in the pages of Pliny for his "Unswept Room," a pavement in which he imitated the droppings from a dinner table. Versions of this design and of the central panel, which showed doves drinking and preening themselves at a bowl, have survived from the Roman age.

Other arts. We may conclude our survey by looking at those arts which are often labeled "minor" – though wrongly, for metalwork and gem engraving, at least, were highly regarded in ancient times; Pliny lists famous artists in both fields, including a gem engraver to whom Alexander gave the exclusive right of cutting his portraits.

In decorative metalwork the most important type was gold and silver plate, whether plain or decorated with incision or repoussé reliefs. Much of this was made for ritual use or for dedication at the sanctuaries of the gods, but as time went on there was an increased demand from private collectors, especially in the Hellenistic age, when Alexander's conquests made available vast quantities of treasure, as well as opening up new sources of the necessary ores. Domestic silverware (ladles, strainers, plain cups and toilet vessels) was a largely Hellenistic development. Throughout our period the main finding places are the barbarian fringes of the Greek world, particularly Thrace and south Russia, where the tombs of native chieftains have yielded treasures of imported or specially commissioned plate. These include richly chased and embossed vessels of various forms, notably libation bowls and animal-head vases. One of the most spectacular treasures, found at Panagyurishte in Bulgaria in 1949, consists of nine gold vessels – four rhyta (pourers), three jugs in the form of women's heads, an amphora, and a libation bowl – decorated in the repoussé technique with scenes from Greek myth or legend (except for the bowl, which has Negro heads in three concentric rings).

Bronze too was used to produce decorative metalwork. The cheek pieces of helmets and shoulder plates of cuirasses were often adorned with embossed reliefs; and decorative handles or appliqués might be attached to plain bronze vases. A particularly sumptuous vessel from a tomb at Dherveni in Macedonia, dated to the late 4th century, has repoussé reliefs on the body, solid-cast figures seated on the shoulder, and elaborate handles embellished with palmettes, volutes and bearded heads; the whole surface, moreover, is gilded, with details picked out in silver. Much humbler are the circular covers hinged to bronze mirrors. The backs of these often carried heads or mythological scenes in relief; while the interiors were sometimes decorated with engravings – cool, economical line drawings which would have stood out dark against the surface. Like all ancient bronzes, these mirror lids were meant to be seen in a bright, burnished condition and not with the patina which coats them today.

Bronze figurines, besides serving as decorative attachments to vases and other objects, were regularly produced as works in their own right. While many were dedicated to the gods, others remained in private possession; popular subjects, such as athletes, dancers, and, in Hellenistic times, hunchbacks and other grotesque figures, clearly suggest a collectors' market. Despite the miniature scale, several of these bronzes, like the Baker dancer in New York and the Negro musician in Paris, are masterpieces.

Above: detail of a gilded bronze vessel from a grave at Dherveni in Macedonia. A satyr takes part in a Dionysiac revel, symbolic of the joys awaiting the initiate in the afterlife. Late 4th century BC. Thessalonica, Archaeological Museum.

Below: scaraboid gem (jasper) signed by Dexamenus (c. 440–430 BC). He might justly feel proud of this head, cut on a stone only 1·6 centimeters wide. Boston, Museum of Fine Arts.

Gold pendant from a tomb at Koul-Oba near Kertch (south Russia), with an embossed relief representing the head of Phidias' Athena Parthenos. One of a pair found by the head of the corpse, it perhaps served as an earring. The disk is 7·2 centimeters in diameter. Mid-4th centuy BC. Leningrad, Hermitage Museum.

flat face with a domed back) and were either set to swivel in a ring or worn as pendants on a necklace or bracelet. But by the late 4th century the immovable ring-stone, oval in shape, was the normal type. For scaraboids the commonest stone was the gray or white chalcedony, while ring-stones included carnelians, jaspers, and, after Alexander's opening of the east, garnets and amethysts. There were also imitations in glass. Thanks to their signatures, we know the names of several gem cutters, the finest being the late 5th-century artist Dexamenus of Chios, whose engravings of a bearded head and a flying heron show an amazing mastery of the exacting technique. In Hellenistic times an important innovation was the cameo, in which the design was worked in relief instead of in intaglio, and artists often exploited a banded stone like onyx to obtain, for example, white figures against a dark brown background. A superb example of the technique, admittedly on a much larger scale, is the Tazza Farnese in Naples, a cup showing an allegory of the fertility of Egypt.

Other forms of production are perhaps, from our point of view, crafts rather than arts (though a Greek would not have recognized this distinction, since the same term, *techne*, covered both). Terracottas include many representations of actors, as well as the attractive Tanagra figurines of elegant ladies in their Sunday best. Much impressive gold jewelry (diadems, necklaces, earrings, bracelets, brooches, finger rings) has survived, including wreaths which simulate oak and laurel leaves, and medallions like the pair from south Russia showing the head of Phidias' Athena Parthenos. Multicolored glassware and relief-decorated pottery were both popular in Hellenistic times.

Finally, special mention may be made of coins. Struck from metal dies which were engraved with the same miniaturist skill as gems (and indeed were sometimes, at least, cut by the very same artists), these often rank as works of art. Outstanding are some of the Sicilian issues of the 5th century and the coin portraits of Hellenistic rulers, notably those of Alexander and of the kings of Bactria and India. Modern coins may not be so artistically produced as these, but they owe their general form to their Greek counterparts. Not only did the Greeks disseminate the use of coins throughout the Mediterranean, they also established the principle that the obverse should be stamped with a head (at first that of a deity, later that of a king), and the reverse with some kind of emblem or commemorative scene. This principle was subsequently adopted by the Romans and transmitted to the monarchies of the modern world. Greek coins are, in fact, almost an epitome of Hellas and its achievement. The issues of Athens, Syracuse and the rest are both one of the most characteristic expressions of the independence of the *polis* and, at the same time, the first chapter in a story which runs through the whole subsequent course of western civilization.

Since they were less in the public view and suffered less from problems of weight and balance than full-scale statues, they often adopted types (the female nude) and poses (the throwing action) in advance of monumental sculpture.

Engraved stones were used as personal seals by the wealthier classes. Initially they were scaraboid in form (a

Further Reading

GENERAL

Andrewes, A., *The Greeks* (London, 1967).
Boardman, J., Griffin, J. and Murray, O. (eds.), *Oxford History of the Classical World* (Oxford, 1986).
Cary, M., *The Geographic Background of Greek and Roman History* (Oxford, 1949).
Crawford, M. (ed.), *Sources for Ancient History. Studies in the Use of Historical Evidence* (Cambridge, 1983).
Finley, M. I., *The Ancient Greeks* (London, 1963; paperback edn. 1966).
Jones, N. F., *Public Organization in Ancient Greece* (Philadelphia, Pa., 1987).
Kitto, H. D. F., *The Greeks* (revised edn. Harmondsworth, 1957).
Levi, P., *Atlas of the Greek World* (Oxford, 1980).
Tarn, W. W. and Griffith, G. T., *Hellenistic Civilisation* (3rd edn. London, 1952; paperback edn. 1966).

ECONOMICS AND SOCIETY

Bieber, M., *The History of the Greek and Roman Theater* (2nd edn. Princeton, N.J., 1961).
Cary, M. and Warmington, E. H., *The Ancient Explorers* (London, 1929; paperback revised edn. 1963).
Casson, L., *Ships and Seamanship in the Ancient World* (Princeton, N.J., 1971).
——, *Travel in the Ancient World* (London, 1974).
Ellis Jones, J., *et al., An Attic Country House* (London, 1974).
Flacelière, R., *Daily Life in Greece at the Time of Pericles* (London, 1965).
Forbes, R. J., *Studies in Ancient Technology* (9 vols., 2nd edn. Leiden, 1964–72).
Glotz, G., *Ancient Greece at Work* (London, 1926).
Harris, H. A., *Greek Athletes and Athletics* (London, 1964).
——, *Sport in Greece and Rome* (London, 1972).
Lacey, W. K., *The Family in Classical Greece* (London, 1968).
Marrou, H.-I., *A History of Education in Antiquity* (London, 1956).
Michell, H., *The Economics of Ancient Greece* (revised edn. Cambridge, 1957).
Nilsson, M. P., *Greek Popular Religion* (New York, 1940).
——, *Greek Piety* (Oxford, 1948).
——, *A History of Greek Religion* (2nd edn. Oxford, 1949).
Nock, A. D., *Conversion* (Oxford, 1933).
Osborne, R., *Classical Landscape with Figures: The Ancient Greek City and its Countryside* (London, 1987).
Parke, H. W., *Greek Oracles* (London, 1967).
Pickard-Cambridge, A. W., *The Dramatic Festivals of Athens* (2nd edn. Oxford, 1968).
Rose, H. J., *A Handbook of Greek Mythology* (6th edn. London, 1958; paperback edn. 1964).
Rostovtzeff, M. I., *Social and Economic History of the Hellenistic World* (3 vols., Oxford, 1941).

POLITICAL HISTORY AND ADMINISTRATION

Bury, J. B. and Meiggs, R., *A History of Greece to the Death of Alexander* (4th edn. London, 1975).
Cary, M., *A History of the Greek World from 323 to 146 B.C.* (2nd edn. London, 1951; paperback edn. 1972).
Hammond, N. G. L., *A History of Greece to 322 B.C.* (Oxford, 1959).
Laistner, M. L. W., *A History of the Greek World from 479 to 323 B.C.* (3rd edn. London, 1957; paperback edn. 1970).
Staveley, E. S., *Greek and Roman Voting and Elections* (London, 1972).
Zimmern, A. E., *The Greek Commonwealth* (5th edn. Oxford, 1947; paperback edn. 1961).

MILITARY

Lawrence, A. W., *Greek Aims in Fortification* (Oxford, 1979).
Snodgrass, A. M., *Arms and Armour of the Greeks* (London, 1967).
Tarn, W. W., *Hellenistic Military and Naval Developments* (Cambridge, 1930).

ART AND ARCHITECTURE

Andronikos, M., *Vergina* (Athens, 1984).
Arias, P. E. and Hirmer, M., *A History of Greek Vase Painting* (London, 1962).
Berve, H., Gruben, G. and Hirmer, M., *Greek Temples, Theatres and Shrines* (London, 1963).
Boardman, J., *Greek Art* (revised edn. London, 1973).
Brommer, F., *The Sculptures of the Parthenon* (London, 1979).
Cook, R. M., *Greek Art. Its Development, Character and Influence* (London, 1972).
——, *Greek Painted Pottery* (2nd edn. London, 1972).
Lawrence, A. W., *Greek and Roman Sculpture* (London, 1972).
——, *Greek Architecture* (3rd edn. Harmondsworth, 1974).
Lullies, R. and Hirmer, M., *Greek Sculpture* (revised edn. London, 1960).
Pollitt, J. J., *Art in the Hellenistic Age* (Cambridge, 1986).
Richter, G. M. A., *The Sculpture and Sculptors of the Greeks* (4th edn. New Haven, Conn., 1970).
——, *Handbook of Greek Art* (7th edn. London and New York, 1974).
Robertson, C. M., *A Shorter History of Greek Art* (Cambridge, 1981).
Robertson, D. S., *Greek and Roman Architecture* (2nd edn. Cambridge, 1943; paperback edn. 1969).
Rolley, C., *Greek Bronzes* (London, 1986).
Strong, D. E., *The Classical World* (London, 1965).
Wycherley, R. E., *How the Greeks Built Cities* (2nd edn. London, 1962).

Acknowledgments

Unless otherwise stated, all the illustrations on a given page are credited to the same source.

A–Z Illustrations, Surrey 92.
Agora Museum, Athens; photo Ekdotike Athenon, S.A., Athens 71 center and bottom right, 72.
American School of Classical Studies at Athens 53, 71 top right, 86 top right, 86 bottom left, 88 top.
Archaeological Museum, Olympia; photo Ekdotike Athenon, S.A., Athens 39 top right, 41 left, 127.
Archaeological Museum, Thessalonica; photo Ekdotike Athenon, S.A., Athens 135 top.
Ardey Verlag, Dortmund from *Der Pergamon Altar* (1959) by Carl Humann 46.
Ardey Verlag, Dortmund from *Chronik der Ausgrabung von Pergamon 1871–1886* (1963) ed. E. Schulte 49 bottom.
Ashmolean Museum, Oxford 23 bottom, 26, 95, 97 top.
Dick Barnard, London 43 bottom right, 62 top left, 67 top right, 68 center, 70, 71 left, 83, 87 left, 115 bottom left, 121 bottom, 131.
Bibliothèque Nationale, Paris 101.
Bodleian Library, Oxford; photo the Warburg Institute, London 23 top.
John Brennan, Oxford 5.
British Museum; photo R. V. Schoder, SJ, Chicago 18 top left.
British Museum; photo Michael Holford 18 top right, 34, 35 left, 44 bottom, 66 bottom, 67 top left, 79 bottom, 84, 85 center, 89 top, 96, 108.
British Museum, Department of Prints and Drawings; photo John R. Freeman, London 21, 29.
H. W. Catling, Athens 93.
A. Conze and others, *Archäologische Untersuchungen auf Samothrake*, (1880); photo R. Wilkins, Oxford frontispiece.
Corpus Christi College, Cambridge 107.
M.D.C. Cuss, Oxford 43 bottom left, 44 top.
Delos Archaeological Museum; photo Ekdotike Athenon, S.A., Athens 116 top.
Deutsches Archäologisches Institut, Athens 38 bottom, 40 bottom, 41 bottom right, 42 bottom left, 43 top, 57 bottom.
École Française d'Archéologie, Athens 114 top right, 118 top.
Ekdotike Athenon, S.A., Athens 8 bottom left, 62, 66 top left, 73 top, 75 left.
J. Ellis Jones, Bangor 90.
Elsevier Archives, Amsterdam 49 top, 85 bottom, 87 top right, 132.
F. Fanelli, *Atene Attica* (1707); photo R. Wilkins, Oxford 25 bottom.
John Fuller, Cambridge 2 left.
Werner Forman Archive, London 64 bottom left, 65 bottom.
Ray Gardner, London 106.
Roger Gorringe, London 17 top, 19 top, 38 top, 39 top left, 42 top right, 55, 59 top, 66 center, 113 left, 114 bottom, 121 top, 125.
E. T. Hall, Oxford 60.
Hannibal, Athens 37, 39 bottom, 40 top, 42 top left.
Robert Harding Associates, London 41 top right, 67 bottom, 68 top right, 113 right, 123.
D. A. Harissiadis, Athens 57 top.
Hermitage Museum, Leningrad; photo Werner Forman Archive 136.
A. A. M. van der Heyden, Amsterdam 11, 13, 20, 33, 52, 64 top left, 69, 76.
Michael Holford Library, London 19 bottom, 65 top, 68 top left, 68 bottom.

Alan Howard, London 2 right.
Istanbul Museum; photo Schwitter Library, Lieli, Switzerland 128.
A. F. Kersting, London 28.
Lesley A. Ling, Manchester 89 bottom right, 110.
Lovell Johns, Oxford 12, 14, 73 bottom, 78, 99.
Howard Loxton, London 9, 115 bottom right, 117 bottom left.
Mansell Collection, London 15, 22, 77, 85 top right, 88 bottom, 126.
Musée du Louvre; photo Maurice Chuzeville, Paris 109, 129 right.
Musée du Louvre; photo Lauros-Giraudon, Paris 87 center right.
Museo Archeologico Nazionale, Naples; photo Mauro Pucciarelli, Rome 16.
Museo Nazionale Romano; photo Mauro Pucciarelli, Rome 130.
Museo Nazionale Romano; photo R. V. Schoder, SJ, Chicago 111.
Museum of Fine Arts, Boston; photo R. V. Schoder, SJ, Chicago 86 top left, 135 bottom.
Muzeum Narodowe, Warsaw 129 left.
National Archaeological Museum, Athens; photo Ekdotike Athenon, S.A., Athens 17 bottom, 74, 82, 85 top left, 89 bottom left, 91, 105, 119, 133.
National Archaeological Museum, Athens; photo R. V. Schoder, SJ, Chicago 61, 64 right, 102, 117 bottom right.
Ny Carlsberg Glyptotek, Copenhagen; photo R. V. Schoder, SJ, Chicago 75 right.
Palestrina Museo Nazionale; photo Mauro Pucciarelli, Rome 81.
Pella Archaeological Museum; photo Ekdotike Athenon, S.A., Athens 134.
Picturepoint Ltd., London 114 top left.
Pitt Rivers Museum, Oxford, by courtesy of the Ministry of Defence (Crown copyright) 58, 59 bottom.
Royal Ontario Museum, Toronto 86 bottom right.
F. Piot, *Monuments et mémoires* (1908); photo R. Wilkins, Oxford 116 bottom left.
Scala, Florence 7.
R. V. Schoder, SJ, Chicago 45, 118 bottom, 124.
G. Speake, Oxford 31 top, 47, 115 top.
Spectrum Colour Library, London 25 top, 48, 51, 97 bottom, 112, 117 top.
Staatliche Antikensammlungen, Munich; photo Caecilia H. Moessner 87 bottom right, 103.
J. Stuart and N. Revett, *The Antiquities of Athens* (1762–1816); photo R. Wilkins 27.
Spyros Tsavdaroglou, Athens 8 top right, 8 bottom right.
Victoria University Library, Toronto 79 top.
R. Wilkins, Oxford 31 bottom, 35 right, 36.

The Publishers have attempted to observe the legal requirements with respect to the rights of the suppliers of photographic materials. Nevertheless, persons who have claims are invited to apply to the Publishers.

For reading parts of the text and making valuable comments I am grateful to Mr. J. Boardman and Dr D. J. Crawford, neither of whom should be held responsible for any mistakes that remain. Mr C. Canby and Dr G. Speake of Elsevier International Projects Ltd. have given much help during the writing and editing of the book, as has Miss Hilary Kay in assembling the illustrations. I am also grateful to Celia Rowe and Pauline Lownsborough for assistance with typing the text; and my wife, Dr Lesley A. Ling, has proved, as always, an unfailing source of guidance and inspiration.

Glossary

Acanthus leaf The spiky leaf of the acanthus plant (*Acanthus spinosus*, otherwise known as "bear's breech" or "architect's plant"), a favorite motif in architectural decoration from the late 5th century onwards, notably in the Corinthian capital. See also **Corinthian Order.**

Acropolis Name given to a hill which formed the nucleus of many Greek cities and had originally been virtually synonymous with the city, serving as a community's stronghold and place of refuge in times of war. In the Classical and Hellenistic periods it often served as a religious sanctuary or a showpiece for splendid buildings. The most famous example, the Acropolis *par excellence*, is that of Athens.

Aeolian Name given to the group of Greek immigrants which settled, after the Dorian invasions, along the northern part of the west coast of Asia Minor. Coming from Thessaly and Boeotia, they retained their own dialect and their primarily agricultural economy.

Aeschylus (525–456 BC) Athenian dramatist, the first of the three great tragedians, a poet of grandeur and deep religious convictions, who preached the supremacy of justice and of the Divine Will. Of about 90 plays which he wrote, 7 survive, including the *Oresteia* (458 BC), the only extant trilogy.

Agora An open space at the middle of a Greek city, which served at once as a marketplace, administrative center and social center. Originally forming a kind of twin nucleus with the acropolis, it gradually became the vital hub of city life and was monumentalized by the construction of colonnades and grand public buildings around it. The Athenian Agora provides an example of unplanned growth; that at Priene, with its rectangular regularity, is a purpose-built city-center.

Alcibiades (c. 450–404 BC) Athenian politician who rose to prominence as leader of the extreme democrats during the Peloponnesian War. Gifted but unscrupulous, he urged the Athenian expedition to Sicily, then, when he was indicted for alleged acts of sacrilege, fled to Sparta and put his services at the disposal of the enemy. Later he changed sides once more and led the Athenian fleet in successful campaigns in the Aegean and Hellespont before he went into final exile in 406 BC.

Amphora Wine-jar, one of the commonest shapes in Greek pottery, a high two-handled pot with a neck considerably narrower than its body. Coarse amphorae, used for the transport of wine, had pointed bottoms for convenience of stacking and narrow necks which could be plugged with clay stoppers. Fine painted amphorae had broader necks and served as decanters. A special class was the Panathenaic amphorae, large jars decorated in the black-figure technique and presented, full of oil, to victors at the Panathenaic games in Athens.

Amphora

Anaxagoras (c. 500–c. 428 BC) Philosopher from Clazomenae who settled in Athens after the Persian Wars. He put forward a theory that all things in the universe were compounded of "seeds" which had been set in motion by a principle which he called "Mind." He also gave the correct explanation of eclipses, though adhering to the old tradition of a flat earth. His new-fangled ideas resulted in an indictment on charges of impiety, which forced him to flee from Athens.

Anthesteria A festival in honor of **Dionysus**, held during three days in February, when the wine-jars were opened and the new wine tasted. The chief day was the day of the tasting, called "Choes" (Jugs), which was attended not only by the adults but also by small children, who were presented with

miniature jugs painted (in Athens at least) with children's games. There was also a drinking contest and a pageant of the marriage of Dionysus. On the third day, a kind of All Souls' Day, pots of cooked fruits were offered to the dead and to Hermes the guide of souls to the underworld.

Apelles (*fl.* c. 330–320 BC) The greatest painter of antiquity, born at Colophon, but probably naturalized as an Ephesian. He was best known for his depictions of feminine beauty (two versions of Aphrodite painted on Cos) and his portraits (Alexander holding a thunderbolt etc.).

Aphrodite Goddess of love, beauty and fertility, though sometimes worshiped in other capacities, for instance as a goddess of the sea or goddess of war. In mythology, the child of Zeus and Dione, and consort of Hephaestus, who exposed her love-affair with Ares by trapping the miscreants in a net and calling the other gods to witness their discomfiture. She seems originally to have come from the east, and one of the main centers of her worship was Cyprus, after which she is often called "the Cyprian." In art she inspired famous nude statues and paintings (the Cnidian Aphrodite by **Praxiteles**, the crouching Aphrodite by Doidalsas, the Aphrodite Anadyomene by **Apelles**).

Apollo A god of many parts, looking after agriculture, flocks and herds, archery, medicine, music and prophecy, generally a symbol of Hellenism and the champion of mankind. Later, in Hellenistic and Roman times, he tended to be identified with the sun-god Helios. Among his attributes the commonest were the lyre and the bow; and his sacred plants were the laurel, used for the wreaths awarded to victors in his games at Delphi, and the palm-tree, under which he was supposed to have been born at Delos. His best-known religious centers were the oracular shrines, of which Delphi was the chief.

Archaic Describes the phase in Greek civilization from the 7th to the early 5th century BC, the period in which the Greeks emerged from their Dark Age and adopted many of their characteristic cultural and political forms.

Archimedes (c. 287–212 BC) One of the greatest mathematicians of all time, born at Syracuse and killed during the Roman sack of the city. His favorite field was the measurement of curvilinear areas and volumes: he established close limits for the value of π (the ratio of a circle's circumference to its diameter) and calculated the ratio of volume between a cylinder and a sphere inscribed within it – an achievement which was commemorated by a carving on his tomb. In other fields he explained the principle of the lever, devised a method of expressing numbers up to an almost inconceivable magnitude, and studied the properties of solid objects floating in liquids (hence his famous discovery of specific gravity).

Ares In mythology the god of war, the son of Zeus and Hera, and paramour of Aphrodite. His province was the rage of battle rather than the finer arts of war represented by Athena, and his worship was never widespread in Greece, though he had an important sanctuary at Thebes and there was a 5th-century temple of Ares in Attica which seems to have been transplanted into the Athenian Agora in Roman times.

Aristarchus (c. 310–c. 230 BC) Mathematician and astronomer from Samos, famous for his discovery that the sun was far larger than the earth and for his view that the earth and all the planets revolved around the sun, while the sun and stars were stationary, the latter being an enormous distance away. His views were rejected by other scholars.

Aristophanes (c. 450–c. 385 BC) Athens' greatest comic playwright, the author of plays such as the *Clouds*, the *Wasps*, the *Birds* and the *Frogs*. An arch-conservative, he attacked democratic politicians (Cleon), modern thinkers (Socrates) and playwrights of advanced views (Euripides), as well as maintaining consistent opposition to Athenian involvement in the Peloponnesian War. The marvelous lyricism and coarseness of his earlier plays were toned down in the later ones, which turned the spotlight from politics to social life, thus presaging New Comedy.

Aristotle (384–322 BC) Philosopher and scientist, born in Chalcidice. He studied in Athens at **Plato**'s "Academy" and later returned to found his own philosophical school, the "Lykeion" (Lyceum), named after the *gymnasion* in which he taught. His greatest achievements were to systematize the knowledge which the Greeks had thus far accumulated and to establish the principle of collecting data as the basis for scientific study. Botany, zoology and other natural sciences may be said to have begun with Aristotle.

Artemis Goddess of wild beasts and childbirth (in which capacity she was often identified with Eileithyia). In mythology the daughter of Zeus and Leto, and twin-sister of Apollo. Her votaries sometimes simulated animals, as for

instance at Brauron in Attica, where little girls called "bears" performed a dance for her. At Ephesus she was identified with an Asian nature-goddess and portrayed as a female with many breasts; but normally she was shown in art as a huntress wearing a short tunic and carrying bow and arrows.

Arundel, Thomas Howard, 14th Earl of (1585–1646) The first great English art-collector. He was fired with enthusiasm for ancient sculpture by a tour of Italy in company with the architect Inigo Jones and subsequently accumulated a splendid collection of statues, busts and inscriptions. Many of these, including fragments of figures from the Great Altar at Pergamum, were collected in Greece and Asia Minor by his agent William Petty. After his death his collection was dispersed by his heirs. Much of it reached the University of Oxford, but some pieces were buried beneath houses and on waste ground in London. One Pergamene sculpture found its way, after various vicissitudes, to a cottage at Worksop in Nottinghamshire, where it was discovered in 1960.

Asclepius A healing god whose worship spread through Greece in the late 5th century BC; his sanctuary at Epidaurus, where patients were cured while they slept, often with a little help from the god's sacred snakes, became a kind of Greek Lourdes. In art he was shown as a mature bearded man with a staff and a snake.

Athena War-goddess and patroness of arts and crafts, later a personification of wisdom. In Classical times she was best known as the patron goddess of Athens, where her grandest temple was that of Athena Parthenos ("the Virgin"), better known as the "Parthenon." The pedimental sculptures depict two of the main stories from her mythology – her birth, fully armed, from the head of Zeus after it had been split by Hephaestus' axe, and her contest with Poseidon for the ownership of Attica.

Babin, Jacques-Paul (died 1699) French Jesuit father who spent much of his life as a missionary in the Turkish Empire. His account of Athens, though marred by his naive and unscholarly approach, was the first extensive survey of conditions in the city to reach western Europe in modern times and inspired **Jacob Spon**, who published it, to undertake his own tour of the Greek world.

Beazley, Sir John Davidson (1885–1970) British art-historian who devoted much of his life to the identification of the painters of Attic red-figured vases and to a parallel study of black-figure painters. The second edition (1963) of his monumental *Attic Red-Figure Vase-Painters* catalogs all the known works of nearly 800 painters; while *Attic Black-Figure*

Vase-Painters (1956) identifies 500 potters and painters, and attributes to them some 10,000 vases. This achievement has transformed the study of Attic vase-painting, and enables archaeologists to recognize the painter or affinities (and therefore the approximate date) of virtually any decorated potsherd.

Carrey, Jacques (1649–1726) French artist from Troyes, a pupil of the royal painter Charles Le Brun, on whose recommendation he was taken to Constantinople by the Marquis de Nointel. Among the work which he carried out for Nointel were drawings of antiquities in Athens, notably the Parthenon sculptures. Several of these drawings, providing valuable evidence for the condition of the sculptures before the Venetian shelling of the Acropolis, found their way to the Bibliothèque Nationale in Paris, where they were bound in a volume in 1811.

Caryatid Statue of a draped maiden serving as an architectural support in lieu of a column. Caryatids are found in several small and ornate Ionic buildings, notably the Erechtheion on the Athenian Acropolis, where six of them adorned the south porch.

Cella The central hall of a Greek temple, containing the cult statue of the deity to which the temple was dedicated.

Cella

Chandler, Richard (1738–1810) British traveler, antiquary and epigraphist. As a graduate of Magdalen College, Oxford, he published *Marmora Oxoniensia*, an edition of the Arundel Marbles in the possession of Oxford University, and was appointed to lead the first Ionian expedition of the Society of Dilettanti (1764–66). He and his companions **Revett** and **Pars** brought back many important archaeological records from Greece and Asia Minor, including drawings of the temples at Priene and Didyma and copies of inscriptions which have since been lost. He also published his diaries of the trip, which reveal him as a keen observer of wild life and social customs in the areas visited.

Cimon (c. 512–449 BC) Athenian general and statesman, he commanded the forces of the Delian League in their operations against the Persians in the 470s and early 460s. His greatest triumph was the Battle of the Eurymedon (468), a crushing victory on both land and sea which gave the confederate navy undisputed control of the Aegean and won over several of the cities of southeastern Asia Minor. At home he pursued a policy of friendship with Sparta, and, with the rise of the anti-Spartan party under **Pericles**, he spent a spell in exile.

Classical In a general sense the term used to describe the whole civilization of the Greeks and Romans. More specifically the period from about 480 BC (the Persian Wars) to about 323 BC (the death of Alexander the Great), the period of Greece's greatest achievements in literature, art and architecture.

Cockerell, Charles Robert (1788–1863) British architect and archaeologist. He spent the years 1810–16 exploring Greece, Asia Minor, Sicily and Italy, during which time he attempted an abortive excavation at Olympia, played a leading part in the international campaigns at Aegina and Bassae, measured the fortifications at Syracuse, and surveyed the remains of the temple of Olympian Zeus at Agrigento. The results of his work were published in a supplement to the *Antiquities of Athens* (1830) and in *The Temples of Jupiter Panhellenius at Aegina and of Apollo Epicurius at Bassae* (1860). In later life he was a distinguished architect, working on such buildings as the Ashmolean Museum at Oxford and the Fitzwilliam Museum at Cambridge.

Conze, Alexander (1831–1914) German archaeologist, director of the Austrian excavations on Samothrace (1873 and 1875) and of **Humann**'s work at Pergamum (1878–86). One of the leading exponents of the more scientific archaeology of the last quarter of the 19th century, he adopted the policy of exposing whole groups of buildings rather than individual monuments and of studying them in their full topographical and historical perspective. The volumes which he edited on the work at Samothrace and Pergamum set high standards of archaeological publication. He also carried out important research on early Greek pottery and Attic grave-reliefs.

Corinthian Order A sub-form of the **Ionic order** in which the traditional volute capital was replaced by a bell-shaped capital decorated with **acanthus** leaves and slender vertical spirals. According to a story recounted by Vitruvius, the capital was invented by the bronze-worker Callimachus, who was inspired by the sight of an acanthus plant growing up around a basket. The earliest Corinthian columns were isolated examples in the interior of temples, but by the late 4th

Corinthian capital

century Corinthian capitals were used on the exterior of small, folly-like structures, and in Hellenistic times they graduated to the exteriors of large religious buildings.

Cornice The uppermost, strongly projecting part of an architectural order, surmounting the frieze. Also a horizontal decorative molding running around the upper wall of a room.

Curtius, Ernst (1814–96) German historian, topographer and archaeologist, the organizer of the excavations at Olympia. After visiting the site in 1839 and 1840, it became one of his life's ambitions to excavate Olympia, and in a famous lecture delivered in Berlin in 1852 he first formulated his plans for the project which was only realized over 20 years later. The arrangement eventually reached with the Greek government whereby the purely scientific purpose of the excavations was stressed and all finds were to be ceded to the host country acted as a model for countless later excavation treaties. Curtius also played an important part in turning the German Archaeological Institute in Berlin into a state institution and founding its branch in Athens.

Cyriac of Ancona (1391–1455) Italian merchant (full name Ciriaco de' Pizzicolli) who spent much of the period from 1418 to 1448 traveling in Italy, Greece and the eastern Mediterranean. His drawings of Greek antiquities and his copies of inscriptions provided the Italian Renaissance with its only significant glimpse of Greek archaeology and inspired certain Renaissance sculptors, notably those of the Rimini school.

Dalton, Richard (1715?–1791) British traveler and draughtsman, later librarian to King George III. On a grand tour in 1749 he executed numerous drawings of antiquities in Greece and Egypt. Those of the monuments in Athens were, along with **Pococke**'s, the most accurate yet produced but were still marred by a lack of precise observation and measurement and by fanciful restorations; they were almost immediately superseded by the work of **Stuart** and **Revett**.

Demeter Greek goddess of the fruits of the earth, particularly corn, and also a divinity of

the underworld. She was generally worshiped in conjunction with her daughter Kore (Persephone), who represented the yearly cycle of the corn. According to the myth, Kore was carried off by the underworld god Hades and only returned under an arrangement whereby she spent part of the year above ground and part of the year below. The rites of the two goddesses were specially associated with Eleusis, where they formed the focus of the most famous mystery religion of the ancient world.

Demosthenes (384–322 BC) Athenian statesman and the greatest orator of antiquity. Having cut his teeth as a pleader and speech-writer in private lawsuits (including one to reclaim his own inheritance), he graduated to public trials and to political life, where he led the party which advocated resistance to Macedonia. His mastery of language and singleness of purpose are nowhere better displayed than in his orations against Philip, the *Philippics*.

Dentil One of a series of small rectangular blocks hanging from the underside of the cornice in the **Ionic order** of architecture.

Deus ex machina In Greek drama, the introduction of a god in the air by means of some form of crane, a device often used to resolve a plot which had reached an impasse.

Dionysus God of the forces of nature, probably deriving from Thrace, whose orgiastic worship swept Greece in the early

Dionysus

first millennium BC. His followers, mainly women, went on to mountainsides and indulged in ecstatic dances during which they tore apart live animals and ate the raw flesh (a rite known as *omophagia*). Later his cult became more respectable and was virtually adopted into the state religion. His festivals in Attica gave birth to drama, and, perhaps under Orphic influence, he became the focus of one of the most successful mystery religions of Hellenistic and Roman times, offering his votaries the prospect of immortal bliss after death.

Dodwell, Edward (1767–1832) British traveler and artist, who spent the years 1801, 1805 and 1806 touring Greece, often in the company of William **Gell**. During his travels he made numerous drawings and watercolors, including some of the Parthenon executed with the aid of a *camera obscura*, and also assembled a large collection of vases and other antiquities, many of which he excavated himself from graves in Attica. Though not an expert archaeologist, he made a number of useful observations on ancient remains, and his *Classical and Topographical Tour through Greece* (1819) is a mine of interesting information about life in early 19th-century Greece and about his own experiences there (including a fight with bandits in the Peloponnese).

Dorian Name given to one of the main tribal divisions of the Greek race. The Dorians were the last of the invaders to arrive in the Greek peninsula, and they settled particularly in the Peloponnese, the southernmost Aegean islands and the southwest corner of Asia Minor. They remained culturally distinct from the other Greeks, for instance in architecture and dialect; and in Sparta and Crete they retained an individual political system in which the subject peoples were serfs and dependants, while the conquerors formed a ruling military class.

Doric Order Style of architecture particularly associated with European Greece and the western colonies. Its most distinctive features, as in all Greek architecture, were embodied in the exterior – simple fluted columns without bases and crowned by cushion capitals, and a frieze consisting of alternate triglyphs and metopes. Proportions tended to be heavy, and the overall effect was strong and austere. The canonical example of a Doric temple is generally considered to be the temple of Zeus at Olympia; the Parthenon is externally Doric but employs unusually graceful proportions and incorporates a number of Ionic elements.

Dörpfeld, Wilhelm (1853–1940) German architect and archaeologist, the most important excavator of the late 19th and early 20th centuries. After being discovered by Friedrich Adler, he joined the staff of the excavations at Olympia, where he established a unique reputation as an interpreter of

building remains. His drawings in the Olympia publication were more careful and more detailed than any yet attempted for ancient architecture. He later brought scientific standards to bear on Schliemann's excavations at Troy and for 25 years was director of the German Archaeological Institute in Athens – a post which he filled with such success that the German Foreign Office protested when he announced his retirement. During this period he was constantly in demand as a consultant to the excavations of the Greek Archaeological Society and carried out his own campaigns at innumerable sites in Greece and Turkey.

Eleusinian Mysteries Religious festival celebrated at Eleusis near Athens each September and focusing, like other mystic religions, upon the initiation of believers into certain secret rites, bringing the promise of a joyous life after death. The mysteries were based on the worship of **Demeter** and her daughter Kore (Persephone), goddesses of corn and of the renewal of life, and included the revelation of holy objects and the acting of a passion play based on the myth of the two goddesses. The initiation of the Mystics (*mystai*) was divided into two grades, the higher one (*epopteia*) taking place a year after the lower.

Elgin, Thomas Bruce, 7th Earl of (1766–1841) British diplomatist and art-collector. Appointed envoy extraordinary to the Ottoman court in Constantinople, and determined to make his embassy "beneficial to the progress of the Fine Arts in Great Britain," he managed to obtain permission to remove antiquities from the Athenian Acropolis. Much of his collection, notably the sculptures which he had taken from the Parthenon, was eventually bought by the British government and put in the British Museum.

Engaged column A column attached to a wall.

Entablature The part of an architectural order which lies above the columns, consisting normally of the architrave, frieze and cornice.

Epinetron A pottery thigh-shield, semi-cylindrical but bull-nosed at one end so as to fit over the knee, used by women to draw out tufts of wool into roves ready for spinning. The *epinetron* (alternatively known as an *onos*)

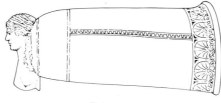

Epinetron

was generally made of coarse pottery, but fine, painted examples, in which the nose is decorated with a modeled bust, are also known.

Eratosthenes (c. 275–c. 194 BC) Head of the Library at Alexandria and the greatest polymath of antiquity. He wrote works on literary criticism, chronology, astronomy, geography, mathematics and philosophy, and composed both epic and elegiac poems. His greatest achievements were in geography, where he realized that all the oceans were one and that the three continents of Europe, Asia and Africa formed an island within them; suggested that the Atlantic might be interrupted by a fourth continent; and calculated the circumference of the earth to within 200 miles of the truth.

Euripides (c. 485–c. 406 BC) The youngest of Athens' three great tragic playwrights and the first to adopt a "modern" approach to drama. He questioned the overriding power of the gods, studied the reaction of the human mind and emotions to given situations, and put a new emphasis on the character and behavior of women. Nineteen plays survive, the greatest being the *Bacchae*, composed shortly before his death in Macedonia.

Fates The Moirai, three goddesses (originally one) who determined a man's destiny, daughters (according to one version of the mythology) of Zeus and Themis. They were generally conceived as three spinners who presided at every birth, one to assign the lot (Lachesis), one to spin the thread of life (Clotho), and one to sever it (Atropos, the inflexible one).

Fluting The vertical channeling with which columns were decorated. In Doric architecture the flutes met in sharp edges (arrises) and were generally 20 in number; in Ionic they were separated by smooth fillets and were generally 24 in number. Some gigantic temples, such as that of Olympian Zeus at Acrages, had flutes wide enough for a man to stand in.

Furtwängler, Adolf (1853–1907) German archaeologist and art-historian, who made his name as cataloger and interpreter of the small finds from the excavations at Olympia. In addition to establishing a relative chronology for the art of the Archaic period, his volumes in the Olympia publication demonstrated the value of first-rate scale-drawings as a means of publishing an exhaustive record of the small objects – especially of the bronzes, where oxidation "causes finer details to disappear in a photograph." As assistant in the Berlin Museums and director of the Antikensammlungen in Munich, he continued to build up an unrivaled knowledge of Greek art and produced fundamental studies on sculpture, vase-painting and ancient gems. His last years were largely dedicated to excavations in Greece, notably at Aegina, where he contracted the fever from which he died.

Gell, Sir William (1777–1836) British traveler who published Greek itineraries, including references to ancient remains, and acted as leader of the second Ionian mission of the Society of Dilettanti. This mission yielded the first ground-plans of the temples at Priene and Didyma – plans which Revett had not attempted in 1764–65 because the structures were too ruinous. Gell and his architects also carried out a survey of the temple of Artemis at Magnesia on the Maeander, which had been discovered by Elgin's private secretary, W. R. Hamilton, in 1803. From 1820 onwards he lived in Rome and Naples, becoming a lion in the British community in Italy, and writing books on the excavations at Pompeii and the topography of Rome.

Geometric A term used to describe the period from about 1050 to about 700 BC, when the most characteristic material evidence from the Greek world is pottery decorated with abstract, largely rectilinear, ornament.

Greater Dionysia The main Athenian festival in honor of **Dionysus**, held in March and attended by visitors from all parts of Greece. The ceremonies focused around the temple of Dionysus of Eleutherae on the south side of the Acropolis and included a splendid procession in which a statue of Dionysus was brought into the city; but the main attraction was the performance, in the neighboring theater, of new lyric choruses, comedies and tragedies, spread over a period of five days.

Gymnasion A sports center incorporating such features as a *palaistra*, running-track, bathrooms, changing-rooms and a store for the oil with which athletes anointed themselves before exercise. But, as physical education was inseparable from intellectual education, the *gymnasia* tended increasingly to become general cultural centers, especially those which served as headquarters of the *ephebeia* (the small finishing-college for well-to-do young men which became a feature of every Hellenistic city). They were accordingly provided with lecture halls and libraries as well as sports facilities.

Hamilton, Sir William (1730–1803) British diplomat and art-collector, best known nowadays as the unfortunate husband of Nelson's paramour Emma. While envoy extraordinary in Naples from 1764 to 1800, he formed two large collections of antiquities, mainly red-figure vases, which were sold in 1772 and 1801, the first being bought by the British Museum. His splendid publications of these collections reflected the standards set for Athenian architecture by **Stuart** and **Revett**.

A consignment of the vases was lost in a shipwreck off the Scilly Isles in 1798 and is currently being retrieved in diving operations.

Heliaia Name given to the citizens of Athens in their judicial capacity, a body of 6,000 from which the *dikasteria* were drawn. Also the building in which courts were held.

Hellenistic Describes the period from the death of Alexander (323 BC) to the Roman conquest of the Greek world (completed in the 1st century BC). Greek rule extended at various times over much of the Middle East, including even northern India. The independent city-states characteristic of the Classical age were now absorbed in or overshadowed by vast kingdoms, while art, literature and philosophy were conditioned by a new cosmopolitan outlook. The period of Greece's greatest achievements in pure and applied science.

Hephaestus God of fire and especially of the smithy, thus patron of smiths and generally of craftsmen. In mythology he was born lame, much to the disgust of his mother Hera, who cast him out of heaven (alternatively he was ejected by Zeus for taking Hera's part in a quarrel); later he was reinstated, married Aphrodite and produced all manner of marvelous works, e.g. the armor of Achilles. His worship was most firmly established in industrial centers, notably Athens, where the temple which he shared with Athena in an important craftsmen's quarter is still well preserved (the "Theseum").

Hera Consort of Zeus and the goddess of marriage and the life of women. She is portrayed in the *Iliad* as a hen-pecking wife, and mythology is full of stories about her bitterness against Zeus's various mistresses and their children. Her most famous sanctuaries were at Argos and Samos.

Herm A religious image consisting of a pillar with the head of a god and a phallus. Generally the god portrayed was Hermes, and the herms were set up at roadsides, at boundaries, in house-courtyards and in exercise-grounds, all of which were protected by that god. The mutilation of the herms in the streets of Athens in 415 BC led to a superstitious panic and a witch-hunt of suspected revolutionaries. In Roman times herms were used as decorative sculptures, carrying the heads of various deities or portraits of famous people.

Hermes The messenger of the gods, in mythology the son of Zeus and Maia. He was also a god of the roadside, protector of travelers and traders, and guide of souls to the underworld. In accordance with these functions he was generally portrayed in art as a herald, wearing a winged cap or a broad-brimmed traveling hat and a pair of sandals and carrying the herald's staff (*kerykeion*); but

there were also images which showed him as a pillar of stone with a head on top and a phallus halfway up. See **Herm**.

Herodotus (c. 484–c. 425 BC) The world's first true historian, the author of an account of the Persian Wars. Born at Halicarnassus, he traveled widely around the Mediterranean, Black Sea, Egypt and the Middle East, collecting information for his book, which brought together a wealth of geographical, ethnological and anecdotal detail concerning the various peoples involved in the wars. His visits to Athens left him with a profound admiration for that city.

Herm

Hoplite The traditional heavy-armed foot soldier of the city-state armies, to whom the Greeks owed their victories over the Persians, and who remained the basis of Spartan military primacy till the 4th century BC. He wore a bronze helmet, breastplate and greaves; carried a heavy elliptical shield; and fought with an iron sword and a 3-meter-long spear. When fighting in closed formation and on level ground, hoplite armies were not easily overcome, but once they became disordered their comparative immobility made them vulnerable to a faster-moving foe.

Humann, Carl (1839–96) German engineer and archaeologist, the discoverer of the Great Altar at Pergamum. Settling in Turkey to convalesce from a respiratory condition, he was fired with an enthusiasm for archaeology by a campaign of excavation on Samos in 1862 and, in the course of his work building roads and railways for the Turkish government, came to realize the importance of the remains on the acropolis at Pergamum. His excavation of the Great Altar and its sculptures in 1878–79 opened a new chapter in the study of Hellenistic art, and his subsequent work at Pergamum and other sites contributed important new information on Hellenistic city architecture.

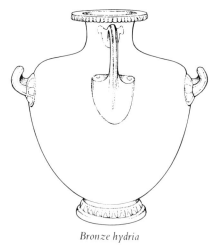

Bronze hydria

Hydria Name given to a jar in which water was fetched from the fountain. It has a vertical handle at the back for dipping and pouring, and two horizontal handles at the sides for lifting.

Intaglio Term used, especially in gem-cutting, to describe an engraved design as opposed to a design in relief.

Ionian Name given to one of the main sections of the Greek people. Expelled from the Greek peninsula by the Dorians in the 11th century BC, they settled in the Aegean islands and central part of the seaboard of Asia Minor, which became known as Ionia. They played an important part in the cultural flowering of the Archaic period, notably in the fields of science, poetry and architecture; and they retained their distinctive dialect, spoken also in Athens, which claimed to be their mother-city.

Ionic order Style of architecture particularly associated with Athens and east Greece. Its columns are taller and slenderer than Doric, have elaborately profiled bases and are crowned by ornate capitals in which the most distinctive feature is the volute-member, which resembles a partly unwound scroll laid across the shaft. The upper parts vary in the Classical period, eastern examples lacking a frieze and having dentils hanging beneath the cornice, Athenian examples dispensing with the dentils and inserting a continuous frieze, generally sculptured. Later the two versions were combined.

Isis The wife of Osiris and a national deity in Egypt. In Hellenistic times her worship was carried, in Hellenized form, over much of the Mediterranean; and it retained its popularity in the Roman period. Like other mystery religions it involved a myth of death and resurrection and required that its novices go through an elaborate ceremony of initiation. Isis received daily services, and her ritual, wherever conducted, involved the use of sacred water from the Nile and of a holy rattle, the *sistrum*. Her main festivals were the Isia in November and the Ploiaphesia (festival of the Launching of the Ship, celebrating the opening of navigation) in March.

Isocrates (436–338 BC) Athenian orator and teacher. He turned the oration into one of the most popular literary forms and set up a school which placed emphasis on the teaching of rhetoric and turned out many successful debaters and politicians, besides making him a fortune. Politically he is notable for his view of Greek culture as a unifying force and for his advocacy of a Panhellenic crusade against barbarian Persia.

Kantharos

Kantharos Name normally given to a type of drinking-cup, 15 to 20 centimeters in diameter, with vertical, ear-like handles. Dionysus is often shown holding one in vase-paintings.

Kottabos A game popular at Greek drinking-parties, in which the player, reclining on a couch, threw a little wine from his cup at a mark, whether an empty basin or little saucers floating in a water-filled bowl or some other more sophisticated variant. The game was regarded as a type of libation and a player often invoked the name of his beloved as he made the cast.

Leake, William Martin (1777–1860) British army officer who took advantage of various missions entrusted to him in Greece and Asia Minor to obtain an unrivaled knowledge of Classical topography. His journeys, including a trek across Asia Minor during which he and his party traveled in the dress of Tartars, were all conducted between 1799 and 1810, and he devoted the latter part of his life to writing up the results of his researches. His most important works are *The Topography of Athens* (1821), *Travels in the Morea* (1830) and *Travels in Northern Greece* (1835).

Lekythos

Lekythos A small flask with a narrow neck, generally used for oil or perfume. The best-known version is the tall slender vessel produced in Athens during the late 6th and 5th centuries BC and associated especially with white-ground decoration. Many of these white-ground *lekythoi*, designed to be left at tombs, were relatively large and might be provided with a false bottom, so that they actually contained much less oil than appearances would suggest.

Lenaia A Dionysiac festival celebrated at Athens in January. Little is known about its rites, except that it included a procession and dramatic productions, chiefly comedies.

Libation A drink-offering to a god, generally poured over an altar.

Kottabos

Lysias (c. 459–c. 380 BC) Athenian speech-writer and son of the wealthy Syracusan shield-manufacturer Cephalus who had settled in Athens under Pericles. His speeches, which include a personal indictment of the murderer of his brother, are notable for the simplicity and precision of their language.

Lysippus (*fl.* c. 340–310 BC) Sculptor from Sicyon, one of the most prolific and versatile of Greek artists. His works included a colossal statue of Zeus at Taras, a group of Alexander's Companions, colossal and miniature statues of Heracles, portraits of Alexander, various athletic statues and a personification of Kairos (Opportunity). Copies of his Apoxyomenos (athlete scraping himself), Agias (a Thessalian all-in wrestler) and Heracles Epitrapezios (Heracles at table) have been recognized; and the Azara bust of Alexander and the Farnese type of Heracles may both be based on originals by him.

Maenad One of the female worshipers of **Dionysus** who roamed in a state of ecstasy through woods and over mountainsides, hunting animals and devouring their raw flesh. They are often shown in vase-paintings, dancing with or fending off satyrs and sileni; they wear ivy wreaths and fawn-skins, and carry animals, snakes and *thyrsoi* (the magic wands of Dionysus).

Magna Graecia A general term for the Greek states of southern Italy. Their acme belongs to the Archaic period, when they produced important philosophers and successful athletes; only Taras retained its importance into late Classical and Hellenistic times.

Megalithic Term used to describe a type of masonry constructed of large stone blocks without the aid of a binding material such as mortar.

Menander (342–291 BC) Athenian dramatist, the best-known exponent of the New Comedy, a type of domestic comedy based on a love-plot and involving certain stock characters, such as the cheeky slave, the profligate young man, the grumpy old man, etc. He produced over 100 plays, but only one, the *Dyskolos* (*Old Misery*), survives in anything like its entirety, thanks to a manuscript which came to light 20 years ago.

Metope The square slab, often sculptured but usually plain, which alternated with triglyphs to form the frieze in Doric architecture.

Muses The goddesses, generally nine in number, who acted as patrons of poetry, literature, music and dance. They had small cults in various parts of Greece and were particularly revered by men of culture. The great philsophical schools at Athens and the state research institute at Alexandria (the so-called "Museum") were organized as religious sects dedicated to the worship of the Muses. Our words "music" and "mosaic" are derived from them. Music was regarded by the Greeks as the most fundamental aspect of culture, the sphere of the Muses *par excellence*; mosaic (i.e. wall mosaic: Latin *opus musivum*) developed from the stone incrustations used to simulate grottoes sacred to the Muses.

Maenads

Myron (*fl.* c. 460–450 BC) Greek sculptor, born at Eleutherae, just inside the border of Attica. In antiquity his most famous works were a bronze cow which stood on the Acropolis in Athens and a statue of the runner Ladas; but his Diskobolos (the discus-thrower reflected in a number of Roman copies) was scarcely less well known. A group of Athena and the satyr Marsyas, reconstructed by **Furtwängler**, has also been attributed to him.

Nemean games Athletic and musical competitions, held every other year, in winter or summer, in the sanctuary of Zeus at Nemea. They became a Panhellenic festival in 573 BC, and the prizes were crowns of wild celery.

Newton, Sir Charles Thomas (1816–94) British archaeologist, the discoverer of the Mausoleum at Halicarnassus. He played a leading part in developing the collections of the British Museum, first as its representative in the Levant during the 1850s, when he excavated at several Greek sites in Turkey (Calymnos, Halicarnassus, Cnidos and Didyma), then as its first Keeper of Greek and Roman Antiquities. During his keepership the Museum obtained grants of over £100,000 to purchase antiquities, as well as receiving material from the excavations which it sponsored on Rhodes, at Cyrene, at Priene and at Ephesus. Later Newton was appointed to the newly created professorship of Classical Archaeology at London University, and played a major role in the inception of the Society for the Promotion of Hellenic Studies (1879) and the British School at Athens (1885), Britain's two leading organs of research into the archaeology of the Greek world.

Olympiad A period of four years beginning with the year of each Olympian festival; as a chronological unit familiar to all Greeks, it became the basis of a system of dating historical events. Thus Pliny dates the *floruit* of the painter Zeuxis to "the 4th year of the 95th Olympiad" – i.e. 397 BC.

Oracle A god's reply to a worshiper's question, or the place where that reply was given. The god's will might be revealed in various ways: e.g. by the appearance of an animal's entrails or the rustling of leaves in a sacred oak-grove. The best-known kind of responses were those given by Apollo through the lips of a man or woman in a state of trance; his chief oracles were at Delphi, Didyma and Klaros.

Orchestra The circular area, literally "dancing-floor," at the center of a Greek theater.

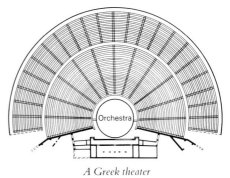

A Greek theater

Orphism A religious movement supposedly founded by Orpheus, the first Greek religion to embody its doctrines in a literature. The Orphics sought, through a complex mythology regarding the formation of the universe and of the human race, to show that man contained something divine and something evil within him; he must strive by purification and righteous conduct to free the soul (the divine part) from the body (the evil part). Only so could he escape after death to a life of happiness. These ideas, which were widely misunderstood in Classical times, exercised considerable appeal in the Roman age.

Ostrakon The Greek word for potsherd, which gave its name to the practice of ostracism, the method used in 5th-century Athens to banish dangerous politicians. If it was decided that an ostracism should be held in a given year, all the people assembled in the Agora and cast their ballots, cut on *ostraka*, against whichever politician they feared most;

and, provided that a quorum of 6,000 took part, the individual who received the greatest number of votes was exiled. The occasion was marked by intricate political maneuverings, as in 417, when two potential victims, Alcibiades and Nicias, joined forces and induced their supporters to banish a third person, Hyperbolus. *Ostraka* were also used for writing tax-lists, school exercises, magical spells etc. in Ptolemaic Egypt.

Palaistra A wrestling-ground, an essential part of the *gymnasion*. It could, however, exist in its own right, surrounded by the necessary ancillary buildings, and is frequently confused with the *gymnasion*.

Panathenaia An Athenian festival in honor of **Athena**, held on her reputed birthday in July, and celebrated every fourth year with particular splendor (the Great Panathenaia). On this occasion the chief event was a procession to take a new robe to the sacred image of Athena on the Acropolis. The robe, which was woven with a picture of the mythical struggle between the gods and the giants, was spread over the mast of a ship set on wheels and was followed by girls carrying sacred implements, by youths leading sacrificial animals, by chariots and by horsemen. This cavalcade is represented on the Parthenon frieze. The rest of the festival consisted of athletic and musical contests.

Pankration A combat event in Greek athletics, a form of all-in wrestling; no holds were barred, so far as we know, save biting and gouging. Like boxing, the *pankration* continued without interruption till one party surrendered.

Papyrus The paper reed, cultivated in ancient times in the Nile Delta. Though used also for the manufacture of boats, sails and cloth, it was grown mainly for the production of the writing material, also called "papyrus," from which most book scrolls were made.

Pars, William (1742–82) British landscape and portrait painter, chosen at the age of 22 to go as artist on Chandler's expedition to Asia Minor. His sensitive watercolors of Greek ruins in their landscapes and his pen-and-wash drawings of Classical sculptures were translated into engravings and published in *Ionian Antiquities* and other books. He later worked on landscapes in Switzerland, Ireland and, with a pension from the Society of Dilettanti, central Italy.

Pausanias (*fl.* c. 150 AD) A Greek from Asia Minor who wrote a *Description of Greece* in 10 books. Composed like a guidebook, it combines an account of the buildings and works of art in each city with learned mythological and historical digressions. The

information which it gives is of inestimable value to modern archaeologists, who have identified, for instance, the monuments of Olympia and the Athenian Agora by reference to it.

Pediment The triangular space formed between the horizontal cornice and the end of any ridged roof in Greek architecture. In Doric buildings the space was often filled with sculpture, a practice which called for much ingenuity on the part of the sculptor, given the shallow pitch of Greek roofs.

Peltast Type of light-armed soldier introduced into Greek armies, perhaps from Thrace, in the late 5th century BC. Named from their small round shields (*peltai*), they originally wore no body-armor and carried light javelins; but, as they became a regular fighting arm alongside heavy infantry in the 4th century, their armaments were improved. They lost importance with the rise of the Macedonian armies.

Pentathlon Unlike the modern pentathlon, the ancient athletic event known by this name comprised jumping (a long-jump), throwing the javelin, throwing the discus, running (a one-length race) and wrestling. The system of scoring is controversial, but the victory was probably awarded on the basis of wins in three events out of the five.

Pericles (c. 495–429 BC) Athenian statesman and leader of the democratic party in Athens. He introduced payment for jury-service and presided over the creation of Athens' maritime empire. His policy of consistent opposition to Sparta led to the Peloponnesian War which broke out in 431 BC. He himself died in the epidemic which ravaged Athens in 430–429. His most lasting legacy is the building program which he promoted on the Acropolis and which produced the Parthenon and the Propylaia.

Peristyle A row of columns surrounding a building or courtyard.

Phidias (active c. 460–c. 430 BC) The greatest sculptor of antiquity, a friend of **Pericles** and supervisor of the building program on the Athenian Acropolis in the 440s and 430s. He seems to have left Athens under a cloud after being charged with pecculation and went to Olympia, where he produced the colossal gold-and-ivory cult-statue of Zeus. The sculptures of the Parthenon probably provide our nearest conception of his style.

Piranesi, Giovanni Battista (1720–78) Italian draughtsman and engraver, famous for his grand and romantic views of ancient remains. Most of his work was done in Rome, but a posthumous volume of prints covers the Greek temples of Paestum.

Plato (c. 429–347 BC) Athenian philosopher, a pupil of **Socrates** and the greatest moral theorist of antiquity. His principal doctrine was the theory of Ideas, universal truths established by induction (e.g. Goodness, Beauty, Justice). He also formulated a picture of the ideal state, a communistic republic whose ruling class should be consistently educated towards a life of higher philosophical thought. His efforts to realize his ideal under Dionysius II at Syracuse were doomed to failure.

Pliny (G. Plinius Secundus, 23–79 AD) Roman soldier, administrator and writer, who composed books on a wide range of topics. The sole survivor is the *Natural History*, an encyclopedia in 36 volumes containing a mass of information loosely subordinated to the theme of natural sciences. Though superficial and uncritical, it sheds important light on Greek art and various aspects of ancient industry and technology. Pliny's scientific curiosity led to his death in the eruption of Vesuvius which buried Pompeii and Herculaneum.

Pococke, Richard (1704–65) English traveler and cleric who spent the years from 1733 to 1740 on grand tours of western Europe, Greece and the Levant. He published an account of his travels in *A Description of the East and Some Other Countries* (1743–45), the second volume of which includes drawings of antiquities in the Greek islands and Athens. His account of Athens, where it struggles free from its dependence on **Spon**, is remarkable for its naivety.

Podium A raised platform: used especially of the high basis beneath certain columnar monuments in Greek and Roman architecture – e.g. the Great Altar at Pergamum, the Mausoleum at Halicarnassus and the standard type of Roman temple.

Polyclitus (active c. 450–c. 420 BC) Sculptor from Argos, famous for his interest in proportions and the high finish of his works. Copies of two of his athletic statues, the Doryphoros and the Diadoumenos, have been identified; but his great gold-and-ivory statue of Hera for the goddess's sanctuary near Argos can only be visualized from devices on coins.

Poseidon Greek god of earthquakes, streams, horses and, more especially, the sea; in mythology the brother of Zeus and Hades, and husband of the sea-nymph Amphitrite. Like other Olympian gods he lost ground with the development of personal and monotheistic religions in late Classical and Hellenistic times.

Praxiteles (*fl.* 360–340 BC) Athenian sculptor, most famous in ancient times for his marble statue of Aphrodite at Cnidos, the first important female nude in the history of Greek sculpture. His statue of Hermes and Dionysus, found at Olympia in 1877, is the only surviving original statue by any of the great Greek masters.

Pullan, Richard Popplewell (1825–88) British architect and archaeologist. Appointed architect to **Newton**'s expedition to Halicarnassus, he produced a hypothetical reconstruction of the Mausoleum and carried out further work at Cos and Cnidos. In the 1860s, sponsored by the Society of Dilettanti, he undertook excavations at three sites in Asia Minor, including Priene. He was later criticized because his drawings did not always distinguish between fact and conjecture, and because he sometimes failed to grasp the full meaning of the evidence; but he was methodical enough by the standards of the mid-19th century, and there can be no doubt that his drawings were generally accurate.

Radiocarbon A radioactive isotope, otherwise known as "Carbon 14," present in all organic matter and useful as an aid to dating in archaeology. Once the organic matter is dead, it loses its radiocarbon content at a steady rate: after about 5,570 years (termed the "half-life"), only half the original amount is left; while after twice that period half the residue (i.e. a quarter of the original quantity) remains; and so on. By measuring the proportion of radioactive to ordinary carbon atoms in a piece of dead matter (e.g. wood or bone) scientists can calculate approximately when it ceased living, i.e. when the tree was felled, or when the animal was killed. The technique is little used in Classical archaeology, since closer dates can usually be arrived at by other means.

Red-Figure Style of pottery decoration with red figures on a black ground, fashionable from the late 6th to late 4th centuries BC. The principal centers of manufacture were Athens and, in the 4th century, south Italy.

Repoussé In metalwork a technique of decoration in which thin plates, disks, walls of vessels etc. are hammered into relief from the reverse side.

Revett, Nicholas (1720–1804) Architect and coauthor, with **James Stuart**, of *The Antiquities of Athens*, which set new standards in the recording of ancient architecture and brought an awareness of the Greek monuments to western Europe. He also acted as architect on **Chandler**'s expedition to Asia Minor, which resulted in the first volumes of *The Antiquities of Ionia*.

Rhyton A "pourer," a drinking- or libation-vessel in the form of a horn or an animal's head with a hole pierced through the lower end to act as a spout. When it was full, the hole had to be kept closed by a finger; for drinking, the

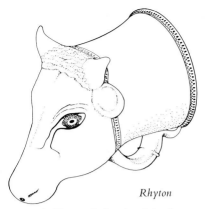

Rhyton

vase was held over the head and the finger released so that the liquid flowed into the drinker's mouth.

Ross, Ludwig (1806–59) German traveler, epigraphist and archaeologist. After a varied early career he became Superintendent of Antiquities in Athens in 1834 and played an important part in the clearing of the Athenian Acropolis and the reerection of its buildings, notably the temple of Athena Nike. That his perceptive observations on the Parthenon foundations and on the history of vase-painting were not fully appreciated, was perhaps due to his independent character. He left Greece in 1845 to take up a professorship at Halle.

Sarapis An Egyptian deity formed from a fusion of the underworld god Osiris and the sacred bull-calf Apis. Though worshiped previously at Memphis, his great successes began in Hellenistic times when Ptolemy I tried to turn him into a common deity of Greeks and Egyptians and succeeded instead in creating a god of healing and protector of seamen whose cult swept the Aegean and western Mediterranean. His cult usually went with that of his consort **Isis**, their son Horus and the conductor of souls Anubis; but Isis also traveled in her own right, retaining her pure-bred Egyptian consort Osiris. Sarapis' famous cult-statue at Alexandria showed him in Greek guise: a bearded Zeus enthroned with a corn measure (symbol of fertility) on his head, a scepter in his hand and the three-headed dog Cerberus (guardian of the underworld) at his feet.

Sarcophagus Coffin, strictly of stone or clay, though the term is also applied to wooden ones. The Greeks used plain sarcophagi in all periods; painted clay sarcophagi were produced in east Greece in the late 6th and early 5th centuries BC; and sculptured stone sarcophagi were made by Greek craftsmen for the kings of Sidon in the 5th and 4th centuries (the most notable example being the "Alexander" sarcophagus). Examples of wooden coffins, often with painted ornament, have survived from south Russia and from Ptolemaic Egypt.

Satyr Play A grotesque drama, with a chorus dressed to represent satyrs. In Classical Athens there was at first one appended to each trilogy of tragedies in the **Greater Dionysia**, but from the mid-4th century this practice was discontinued, a single satyr play being staged at the beginning of the festival. Aeschylus, Sophocles and Euripides all wrote satyr plays; but the *Cyclops* of Euripides is the only surviving example, apart from a fragment of the *Ichneutae* of Sophocles.

Satyrs Spirits of the woods and hills, bestial in behavior and part-bestial in appearance, who came to form part of the circle of Dionysus. In the 5th century BC they were shown in art as bearded, with horses' ears and tails; but from the 4th century they were distinguished from the Sileni, being young with some of the characteristics of goats, while the Sileni were old with horses' traits.

Sarapis

Scaraboid A type of gem with a flat oval face and a domed back. This shape, which was chiefly popular in the Classical period, was a simplified form of the scarab, a gem cut in the form of a dung-beetle (Latin *scarabaeus*) with the design engraved on the underside.

Scopas (*fl.* c. 370–350 BC) Architect and sculptor from Paros, said to have been connected with three of the major building projects of the 4th century. He was architect of the temple of Athena Alea at Tegea, as well as the sculptor of two statues inside it; he worked on some of the sculptures of the Mausoleum at Halicarnassus; and he carved the reliefs on one of a series of sculptured column drums in the temple of Artemis at Ephesus. No work of his can be identified with confidence, but possible echoes of his style suggest that he was a sculptor of passion.

Socrates (469–399 BC) Athenian philosopher, who diverted speculation from the nature of the universe to the question of morality. His conversations with the young men of his city, reflected in the writings of **Plato** and Xenophon, sought to establish the kind of truth which should determine the conduct of men: e.g. what is beautiful and what is ugly? what is meant by just and unjust?

Sophocles (c. 496–406 BC) The second of the three major Athenian tragic playwrights. He introduced a third actor to supplement the two actors used by **Aeschylus**, and reduced the role played by the chorus, the primary element in Greek drama. Of his seven surviving plays, concerned mainly with the study of human characters in tragic situations, the most famous is *Oedipus Rex*.

Spon, Jacob (1647–85) French doctor and antiquary from Lyons, who wrote a book on the antiquities of his own city before graduating to those of Greece. He spent the years 1675 and 1676 touring Greece and Asia Minor with George **Wheler** and brought back a large collection of inscriptions, manuscripts and coins. His account of the tour contains much valuable information on the Greek monuments and is written with a discernment and degree of scholarship unusual in his time. He was later forced to leave France by the revocation of the Edict of Nantes.

Stackelberg, Otto Magnus, Baron von (1786–1837) Esthonian painter and archaeologist, who traveled in Greece and Turkey from 1810 to 1814 and was one of the international brotherhood of antiquaries who excavated the temple of Apollo at Bassae. His account of the work and drawings of the frieze appear in *The Temple of Apollo at Bassae in Arcadia* (1826). Despite several bouts of illness and capture by pirates (who tore up his drawings), he managed to produce many sensitive paintings of Greek life and landscape. He later lived in Rome, where he drew the recently discovered Etruscan tombs at Tarquinia.

Stadion The Greek running-track, a rectangular area about 200 meters long and from 25 to 40 meters wide. Also the name given to the single-length race (and to the measure of distance on which it was based). In longer races the contestants had to run to and fro along the track, rounding a turning-post at each end. Spectators were accommodated on banking or natural slopes at either side.

Stoa Name given to a type of building which consists basically of a colonnade, closed at the back. It might be single-storied or two-storied, might have a row of shops or offices in the back half, and might turn at right angles to form two or more arms.

Stoicism Philosophical teaching of the school or sect founded by Zeno about 300 BC and known as the "**Stoa**" after the public hall in Athens where he and his successors used to teach. The Stoics believed in a Universe ruled by a Supreme Power and taught that Virtue (which to them consisted in living in harmony with Nature, i.e. the Supreme Power) was the only good.

Stratification The principle of classifying excavated material by layers (successive deposits), a fundamental tool in archaeological research. As, in a straightforward situation, lower layers will be earlier in date and higher layers will be later, it is possible to establish a relative chronology of the objects found in them; and, if one or two of these objects are capable of an absolute dating, approximate dates will be provided for the other objects and for the deposition of the layers themselves. If such layers correspond to particular events (e.g. the erection or destruction of a building), they will thus provide dates for those events.

Stuart, James (1713–88) British painter and architect, often known as "Athenian Stuart." With **Nicholas Revett** he was responsible for the publication of *The Antiquities of Athens*, which brought the fashion of Greek-style architecture to England and set a precedent for the systematic recording of Greek buildings by modern archaeologists. He himself accepted several commissions to design houses in the "Grecian" style, and the fame which he acquired led to a rift with Revett, who felt that his contribution to the *Antiquities* had been undervalued.

Stucco Plaster based on lime and an additive such as marble-dust, used primarily for surfacing coarse stone in architecture and sculpture, but also adapted in Hellenistic times to produce decorative work in relief on walls and similar surfaces.

Terracotta Baked clay, the characteristic material for making cooking vessels and tableware; also used for roof-tiles, sculptors' models, relief plaques and statuary, especially figurines (which may be referred to simply as "terracottas").

Themistocles (c. 528–c. 462 BC) Athenian statesman and chief architect of Athens' naval power. He persuaded his fellow citizens to devote revenue from the silver mines at Laureion to the building of warships, played an important part in the Greek naval victory over the Persians at Salamis, and defied the wishes of Sparta by rebuilding the Athenian fortifications demolished by the invaders. Later his anti-Spartan policy lost favor and the Athenians sent him into exile.

Thesmophoria A festival held at Athens and elsewhere in Greece about October, in honor of **Demeter**, attended only by women. Its main purpose was to promote the fertility of the corn which was about to be sown.

Thetes Wage-laborers, in particular the lowest of the Athenian census-classes, those whose annual income was less than 200 *medimnoi* (10,350 liters) or corn, or the equivalent in other produce or money. They were formally ineligible to hold magistracies, but from the mid-5th century BC they were in practice admitted to all offices. They generally served as sailors and light-armed troops in time of war.

Tholos A circular building with a conical roof and, generally, a colonnaded exterior. It could serve various functions: examples at Delphi and Epidaurus were probably religious buildings, as was the Philippeion at Olympia (a shrine to the Macedonian royal family); but the Tholos in the Athenian Agora was the headquarters of the presidents of the city Council.

Thucydides (c. 460–400 BC) The historian of the Peloponnesian War and arguably the greatest historian of antiquity. Combining impartiality with a relentless desire to get at the truth, he also sought to establish the causes underlying the political actions of states. His own experiences as an Athenian general in the first years of the war made him peculiarly fitted for his task.

Tournefort, Joseph Pitton de (1656–1708) French botanist, professor of botany in the Jardin des Plantes at Paris, and member of the Académie des Sciences. Charged by Louis XIV with a mission to study the plants, natural history, geography, customs, religion and trade of Greece, Asia and Africa, he toured the Greek islands and made numerous observations on their botany and antiquities. These are summed up in his book *Relation d'un voyage du Levant* (1717).

Trapezites A money-changer, so named because he originally sat behind a table (*trapeza*). Money-dealing gradually became more sophisticated, especially with the general increase in travel and the greater diffusion of coinage in Hellenistic times, and money-changers came to take on many of the financial transactions characteristic of modern banking.

Treasurers Name given to the Athenian officials (*Hellenotamiai*: in full "Treasurers of the Greeks") who received the tribute paid by members of the Delian League, later the Athenian Empire. They formed a board of ten recruited annually, perhaps by election, and eventually became the most important financial magistrates in Athens, disbursing money for the needs of the Generals, for shipbuilding, for public works and for the payment of jurors. The office was abolished with the fall of the Empire in 404 BC.

Trieres (trireme) A galley rowed by three superimposed banks of oarsmen, one to each oar. The standard Greek warship of Classical times, dependent in battle (like all Greek warships) on maneuvering into a position to ram its opponent. Owing to the lack of space on board and the difficulty of carrying enough food and water for the complement of about 200 men, the trireme had to keep close to land and was generally beached at night.

Triglyph A decorative element used, in alternation with metopes, in the frieze of the **Doric order**. A vertical oblong, generally twice as high as it was wide, it was carved into three vertical fillets. There is much controversy as to the origin of the decorative forms in Doric architecture, but it is possible that they reflected structural elements in earlier timber buildings, in which case the triglyphs may have been inspired by the ends of wooden ceiling beams.

Tripod A three-legged seat or stand, especially the sacred seat at Delphi on which the Pythian priestess took her position to deliver the oracles of Apollo. Tripods were frequently dedicated to Apollo and awarded as prizes in athletic and musical competitions.

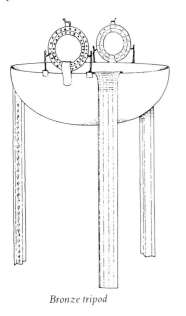

Bronze tripod

Tyche A personification of fortune, referred to by various Archaic and Classical poets, but acquiring importance as a goddess only in Hellenistic times, when she became the patroness of several cities. Eutychides' famous statue of the Tyche of Antioch showed her wearing a crown which simulated the walls of the city.

Vernon, Francis (1637?–1677) English traveler who visited Greece in 1675 and narrowly escaped being shot by Turkish soldiers while drawing in the Odeion of Herodes Atticus in Athens. Apart from an article in the *Philosophical Transactions* of 1676, he left only notebooks of his journeys, being murdered by Arabs in Persia before he could return to England.

Vitruvius Roman architect and military engineer active in the second half of the 1st century BC and best known for his treatise on architecture in ten books. His outlook on architecture is essentially traditionalist (he regretted many contemporary developments), and he is an invaluable source of information about Greek, especially Hellenistic, building practice. The recent theory that he should be identified with Caesar's engineer Mamurra, reviled by the poet Catullus, is probably to be rejected.

Volute Coil-like form popular in architectural decoration and in the decorative arts. Its best-known manifestation is the scroll member in the Ionic capital.

Wheler, Sir George (1650–1723) English traveler and cleric, famous for his tour of Greece and Asia Minor with Jacob **Spon**. Like Spon he brought back a collection of manuscripts, marbles and coins; the manuscripts went to Lincoln College, Oxford, the marbles to Oxford University, and the coins to the Dean and Chapter of Durham Cathedral. Wheler's account of his journeys is largely a doing-into-English of Spon's.

White-ground Style of pottery decoration, used especially for Attic funerary oil-flasks, in which figures and ornaments were painted in a relatively wide range of colors against a white background. It appears alongside red-figure work from the second to the last quarter of the 5th century BC.

Wiegand, Theodor (1864–1936) German archaeologist who specialized in the organization of large-scale excavations, with a special emphasis on building history and town-planning. He directed vast programs of work at Priene, Miletus, Didyma and Pergamum, training teams of architectural historians who collaborated on exemplary multivolume publications. He also carried out work on Near Eastern sites, e.g. Baalbek, and during World War I used aerial photography to record archaeological remains in Palestine and the Sinai peninsula.

Winckelmann, Johann Joachim (1717–68) German art-historian who began life as the son of a shoemaker in Prussia and graduated to be the librarian of cardinals, superintendent of antiquities in Rome and Europe's foremost authority on Classical art. Regarded by many as the true founder of art-history, he was the first to stress "the need of distinguishing between various epochs and tracing the history of styles in their gradual growth and decadence." He thus came to evaluate the Greek contribution to Classical art: "The purest sources of art are opened up: fortunate the man who finds and savors them. To seek these sources means going to Athens."

Wood, John Turtle (1821–90) English architect and archaeologist who went to Turkey as architect to the Smyrna and Aidin railway and ended up hunting for the temple of Artemis at Ephesus. The story of his long search, related in his *Discoveries at Ephesus* (1877), makes compulsive reading but would horrify any self-respecting archaeologist of today.

Volute

Zeugitai The third census-class in the Athenian state, those with an annual income between 200 and 300 *medimnoi* (10,350 and 15,550 liters) of corn, or the equivalent in other produce or money – i.e. an income which enabled them, in theory, to keep a pair of oxen (*zeugos*). They formed the bulk of the heavy infantry in time of war. Though at first eligible only for minor magistracies, they were admitted to the Generalship in the late 6th century BC and to the Archonship in 457.

Zeus King of the gods, thought originally to have been a weather-god. In Classical times he was the highest civic god, and was worshiped in several different capacities – e.g. as guarantor of the sanctity of oaths and as protector of political freedom. But his appeal to the ordinary man diminished as the worship of gods who took a more personal interest in their followers (and set higher moral standards) gained ground. In the Hellenistic period he was identified by the Stoics with their Supreme Power. See **Stoicism.**

Index